THE
GREAT TOWNS
OF
OREGON

*The Guide to
the Best Getaways
for a Vacation or a Lifetime*

DAVID & JOAN VOKAC

WEST PRESS

Publisher's Cataloging-in-Publication
(Provided by Quality Books, Inc.)

Vokac, David, 1940-
 The great towns of Oregon: the guide to the best
getaways for a vacation or a lifetime/David & Joan
Vokac. – 1st ed.
 p.cm.
 Includes index.
 ISBN-13: 978-0-930743-09-3
 ISBN-10: 0-930743-09-1

 1. Oregon–Guidebooks. 2. Cities and towns, Oregon–
Guidebooks. 3. Oregon–History, Local. I. Vokac,
Joan, 1948- II. Title

F874.3.V63 2005   917.9504'44
                         QBI05-600047

First Edition
1 2 3 4 5 6 7 8 9 10
Manufactured in the United States of America

Preface

Is it possible to leave the city without leaving its amenities behind? To be as close as a stroll to natural grandeur, while enjoying the comforts of civilization like cultural experiences, gourmet cuisine, and romantic lodgings? In the great towns featured in this guidebook, the answer is emphatically *yes*!

Here are Oregon's getaway towns most favored by nature and civilization. All are proud of their unique locales and heritage–and generous in sharing their bounty. Collectively, they celebrate the diversity and delights of a renowned region.

This guidebook expands on material originally presented in the premier sourcebook *The Great Towns of America*. For the nine Oregon towns that were featured among the nation's top 100, information has been expanded and updated. Nine additional communities that were prime contenders are now also featured. While sharing proximity to exciting regional attractions and amenities, each of these eighteen special places beckons as a scenic, civilized destination beyond the hustle and bustle of Oregon's cities.

Whether you're seeking a distinctive vacation or a new lifestyle, *The Great Towns of Oregon* is intended to serve as the ultimate guide to the foremost recreation and leisure getaways in this remarkable region. All of the best restaurants, attractions and lodgings are systematically described and rated for each locality. Weather, crime, and other key livability features are quantified and ranked. As a new highlight, in addition to ranking towns by Quality of Life and by Housing Cost, the Vokac Index of Livability and Affordability© presents a unique ratio revealing the relationship between Quality of Life and Housing Cost...with surprising results!

In one year of full-time, independent effort, we personally visited each feature in every great town. No payments were accepted. Thus, every listing is described and rated on merit alone. As a result, we believe that this guide is honest and accurate, with consistent, detailed information about the foremost getaways throughout Oregon.

For everyone who wonders what special places and pleasures await beyond Oregon's cities, *The Great Towns of Oregon* has answers. All the information you need to create a memorable visit...or to explore relocation...tailored to your time, finances, and desires is in this guidebook.

The
Great Towns
of
Oregon

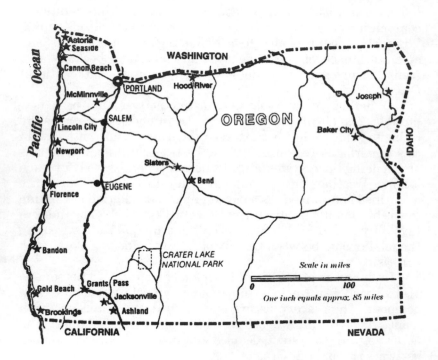

Contents

Introduction

Picture sandy ocean beaches; a rockbound sheltered harbor; flourishing vineyards; emerald-green rain forests; or majestic mountains. Now, imagine human-scaled towns, with style and pleasures normally found only in cities, in the midst of these idyllic settings. Welcome to *the Great Towns of Oregon*.

This is the only detailed guidebook focused on all of Oregon's towns most favored with both urban charms and picturesque surroundings. It was written to help you discover famous and little-known places that make the region remarkable, and enjoy them to the fullest. The book updates and expands material in the premier guide, *The Great Towns of America*.

A wealth of new information is presented in several ways that set this guidebook apart. (1) All of the best attractions, restaurants, and lodgings (instead of random features) in every locale are identified, described and rated. (2) Attention is focused on recreation and leisure pursuits of interest to adventurous adults and couples. (3) Intimate details are presented for more than one thousand romantically oriented bedrooms in exceptional lodgings. (4) The likelihood of good weather is rated for each month in every locale, and supporting data are provided. (5) Websites are included where available. (6) Visitors and dreamers inspired to consider relocating to a great town will relish exclusive quality of life and affordability data and ratings for each town.

The contents and format are designed to quickly provide all of the information you want to get the most from these exciting destinations within your time, finances, and interest.

Great Towns

A "great town" is defined as a locality apart from major cities with both scenic appeal and memorable leisure-time features.

Size, location, natural setting, and leisure appeal were used in a sequential process of elimination. All communities under 100,000 in population were considered. Places with no clear separation from major cities (hence no independent identity) were eliminated. So were towns lacking major cultural attractions, restaurants and lodgings, or more than a few miles from usable water bodies, dramatic landforms, and/or luxuriant vegetation.

Eighteen exceptional locales were found along the rugged coast, in fertile valleys, near mountains, by crystal-clear lakes, and among fruitful vineyards. Collectively, they are Oregon's prime sources of getaway excitement. Individually, each has highlights that make it a worthy destination for a delightful weekend or a lengthy vacation. A full chapter devoted to each locality addresses all natural and cultural attractions; restaurants; and lodgings. The "quality of life" chapter, comparing key livability and affordability factors, may tempt you to stay even longer.

Weather Profiles–the "Vokac Weather Rating"

Weather plays a crucial role in recreation and leisure, and in successful vacations. Because of this, detailed weather information is presented for great towns throughout Oregon. The copyrighted weather profiles for each of the eighteen locales are the most complete in any travel guidebook.

The "Vokac Weather Rating" © (VWR) measures every town's probability of "pleasant weather"–i.e., warm, reasonably dry conditions suitable for outdoor recreation by anyone dressed in light sportswear. Average high and low temperatures, rainfall, and snowfall for each month (plus the frequency of precipitation) are correlated. Typical weather that can be expected each month is then rated on a scale from "0" to "10." A "0" signifies adverse weather with almost no chance that shirt-sleeves and shorts will be comfortable. Every increment of one on the VWR scale represents a 10% greater chance of pleasant weather. For example, a "5" is used where there is a 50% chance that any given day in the month will be pleasant. A "10" pinpoints "great" weather, with warm, dry days almost 100% assured. An easy-to-follow line graph is used to display the month-to-month VWR. Generally, ratings of "7" or above indicate a high probability of desirable conditions for outdoor activity. Ratings of "4" or less suggest increasing likelihood that the weather will restrict some outdoor ventures and/or require special clothing.

As an added convenience, each month of the weather graph has been subdivided into four segments roughly corresponding to weeks. Readers interested in "fine-tuning" the VWR will find the smaller segments helpful. For example, if the ratings for September and October are "10" and "6," the position of the connecting line during the last week of September indicates an "8" rating. The implication is that weather during that week will normally still be "very good" but no longer "great."

Attractions

A hallmark of all great towns is that each has a favored natural setting. Every distinctive attraction in and around each locality is described. Included are leisure-time destinations of special interest to adults–like wineries, remote beaches and hot springs–as well as family-oriented places. All kinds of outdoor recreation–bicycling, ballooning, horseback riding, fishing

7

charters, etc.–are also described, and key sources for equipment rentals and guides are named. As an added convenience, popular categories of attractions are listed alphabetically under general headings such as "boat rentals," "warm water features" or "winter sports."

Restaurants

Sampling various styles of fresh regional foods is one of the joys of travel. While ubiquitous chains dominate most cities, almost all great towns embrace instead their celebrated and aspiring restauranteurs and chefs who contribute unique talents to the community's cultural milieu in one-of-a-kind dining places.

In this book, food and atmosphere (including scenic views) are uniformly described for all of the most noteworthy restaurants from mom-and-pop cafes to temples of haute cuisine. Service is not discussed, because it can vary so much even on a given day.

For each restaurant, the price range is summarized. Meals served *(B=breakfast, L=lunch, D=dinner)* are identified. Days closed are noted but may vary seasonally.

Lodgings

Many of Oregon's most luxurious resorts, significant historical inns, and gracious bed-and-breakfasts are found in great towns where lodgings often have a long and glorious past. This guidebook's emphasis is placed on unique, significant, or homey accommodations instead of omnipresent chain motels and humdrum hotels clustered near freeway offramps. Clean, comfortable budget lodgings are also included for cost-conscious travelers. As an additional trip planning aid, each locality is summarized in terms of its: overall number and quality of lodgings; busiest season (prime time); and average percentage by which rates are reduced off-season.

All leisure-oriented amenities available at each lodging are described, whether natural (like a location on a beach or in a forest) or manmade (i.e., outdoor pool, tennis courts, restaurants, etc.). Where available, toll-free phone numbers and website information are provided.

The overall quality of an average bedroom in every lodging is rated according to the authors' six-level hierarchy. The following descriptive terms are consistently used: humble (frayed or no-frills); plain (or simply furnished); comfortable (or nicely furnished); attractive (or well-furnished); beautiful; and luxurious. All major room features–fireplace, balcony, etc.–are also identified. The cost of rooms is summarized.

Introduction

As a unique bonus, nearly one thousand bedrooms with special views and/or features are highlighted. Exceptional rooms or suites (starting with the best) in the foremost resorts, inns, etc. in each town are identified by room number (or name) and described.

Location

Because great towns are inevitably compact, street maps are seldom necessary. To help you locate any listing without a map, all addresses are referenced according to a street number plus distance (to the nearest mile) and direction from downtown. The term "downtown" covers all features within roughly one-quarter mile of the busiest portion of a town's main business district.

Ratings

Features listed in *The Great Towns of Oregon* collectively represent the highlights that contribute most to each town's appeal. All features are rated. Three levels of quality are reflected in the ratings. (1) A star preceding an entry indicates an especially worthwhile source of a product or service worth going out of the way for. (2) An entry is included, but not starred, if it is a notable (but not exceptional) source of a product or service. (3) Many features and activities were evaluated, but not included, if they were judged to be of only average or lower quality or readily available in numerous other places.

Each feature was personally evaluated by the authors. No payments were accepted. As a result, each listing is described on merit alone, and solely reflects the authors' judgment.

Rating information is somewhat perishable in any guidebook. However, the single-star rating system can help simplify your selection of attractions, restaurants, and lodgings. In addition to the star, the authors' opinion regarding each feature's relative importance is further indicated by the length of its description.

Prices

Comparable information is provided about the relative cost of every restaurant and lodging. Because prices change with the economy, it is impossible to know how long specific rates will be in effect. However, relative price levels usually remain constant. For example, a "low-priced" motel (with rooms costing less than $70 in 2005) can be expected to remain a relative bargain in later years when compared to other lodgings–even though the actual price of a room increases–because the other lodgings in that area will typically increase their prices by about the same percentage as the bargain motel. Similarly, a restaurant will usually continue in its relative price category as years go by.

Restaurants: A basic price code was designed to provide a comparable summary of the cost of an average meal at each restaurant. The code is used for all listed restaurants in all locales. Four categories are used to define the cost per person for a "normal" dinner (with soup or salad and an average-priced entree) not including tip, tax, or beverage for the meal. The categories and related prices are: *Low:* under $12; *Moderate:* $12 - $19; *Expensive:* $20-29; and *Very Expensive:* $30+.

Lodgings: A comparable summary of the cost of a room at each lodging in every town is also presented. Cost is summarized in a category that reflects prevailing rates during "high season" (summer on the coast and mountains, and spring through fall in the inland valleys). Where two categories of rates are noted, rooms in the lodging are available in both price ranges. Nowadays, travelers should feel free to negotiate the price of a room since most lodgings offer discounts from "regular (rack) rates" to members of auto clubs, business travelers, government employees, military personnel, retirees, and others. The categories of comparable "rack rates" are as follows: *Low:* under $70; *Moderate:* $70-100; *Expensive:* $100-200; and *Very Expensive:* over $200.

Livability of Great Towns

For those who are enchanted by the charms of a particular great town, the final chapter provides key data for each community. Comparable indicators are presented for *weather*, *crime*, *overall livability*, and *housing cost*, plus *basic facilities* and *downtown vitality*. Tables rank livability of each great town compared with the others, and with Portland. As a bonus, the unique **Vokac Index of Livability and Affordability**© is presented, revealing where you can get the most Quality of Life for the housing cost.

Some Final Comments

All information has been carefully checked, and is believed to be up-to-date and accurate. To assure that the reader can continue to get current information, the internet website for each facility (where available) is identified. No malice is intended or implied by the judgments expressed, nor by the omission of any facility or service.

The authors hope that *The Great Towns of Oregon* will encourage you to discover and experience their special pleasures, and welcome your comments and questions c/o West Press.

www.greattowns.com

Ashland

Ashland is a great Western crossroads of culture and recreation. One of America's finest theatrical complexes and Shakespearean festivals, and a flourishing university, are driving forces. In a luxuriant mixed forest high on the southern rim of the Rogue River country, the town overlooks a broad pastoral valley surrounded by impressive peaks. Complementing the lovely natural setting is one of the mildest climates in the Northwest. Weather is normally warm and dry from spring through fall, when roadside stands display a bountiful harvest of regional produce.

A year after gold was discovered in nearby Jacksonville in 1851, Ashland was founded. It grew slowly with a sawmill and flour mill as the main industries, along with railroading, fruit growing, and lumbering. In 1935, a professor at the local college, Angus Bowmer, won support for using an abandoned Chatauqua site downtown for a Shakespearean production as part of a celebration. Success soon led to the organization of the Oregon Shakespearean Festival Association. In the past seventy years the town has become renowned for its world-class theater complex.

Today, the Festival runs most of the year in three fine theaters offering a wide range of productions. Spectacular Lithia Park and the heart of town adjoin the Festival grounds. Nearby specialty shops and galleries feature regional arts, crafts, and gourmet foods. Fine restaurants are plentiful, as are lodgings, including a stellar array of romantic bed-and-breakfast inns that delight theater-goers and outdoor enthusiasts here to enjoy nearby rivers, lakes, and mountains, and the mild four-season climate.

WEATHER PROFILE

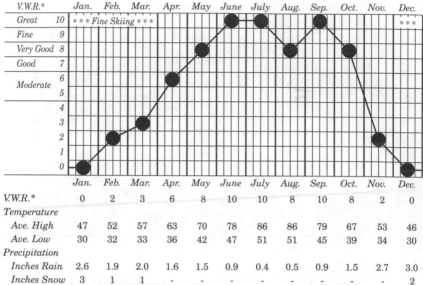

V.W.R.*		Jan.	Feb.	Mar.	Apr.	May	June	July	Aug.	Sep.	Oct.	Nov.	Dec.
Great	10	*** Fine Skiing ***											***
Fine	9												
Very Good	8												
Good	7												
Moderate	6												
	5												
	4												
	3												
	2												
	1												
	0												

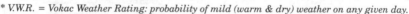

	Jan.	Feb.	Mar.	Apr.	May	June	July	Aug.	Sep.	Oct.	Nov.	Dec.
V.W.R.*	0	2	3	6	8	10	10	8	10	8	2	0
Temperature												
Ave. High	47	52	57	63	70	78	86	86	79	67	53	46
Ave. Low	30	32	33	36	42	47	51	51	45	39	34	30
Precipitation												
Inches Rain	2.6	1.9	2.0	1.6	1.5	0.9	0.4	0.5	0.9	1.5	2.7	3.0
Inches Snow	3	1	1	-	-	-	-	-	-	-	-	2

* V.W.R. = Vokac Weather Rating: probability of mild (warm & dry) weather on any given day.

BASIC INFORMATION

Population: 19,522
Elevation: 1,951 feet
Location: 280 miles South of Portland
Airport (regularly scheduled flights): Medford - 20 miles

Ashland Chamber of Commerce   (541)482-3486
   downtown at 110 E. Main St. (Box 1360) - 97520
   ashlandchamber.com
Southern Oregon Reservation Center (541)488-1011 (800)547-8052
   Box 477 - 97520   sorc.com

ATTRACTIONS

★ *Bicycling*
Bicycles may be rented by the hour or longer to explore many miles of separated bikeways and scenic byways in the lush, gentle Bear Creek valley. Dirt bike enthusiasts will enjoy the twenty-four-mile loop road to Mount Ashland.

Adventure Center   *(541)488-2819   (800)444-2819*
downtown at 40 N. Main St.   raftingtours.com
Bear Creek Bicycle   *(541)488-4270*
just N at 1988 Hwy. 99 N   bearcreekbicycle.com
Siskiyou Cyclery   *(541)482-1997*
2 mi. S at 1729 Siskiyou Blvd.   siskiyoucyclery.com
Cascade-Siskiyou National Monument   *(541)618-2200*
18 mi. SE on Hwy. 66
www.or.blm.gov/csnm
Hiking on a portion of the Pacific Crest Trail is a highlight of this young monument, created primarily to preserve the area's outstanding botanical diversity.

★ **Downtown**
downtown along Main St.
One of America's foremost strolling districts is downtown Ashland anchored by Lithia Park (see listing) and a verdant triangular plaza with drinking fountains where you can contrast city water with lithia water from nearby mountains (it *is* different). Distinctive specialty shops feature products relevant to this region, from Oregon gourmet food and wine, arts and crafts, books, and music (including listening stations) to recreation gear.

★ **Emigrant Lake Recreation Area**   *(541)774-8184*
5 mi. E on Hwy. 66
The nearest major water body to town is a scenic reservoir which has a swimming area and waterslide, plus boating (including rentals), wind-surfing, water-skiing, and fishing. Shaded picnic areas and an improved campground are also provided.

★ **Harry and David**   *(541)776-2277   (800)547-3033*
12 mi. N (via I-5 & Barnett Rd.) at 1314 Center Dr. - Medford
harryanddavid.com
A Rogue Valley tradition since 1934 continues in a colorful market showcasing luscious Comice (the deservedly renowned "Royal Riviera") pears and a cornucopia of other locally grown fruit. Northwestern gourmet products, crafts and clothing are also sold. Nearby is the packing plant and headquarters for the international distribution of gourmet food baskets and boxes. Next door is one of **Jackson & Perkins'** (jacksonandperkins.com, (800)872-7673) multicolored rose test gardens where you can see thousands of roses and hundreds of varieties in seasonal bloom.

★ **Lithia Park**   *(541)488-5340*
   downtown along Ashland Creek on Pioneer St.
   One of the nation's grandest achievements among town parks
   borders the theater complex and extends for nearly a mile along
   Ashland Creek. The National Historic Landmark includes an
   enchanting forest sheltering formal rose and rhododendron
   gardens, a landscaped pond with resident swans, meandering
   pathways, a band shell, tennis courts, imaginative play equipment,
   emerald-green lawns, playing fields, and secluded picnic sites.

★ **Oregon Shakespeare Festival**   *(541)482-4331*
   downtown at 15 S. Pioneer St.
   osfashland.org
   After seventy years, the Oregon Shakespeare Festival is world-
   famous. From February through October, the Tony Award-
   winning complex features major plays by the Bard and others in
   three splendid theaters. The outdoor **Elizabethan Theatre**, with
   a stage and auditorium in keeping with the original Globe
   Theatre of Shakespeare's time, has evolved through a multi-
   million dollar renovation and enhancement. The indoor 600-seat
   Angus Bowmer Theatre and the intimate 350-seat **New
   Theatre** assure ideal playing spaces for any production. Guided
   backstage tours let visitors see what goes on behind the scenes at
   the Festival's theaters. At the Exhibit Center, you can touch
   props and try on costumes. The **Tudor Guild Shop** offers a
   wealth of gifts related to Elizabethan times and Ashland.

★ **Rogue River National Forest**   *(541)482-3333   (866)296-3823*
   3 mi. SE (on US 66) at 645 Washington St.
   www.fs.fed.us/r6/rogue-siskiyou/
   National Forest lands bordering Ashland and beyond have
   unlimited opportunities for hiking, fishing, boating, camping, and
   (in winter) alpine and cross-country skiing. The Pacific Coast
   Trail traverses Mt. Ashland within ten miles of town. The
   Ashland Ranger District Welcome Center has a large selection of
   trail guides, books and maps.

★ **Science Works Hands-On Museum**   *(541)482-6767*
   1 mi. E at 1500 E. Main St.
   scienceworksmuseum.org
   Southern Oregon now has a large state-of-the-art science museum
   with visitor-friendly high-tech exhibits, "Science Live!"
   performances and demonstrations, and hands-on displays for all
   ages. Don't-miss exhibits include "Bubble-ology Room," "Hall of
   Illusions," "Motion Commotion," and "Pedal Power Railroad,"
   among dozens of fascinating opportunities to amaze yourself with
   scientific phenomena in the world around us. Of added interest
   are special events that occur throughout the year.

★ **Southern Oregon University**   *(541)552-6346*
   1 mi. S at 1250 Siskiyou Blvd.
   www.sou.edu
Chartered in 1926, this is the largest university in Southern
Oregon. Enrollment is about 5,500. Impressive buildings on
tranquil, tree-shaded grounds include a large contemporary student
union, and two theaters presenting several plays each year.

Warm Water Feature

★   **Lithia Springs Resort & Gardens**   *(541)482-7128*
   2 mi. N at 2165 W. Jackson Rd.
   ashlandinn.com
At the tranquil **Waterstone Mineral Springs Spa**, guests can
enjoy lithia springs water in two-person tubs, and (next year) relax
in outdoor gardens with a large soaking tub, cold plunge and sauna.
A wealth of organic spa products is sold. Treatments include
traditional and newer procedures like hot rock therapy.

★ *Wineries*
   sorwa.org
These wineries are the best producers of Northwestern wines at
this end of the Rogue Valley appellation (see Jacksonville and
Grants Pass for other major nearby wineries). Each has a stylish
tasting area, wine and gift shop, and tours.

   Ashland Vineyards   *(541)488-0088*   *(800)494-6363*
   2 mi. E at 2775 E. Main St.
   ashlandvineyards.com

   Paschal Winery   *(541)535-7957*   *(800)446-6050*
   5 mi. NW at 1122 Suncrest Rd. - Talent
   paschalwinery.com

   Weisinger's Vineyard   *(541)488-5989*
   4 mi. S at 3150 Hwy. 99 South
   weisingers.com

Winter Sports

★   **Mt. Ashland Ski Area**   *(541)482-2897*
   18 mi. SW via I-5 & Mt. Ashland Rd.
   mtashland.com
Southern Oregon's only major ski area provides access to the
higher slopes of the mountain that crowns the skyline to the
south of Ashland. The average annual snowfall is 300 inches. The
vertical drop is 1,150 feet and the longest run is one mile.
Elevation at the top is 7,533 feet. There are four chairlifts. All
basic services, facilities, and rentals are available at the base for
downhill and cross-country skiing and snow-boarding. A retail
shop with some unique gifts; a cafe; coffee and lunch bar; and
lounge featuring regional microbrews are at the base, but no
lodgings. The skiing season is usually late November into April.

RESTAURANTS

Alex's Plaza Restaurant   *(541)482-8818*
downtown at 35 N. Main St.
mind.net/alexs/
L-D. No L Mon.   *Expensive*
Diverse Northwestern specialties are served in a handsome
upstairs dining room, or in a firelit lounge overlooking a snazzy
backbar. The three tables on a little balcony provide the best view
of the plaza while out back, alfresco diners overlook Lithia Creek.

★ **Amuse**   *(541)488-9000*
downtown at 15 N. First St.
amuserestaurant.com
D only. Closed Mon.-Tues.   *Very Expensive*
Amuse is one of the most outstanding restaurants in Southern
Oregon. New Northwestern cuisine is showcased in innovative
creations like black truffle-roasted game hen with fingerlings,
kale and celery root remoulade, and desserts made here like warm
bittersweet chocolate truffle cake with coffee ice cream. Intimate
dining areas with closely spaced tables set with full linen reflect
casual sophistication that complements fine cuisine.

Apple Cellar Bistro   *(541)488-8131*
3 mi. SE at 2255 Hwy. 66
B-L-D.   *Expensive*
An imposing array of baked goods is displayed in this large
bakery/cafe. They complement light American fare served in
bright, casual indoor and outdoor dining areas.

Arbor House International Restaurant   *(541)535-6817*
5 mi. N at 103 W. Wagner Creek Rd. - Talent
D only. Sun. brunch. Closed Mon. No D Sun.   *Moderate*
An eclectic selection of international dishes is featured in a cozy
converted cottage that has served as a restaurant for more than
a quarter of a century.

★ **Ashland Springs Hotel**   *(541)488-1700*
downtown at 212 Main St.
ashlandspringshotel.com
L-D. Plus afternoon tea on Sun.   *Expensive*
The hotel's dining room, **Larks-Home Kitchen Cuisine**, opened
in spring 2005 as "a celebration of Oregon–its farms, orchards,
vineyards, chocolatiers and charm." Consider the house
salad–local organic greens, dried cranberries and candied
hazelnuts with marionberry vinaigrette; or grilled wild salmon
with horseradish cream and Oregon hazelnut wild rice. Each
delicious dish is skillfully prepared from scratch, and served amid
warm, casually elegant surroundings. The **Chocolate Cafe**
features chocolate drinks and desserts in the late afternoon.

BJ's Ice Cream   *(541)482-4794*
  downtown at 199 E. Main St.
A wide assortment of rich ice creams in many flavors is featured
in cones, cups, sundaes, shakes, malts, sodas and floats that can
be enjoyed at a few tables indoors or on a patio fronting on main
street, or to go.

Beasy's on the Creek   *(541)488-5009*
  downtown at 51 Water St.
  beasysrestaurant.com
  L-D.   *Expensive*
Contemporary American dishes include corn-raised steaks served
with mushroom and marsala wine sauce, and some creative
seafood dishes like lobster ravioli in lemon cream sauce. Meals are
served in a simply stylish setting enhanced by a fireplace and a
view (shared by an umbrella-shaded deck) overlooking the
Ashland Creek, downtown, and mountains.

The Breadboard Restaurant & Bakery   *(541)488-0295*
  1 mi. N at 744 N. Main St.
  B-L.   *Moderate*
The Breadboard is a long-established destination for morning
meals like assorted omelets and scrambles backed by housemade
organic cinnamon rolls. Some of the comfortable booths provide
an appealing view of distant Grizzly Peak.

Brothers' Restaurant   *(541)482-9671*
  downtown at 95 N. Main St.
  B-L.   *Expensive*
One of Ashland's oldest breakfast venues continues to feature all
kinds of omelets and scrambles that can be enjoyed with
homemade scones or (on weekends) luscious cinnamon rolls. The
extensive lunch menu includes piled-high deli sandwiches on rye.
The casual cafe has small dining areas upstairs and down.

★ **Chateaulin Restaurant**   *(541)482-2264*
  downtown at 50 E. Main St.
  chateaulin.com
  D only.   *Very Expensive*
Classical and creative French dishes star in Chateaulin, the
region's premier dinner house. Everything from full gourmet
meals to light cafe fare is expertly prepared with seasonally fresh
ingredients and an emphasis on top-quality regional ingredients,
many organically grown and direct from local farms and ranches.
Housemade desserts are exquisite, too. The polished wood-
trimmed dining areas and bar are inevitably crowded with
theater-goers and others here to enjoy cosmopolitan cuisine and
ambiance. A first-rate wine and gourmet shop adjoins, complete
with Northwestern wine and cheese tasting daily.

Creekside Pizza Bistro   *(541)482-4131*
downtown at 92½ N. Main St.
L-D.   *Moderate*
Pizza, sandwiches, salads and appetizers are served in a shaped-up cafe (new in mid-2005) with a pool table. The most notable feature is the multilevel dining decks adjoining Lithia Creek.

Geppetto's   *(541)482-1138*
downtown at 345 E. Main St.
B-L-D.   *Moderate*
House specialties include a three-mushroom scramble with spinach and gorgonzola, a salmon omelet, housemade fruit-and-nut-bread french toast, or all kinds of designer pancakes. Contemporary dishes like buffalo burger or lamb sausage burger are featured later along with housemade desserts served in a casual long-established cafe and dining room.

Greenleaf Restaurant   *(541)482-2808*
downtown at 49 N. Main St.
greenleafrestaurant.com
B-L-D.   *Moderate*
All sorts of American standards and some nifty creations like apple-cinnamon pancakes, or seed 'n nut waffle, are served in a shaped-up deli cafe at booths, and, on warm days, upstairs on a dining balcony overlooking Lithia Creek.

★ **Hardware Cafe**   *(541)482-0855*
just E at 340 A St.
B-L. Closed Sat.-Sun.   *Moderate*
Peerless pecan cinnamon rolls, orange bear claws, raspberry scones, and jalapeño cheddar bagels are among the wondrously creative and traditional pastries and breads made and displayed here. Enjoy them with coffee at a few tables, or to go, at this decidedly casual, tucked-away tribute to morning delights.

★ **Hong Kong Bar**   *(541)488-5511*
downtown at 23 N. Main St.
D only.   *Expensive*
One of Oregon's most sophisticated Oriental restaurants opened in 2002 on the plaza. Exquisite attention is given to each dish described on a menu featuring creative adaptations of Southeast Asian specialties. The preparations and presentations (including desserts like macadamia nut pie) are pleasing to both the eye and the palate. Stellar cuisine is complemented by an informally posh firelit dining room with a view of the plaza. A cozy upscale Oriental bar adjoins.

Il Giardino Cucina Italiana   *(541)488-0816*
downtown at 5 Granite St.
D only.   *Expensive*

Ashland's long-standing Italian restaurant continues to offer traditional Italian fare like linguine many ways in a casual little trattoria.

Key of "C" Coffee House   *(541)488-5012*
downtown at 116 Lithia Way
B-L.   *Moderate*
A tasty assortment of (varies daily) bagels, scones, muffins, and other morning delights is made and displayed in this fun, funky coffeehouse. Quality baked goods made here are served with a full range of hot drinks.

★ **Lela's Bakery & Cafe**   *(541)482-1702*
just E at 258 A St.
lelascafe.com
L-D. Closed Sun.-Mon.   *Expensive*
Lela's makes outstanding breads and desserts to enhance fine Northwestern cuisine prepared with fresh, seasonal ingredients of the region. The chef's creativity and skill is apparent is every dish (like pear/walnut salad, or pan-roasted pork chop with roasted sweet chilis). A display case full of luscious desserts and contemporary wall art add appeal to this sophisticated restaurant.

Lithia Fountain & Grill   *(541)488-0179*
downtown at 303 E. Main St.
L-D.   *Moderate*
A regional specialty, Umpqua ice cream, is featured in many flavors in shakes, floats, malts and sundaes served at a snazzy polished-stone counter with chrome stools or at trim metal chairs and tables in a restored historic building.

★ **Monet Restaurant**   *(541)482-1339*
downtown at 36 S. Second St.
mind.net/monet
D only. Closed Sun.-Mon.   *Expensive*
Traditional very French cuisine like escargots share the menu with updates like sautéed pork tenderloin with raspberry sauce, plus refined vegetarian dishes and housemade desserts. In the posh dining room, the mood is Monet. Outside, dine in Monet's garden.

★ **Morning Glory**   *(541)488-8636*
downtown at 1149 Siskiyou Blvd.
morninggloryrestaurant.com
B-L.   *Expensive*
Northwestern breakfasts are the specialty of Morning Glory, where dishes like smoked salmon scramble or sourdough blueberry pancakes can be very good. A transformed cottage with a firelit front waiting area and patio dining and a garden contribute to the charm of this popular little breakfast haven.

★ **Munchies**   *(541)488-2967*
  downtown at 59 N. Main St.
  B-L-D.   *Moderate*
For delightful desserts, don't miss Munchies. Displayed in cases
by the entrance, mile-high pies, cakes and assorted cookies are as
good as they look. Breakfast pastries made here are also fine,
along with scrambles and other casual American fare served in a
congenial cellar.

★ **New Sammy's Cowboy Bistro**   *(541)535-2779*
  3 mi. N at 2210 S. Pacific Hwy. - Talent
  D only. Closed Mon.-Wed.   *Very Expensive*
The valley's most unusual dining experience features innovative
American dishes expertly prepared and served in a quirky cottage.
The food has a major following.

  Oak Tree Northwest Restaurant Bar & Grill *(541)488-1434*
  3 mi. SE at 2510 Hwy. 66
  B-L-D.   *Moderate*
Butterhorns and biscuits, and specialties like corned-beef hash,
sweet potato pancakes, or mile-high banana cream pie, are made
here. Comfortable booths are backed by woodsy decor in the coffee
shop. A casual bar and grill with pool tables adjoins.

  Omar's   *(541)482-1281*
  1 mi. SE (on Hwy. 99) at 1380 Siskiyou Blvd.
  L-D. No L Sat. & Sun.   *Moderate*
Omar's is Ashland's oldest continuously operating restaurant
and lounge. Charbroiled steaks, fresh seafood and homemade
desserts have been crowd-pleasers for more than half a century.
The local landmark has two comfortable dining areas and a cozy
lounge.

★ **Pasta Piatti**   *(541)488-5493*
  downtown at 358 E. Main St.
  pastapiatti.com
  L-D.   *Moderate*
Since early 2004, crowds have been flocking the Pasta Piatti for
"New World Italian" cuisine. Outstanding house ciabatta, Oregon
coast blue mussels, and Dungeness crab ravioli are among
creative soups, salads, pastas, artisan-crust whole-wheat flour
pizzas, special house entrees like pan-roasted perch with grilled
artichokes, and dessert like lemon curd or triple espresso gelato.

★ **Peerless Restaurant**   *(541)488-6067*
  just SE at 265 Fourth St.
  peerlesshotel.com
  D only. Closed Sun.-Mon.   *Very Expensive*
The Peerless Restaurant is one of Southern Oregon's best fine
dining experiences. A talented chef dedicated to obtaining peerless

products from local farms and ranches has developed an exciting menu of creative Northwestern cuisine. Creations like Manila clam and asparagus salad, or roast leg of lamb with fiddlehead ferns and a rosemary reduction, and housemade chocolate peanut butter truffle tart are served in a cosmopolitan, simply elegant dining room, and weather permitting, in a garden court.

Standing Stone Brewing Company   *(541)482-2448*
   downtown at 101 Oak St.
   standingstonebrewing.com
   L-D.   *Moderate*
Ashland's first (1997) premium brew pub features breads and desserts made here, along with contemporary American pub grub like buffalo burger, wood-fired pizzas, calzone and some distinctive entrees like alder-plank salmon filet or braised lamb shank. Diners in the pub and back room overlook stainless-steel kettles. Out back is a mountain-view dining deck.

Tabu   *(541)482-3900*
   downtown at 76 N. Pioneer St.
   taburestaurant.com
   L-D.   *Moderate*
Nuevo Latino food includes appropriately spiced fish tacos, gazpacho and other "small plates" that go beyond traditional Spanish or border fare. Cozy, casual dining rooms complement the young upstairs restaurant's distinctive offerings.

★ **Thai Pepper**   *(541)482-8058*
   downtown at 84 N. Main St.
   L-D. L varies seasonally.   *Moderate*
Chicken sate with peanut sauce or tiger shrimp curry with fresh pineapple and spearmint typify diverse classic and innovative Thai dishes offered in a convivial downstairs dining room. Better yet, in good weather, guests can enjoy dining deck's adjoining lush vegetation along Lithia Creek.

The Village Baker   *(541)488-9130*
   downtown at 372 E. Main St.
   B-L.   *Moderate*
A wide assortment of artisan breads is made and displayed along with selected pastries in this to-go bakery with a comfortably funky little eating area by the display cases.

★ **The Wild Goose**   *(541)488-4103*
   3 mi. SE (near I-5) at 2365 Ashland St.
   B-L-D.   *Moderate*
Pastries or buttermilk biscuits made here can be enjoyed with all kinds of scrambles or design-your-own omelets for breakfast. A good selection of all-American fare for lunch and dinner is served in a comfortable coffee shop or a busy bar in back.

★ **The Winchester Inn**   *(541)488-1115*
  downtown at 35 S. Second St.
  winchesterinn.com
  D only. Sun. brunch. Closed Mon.-Tues.   *Expensive*
Contemporary American cuisine is given distinctive stylings in dishes like asparagus-parmesan puffed pastry rolls, Dungeness crab beignets or warm mushroom salad dressed with walnut-lime vinaigrette, along with luscious desserts (some featuring fresh seasonal fruits of the region). A long-established favorite among Ashland's gourmet restaurants now also features a posh wine bar in the lavishly restored Victorian mansion overlooking colorful flower gardens from spring through fall.

LODGINGS

Lodgings are plentiful, including one of America's great concentrations of premium bed-and-breakfast inns. Nearby Medford is the source for inexpensive highway-front motels. High season is late spring to early fall. Winter rates are often reduced as much as 30%.

★ **A Midsummer's Dream**   *(541)552-0605*
  1 mi. SE at 496 Beach St. - 97520
  amidsummer.com
  5 units   *(877)376-8800*   *Expensive-Very Expensive*
An elegant Victorian home in a quiet garden district was (in 2001) skillfully transformed into a delightfully romantic bed-and-breakfast. Full breakfast is complimentary. Each beautifully furnished suite has a glass-block shower, two-person whirlpool, gas fireplace, high-tech extras and a king bed.
  "Othello"–unique see-through gas fireplace
    in view of two-person whirlpool.
  "Romeo"–cottage suite with refrigerator and
    complimentary snacks, corner two-person whirlpool.
  "Desdemona"–spacious, walk-in glass-block shower,
    in-bath sauna, two-person whirlpool.

★ **Ashland Creek Inn**   *(541)482-3315*
  downtown at 70 Water St. - 97520
  ashlandcreekinn.com
  7 units   *Expensive-Very Expensive*
Ashland Creek Inn has a peerless park-like setting next to tranquil Lithia Creek. The Plaza and theaters are a short stroll from the tree-shaded little bed-and-breakfast. A multicourse gourmet breakfast is complimentary. Each spacious unit is beautifully furnished with an eclectic mix of international art and antiques and has a kitchen, private deck by the creek, private bath, and queen or king bed.

★ **Ashland Springs Hotel**   *(541)488-1700*
downtown at 212 E. Main St. - 97520
ashlandspringshotel.com
70 units   *(888)795-4545*   *Expensive-Very Expensive*
The Ashland Springs Hotel is the premier lodging landmark in
the heart of town. The fully restored nine-story "skyscraper"
(circa 1925) is now a tasteful small hotel with a dramatic lobby, a
garden courtyard, a (nearby) fitness center and (fee) spa, and
Lark's (see listing). Full breakfast is complimentary. Well-
furnished rooms range from compact to spacious and have all
contemporary facilities including mini-refrigerators and two
double, queen or king beds. Most have fine views of town and
surrounding hills and mountains.

Bard's Inn - Best Western   *(541)482-0049*
downtown at 132 N. Main St. - 97520
bardsinn.com
89 units   *(800)528-1234*   *Moderate-Expensive*
Theaters are a pleasant stroll from this contemporary motel with
a pool and whirlpool. Expanded Continental breakfast is available
in the adjacent cafe/lounge. Each pleasant room is well furnished
and has two queens or king bed. Two have an in-room whirlpool.

Cedarwood Inn   *(541)488-2000*
2 mi. SE (on Hwy. 99) at 1801 Siskiyou Blvd. - 97520
brodeur-inns.com
58 units   *(800)547-4141*   *Moderate-Expensive*
Amenities in this long-established modern motel include an
outdoor pool, covered soaking pool, steam room and sauna. Each
spacious, comfortably furnished room has a queen or king bed.
Kitchens are available.

Coolidge House   *(541)482-4721*
just N at 137 N. Main St. - 97520
coolidgehouse.com
6 units   *(800)655-5522*   *Moderate-Expensive*
A handsome Victorian home (circa 1875), on the National Historic
Register, has been skillfully transformed into a gracious bed-and-
breakfast amid colorful gardens. Full breakfast is complimentary.
Each room is beautifully furnished and has a queen or king bed.
Two also have a gas fireplace and whirlpool bath.

★ **Country Willows B & B Inn**   *(541)488-1590*
2 mi. SE at 1313 Clay St. - 97520
willowsinn.com
9 units   *(800)945-5697*   *Expensive-Very Expensive*
Country Willows Bed-and-Breakfast Inn is enchanting. A
Victorian farmhouse, a cottage and barn on a peaceful hillside
share luxuriant grounds with a view pool, whirlpool, and forest

trails. Full gourmet breakfast and bicycles are complimentary. Each beautifully furnished room has a private bath and extra amenities, serene Northwest decor touches, garden or mountain views, and queen or king bed.

"Pine Ridge Suite"–extra large, private patio, two-person whirlpool, two-person open shower, gas fireplace in view of king bed.
"Hayloft Suite"–gas fireplace in living room, private
deck, large whirlpool and shower, upstairs king bed.

Knights Inn Motel   *(541)482-5111*
3 mi. SE (near I-5) at 2359 Hwy. 66 - 97520
brodeur-inns.com
40 units   *(800)547-4566*   *Moderate*
Knights Inn offers a choice of single or two-level motel rooms around a pool and whirlpool (the first-rate **Wild Goose** cafe adjoins). Each nicely furnished room has a microwave and refrigerator and a choice of two queen or king bed.

★ **Lithia Springs Resort & Gardens**   *(541)482-7128*
2 mi. N at 2165 W. Jackson Rd. - 97520
ashlandinn.com
24 units   *(800)482-7128*   *Moderate-Expensive*
Lithia Springs Resort & Gardens is one of the Pacific Northwest's most romantic getaways. The gracious contemporary inn is on spectacularly landscaped grounds including ponds and a stream. Tucked away at the base of a forested hillside, the site includes a natural warm spring that is the keystone for the sublime full-service **Waterstone Mineral Springs Spa** (see listing). A gourmet breakfast, local wine and treats are complimentary, and limited food service and drinks are available in the stylish lounge. Each estate room, cottage, or suite is individually beautifully furnished and has a queen or king bed. Almost all feature a refrigerator and an in-room two-person whirlpool with the added benefits of on-site mineral spring water.

"The Water Tower"–very private, romantic large heart-shaped
whirlpool, private balcony with garden view, king bed.

Morical House Garden Inn   *(541)482-2254*
1 mi. N at 668 N. Main St. - 97520
garden-inn.com
8 units   *(800)208-0960*   *Expensive*
An 1880s farmhouse has been transformed into a stylish bed-and-breakfast inn amid tranquil, luxuriant gardens. Full breakfast and afternoon refreshments are complimentary. Each beautifully furnished room has a private bath, understated elegance including some quality Victorian appointments, and queen or king bed.

#9–private view deck, two-person corner whirlpool
and open shower, king bed.

24

★ **Mt. Ashland Inn**   *(541)482-8707*
  16 mi. S at 550 Mt. Ashland Rd. - 97520
  mtashlandinn.com
  5 units   *(800)830-8707*   *Expensive*
This four-story log inn is nestled in the pines near the Mt. Ashland Ski Area. Hearty breakfast, afternoon beverages and cookies are complimentary as are the sauna and whirlpool. Cedar log interiors, handicrafts, antiques, and mountain views distinguish each well-furnished room. There are no phones or TVs, but each cozy room has a large private whirlpool tub with a view, and a gas fireplace in view of a queen or king bed.
  "Sky Lakes Wilderness Suite"–view of Mt. Shasta, two-person
    whirlpool, river-rock gas fireplace in view of king bed.

★ **The Peerless Hotel**   *(541)488-1082*
  just SE at 243 Fourth St. - 97520
  peerlesshotel.com
  6 units   *(800)460-8758*   *Expensive-Very Expensive*
A small hotel, built in 1900, has been lovingly restored and is now on the National Historic Register. Full breakfast in the outstanding dining room (see listing) and evening sherry are complimentary. Each room is beautifully furnished with an eclectic mixture of antiques, a private bath, and queen bed.
  "Suite 7"–panoramic town/mountain view, small private
    balcony, two-person whirlpool, four-poster queen bed.
  "Suite 3"–sitting room with gas wood stove, his-and-hers
    clawfoot tubs, antique queen bed.

★ **Plaza Inn & Suites at Ashland Creek**   *(541)488-8900*
  downtown at 98 Central Av. - 97520
  plazainnashland.com
  91 units   *(888)488-0358*   *Expensive*
The Plaza and theaters are a short stroll from this delightful contemporary small hotel overlooking Ashland Creek. A view whirlpool, exercise room, expanded Continental breakfast and gourmet evening treats and beverages are complimentary. Each beautifully furnished unit has all contemporary amenities plus extras, a microwave, refrigerator, and queen or king bed.
  "Spa King" (6 of these)–spacious, creekside views,
    in-bath two-person whirlpool, two queens or king bed.
  "Fireplace King" (2 of these)–spacious, mountain views,
    remote-control gas fireplace in view of king bed.

Relax Inn   *(541)482-4423*
  3 mi. SE (by I-5) at 535 Clover Lane - 97520
  20 units   *(888)672-5290*   *Low*
This shaped-up single-level older motel by the freeway has a small pool. Each compact, simply furnished room has a queen bed.

★ **Romeo Inn**   *(541)488-0884*
   just S at 295 Idaho St. - 97520
   romeoinn.com
   6 units   *(800)915-8899*   *Expensive*
A charming Cape Cod-style house is now a grand bed-and-breakfast inn set amid noble trees on an expansive lawn. Luxuriant grounds with an English garden theme also include a tranquil pool and whirlpool. A full gourmet breakfast plus snacks and refreshments later are complimentary. Each spacious room is beautifully furnished with a blend of antiques and traditional decor, a private bath, all contemporary amenities plus extras, and a king bed.
   "Stratford Suite"–mountain views, in-room two-person
      whirlpool, gas fireplace.
   "Cambridge Suite"–private garden, gas fireplace,
      two-person shower.

★ **The Winchester Inn**   *(541)488-1113*
   downtown at 35 S. Second St. - 97520
   winchesterinn.com
   19 units   *(800)972-4991*   *Expensive-Very Expensive*
Spectacular tiered gardens distinguish this bed-and-breakfast inn built around a restored Victorian on the National Register. Amenities include an elegant restaurant (see listing), a plush recently added wine bar featuring tasting flights of regional wines, and a gift shop. A full breakfast, beverages, daily treats and fresh flowers are complimentary. Authentic period decor blends with contemporary conveniences, and each beautifully furnished room has a queen or king bed.
   "Fordyce Suite"–overlooks garden, wet bar/refrigerator,
      two-person whirlpool in marble bath, gas fireplace, king bed.
   "Eleanor Rose Suite"–spacious, refrigerator, in-bath
      two-person whirlpool, gas fireplace, king bed.
   "Barbara Howard Suite"–sitting area with gas fireplace, in-
      bath two-person whirlpool and two-person shower, king bed.

★ **Windmill Inn & Suites of Ashland**   *(541)482-8310*
   3 mi. SE (near I-5) at 2525 Ashland St. - 97520
   windmillinns.com
   230 units   *(800)547-4747*   *Expensive*
Ashland's biggest lodging is a contemporary three-story complex with a large pool and whirlpool in a landscaped courtyard, two tennis courts, jogging path, fitness room, and complimentary bicycles and expanded Continental breakfast. Many of the spacious, well-furnished rooms have a private view balcony or patio, microwave and refrigerator, and two doubles, queen or king bed.

Astoria

Astoria is the cradle of civilization in the Pacific Northwest. The town has prospered from a dramatic location between high forested hills and the mighty Columbia River near its outlet to the Pacific Ocean. In this favored locale, it's not surprising that this was once the "salmon canning capital of the world." The lively downtown still meets the needs (from bawdy and basic to upscale) of mariners and loggers as well as visitors.

Lewis and Clark wrote about the very wet winter of 1805-6 at the nearby site of Fort Clatsop. The oldest permanent American settlement west of the Rocky Mountains dates back to the erection of Fort Astoria in 1811. John Jacob Astor chose this townsite as the westernmost of his fur trading posts extending back to St. Louis. Fishing, canning, and maritime activities were Astoria's most important industries, along with logging, for well over a century. The completion of the Astoria Column in 1926 with its observation deck overlooking the Columbia River, the waterfront's striking Maritime Museum in 1962, and the graceful bridge to Washington in 1966, each reinforced Astoria's growing role as a travel destination.

Today, Astoria is endowed with one of Oregon's greatest collections of buildings on the National Historic Register. Many Victorian structures now house museums, restaurants and lodgings. Recent complete restoration and upgrade of the Hotel Elliott heralds the emergence of upscale tourism while the history, architecture, natural grandeur, and maritime industries continue as key ingredients to Astoria's bright future.

Astoria

WEATHER PROFILE

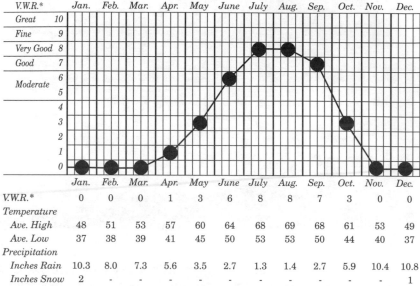

V.W.R.*	Jan.	Feb.	Mar.	Apr.	May	June	July	Aug.	Sep.	Oct.	Nov.	Dec.
V.W.R.*	0	0	0	1	3	6	8	8	7	3	0	0
Temperature												
Ave. High	48	51	53	57	60	64	68	69	68	61	53	49
Ave. Low	37	38	39	41	45	50	53	53	50	44	40	37
Precipitation												
Inches Rain	10.3	8.0	7.3	5.6	3.5	2.7	1.3	1.4	2.7	5.9	10.4	10.8
Inches Snow	2	-	-	-	-	-	-	-	-	-	-	1

* V.W.R. = Vokac Weather Rating: probability of mild (warm & dry) weather on any given day.

BASIC INFORMATION

Population: *9,813*
Elevation: *18 feet*
Location: *96 miles Northwest of Portland*
Airport (*regularly scheduled flights): Portland - 100 miles*

Astoria-Warrenton Chamber of Commerce   (503)325-6311
  just W at 111 West Marine Dr. (Box 176) - 97103   (800)875-6807
  oldoregon.com

ATTRACTIONS

★ **Astoria Aquatic Center**   *(503)325-7027*
   downtown at 1997 Marine Dr.
   swimastoria.com
Astoria Aquatic Center is one of the finest aquatic centers in any town in America. Features include a 25-meter lap pool, a recreation pool with an unusual sprinkler, hot tubs, a 100-foot open waterslide, and a small "lazy river," all under one roof. Travelers are welcome to enjoy all of the facilities with a one-day pass.

★ **Astoria Bridge**
   just NW on Hwy. 101
Oregon is connected to Washington via this 4.1 mile bridge across the mouth of the Columbia River. Completed in 1966, the 1,232-foot-long main span is the longest "continuous truss" in the world. It provides a spectacular "Erector Set" backdrop to downtown Astoria.

★ **Astoria Column**   *(503)325-2963*
   1 mi. SE
   astoria-usa.com
Crowning Coxcomb Hill, 600 feet above the Columbia River, is a 125-foot-high monolith (circa 1926) that commemorates the exploration and settlement of the area. The 360° view of the nearby ocean, river and mountains from the encircling observation platform at the top (reached by 164 steps in a spiral staircase) is breathtaking–on a clear day.

★ **Astoria Waterfront Trolley**   *(503)325-6311*
   downtown at 1095 Duane St.
   old300.org
A painstakingly restored 1913 streetcar travels on steel rails for four miles along Astoria's historic waterfront in summer, and on fall weekends. Guided and narrated tours have made this a very popular way to learn about the picturesque town and the adjoining Columbia River.

Bicycling
Astoria is located on the Bicentennial Trail which extends across the continent to Williamsburg, Virginia. Two local loops southeast of Astoria (Youngs River Falls and Walluski Loop) are 18 and 88 miles, respectively. Nearby Fort Stevens State Park maintains more than seven miles of paved scenic bicycle trails near the ocean. For information, limited rentals, sales and service, contact:
   Bikes & Beyond   *(503)325-2961*
   downtown at 1089 Marine Dr.
   bikesandbeyond.com

Boat Ride
Columbia River Discovery Tours *(503)325-6700 (866)717-1206*
just W at 354 Industry (West End Marina)
Guests can enjoy a two-hour fully narrated river cruise along the downtown waterfront aboard the charter vessel "Shamrock." Longer trips of three hours are also scheduled subject to weather and tide conditions.

★ **Columbia River Maritime Museum**   *(503)325-2323*
downtown at 1792 Marine Dr.
crmm.org
A large post-modern complex on the waterfront is an award-winning maritime showcase with panoramic windows overlooking the vast river. Displays related to the history of the Columbia River and the Northwest include a wide range of artifacts, photos, and ship models, plus interactive and hands-on exhibits. A tour of the lightship Columbia, the last sea-going lighthouse on the West Coast, is a highlight. Open daily 9:30-5.

★ *Fishing Charters*
The Columbia River mouth has long been famous as one of the major sport fisheries in the Northwest. Salmon still reign as the ultimate catch—up to 60 pounds—but steelhead, sturgeon and tuna are also popular. Numerous guides operate morning, afternoon and evening fishing charters on boats carrying from six to twenty-four passengers. Among the largest and best in the area are:
ABC-Astoria's Best Charters *(503)338-6700 (866)914-6700*
astoriasbestcharters.com
Charlton Deep Sea Fishing   *(503)861-2429*
ifish.net
Pacific Salmon Charters   *(360)642-3466*   *(800)831-2695*
pacificsalmoncharters.com

★ **Flavel House Museum**   *(503)325-2203*
downtown at 441 8th St.
An elegant 1885 Queen Anne-style mansion has been restored with elaborate displays of furnishings and artifacts of the period. Expansive grounds are beautifully landscaped and include original trees dating from the 1880s, like a towering sequoia. The carriage house serves as the visitor center and includes a notable collection of regional books and gifts.

Food Specialties
Bruski's Dock   *(503)325-2470*
downtown at 80 11th St.
All sorts of fresh and canned crustaceans and fish can be purchased in this tiny takeout with a couple of picnic tables in front overlooking the colorful nautical scene.

★ **Josephson's**   *(503)325-2190   (800)772-3474*
just W at 106 Marine Dr.
josephsons.com
Josephson's maple-smoked salmon is some of the best smoked fish
in America. Alderwood, maple, and other hardwoods are used for
gourmet-processed Pacific Northwest chinook and coho salmon.
Samples are generously offered. One of Oregon's oldest and finest
commercial smokehouses also sells other seasonally available fish
and shellfish by the pound and in gift packs for shipment
worldwide.
Fort Astoria   *(503)325-6311*
downtown at Exchange & 15th Sts.
This small park has a re-creation of a corner of the 1811 fort–the
first permanent American outpost west of the Mississippi River.
★ **Fort Clatsop National Memorial**   *(503)861-2471*
6 mi. S near Hwy. 101
The grounds showcase a log replica of the fort built by Lewis and
Clark during the winter of 1805-6. There is also a visitor
center/museum and trails to the park's rain forest and wetlands.
During the summer, a living history program portrays the
equipment, clothing and lifestyle of the expedition.
★ **Fort Stevens State Park**   *(503)861-2000   (800)551-6949*
12 mi. W via Hwy. 101 & Fort Stevens Hwy.
visitfortstevens.com
Fort Stevens was built on Oregon's northwestern tip (where the
Columbia River empties into the Pacific Ocean) to guard against
a Confederate attack–that never came. But, in World War II, Fort
Stevens became the only U.S. mainland fort to come under enemy
fire (Japanese) since 1812. The wreck of the Peter Iredale (a
century-old English four-masted sailing vessel) protrudes from
the sandy beach near a popular campground. In addition to the
Fort Stevens Museum, there are numerous historical buildings
(including an ocean-view tower at the jetty). The extensive,
relatively flat grounds also include miles of sandy beaches and
nine miles of bike paths, a full-service campground and picnic
sites. Viewing platforms at the South Jetty give visitors a fine
view of ocean-going ships "navigating the bar" where frequent
enormous swells can complicate passage between the river and
the ocean.
Shively Park
1 mi. SE via 15th St. & Williamsport Rd.
Shively Park is a luxuriant stand of old-growth hundreds-of-years-
old cedars preserved in a semi-wilderness park with hiking trails
into luxuriant woodlands and fern grottoes that belie the
surrounding city.

RESTAURANTS

★ **Baked Alaska**   *(503)325-7414*
  downtown at 1 12th St.
  bakedak.com
  L-D.   *Expensive*
For the best panoramic river view in Astoria, Baked Alaska is the
place to dine. Traditional and creative Northwestern cuisine is
presented on a wide-ranging a la carte menu. Dishes like Alaskan
king crab legs with drawn thyme butter or ginger duck legs
compete with fine Columbia River panoramas from the
restaurant's location on the water.

Bowpicker Fish & Chips   *(503)325-3731*
  downtown at corner of 17th & Duane Sts.
  L only.   *Moderate*
A jaunty little Columbia River gill net boat has been transformed
into the cutest tuna fish 'n chips walk-up in the region. Eat here
at a few casual picnic tables overlooking the nearby nautical
scene, or to go.

Cafe Uniontown   *(503)325-8708*
  just W at 218 W. Marine Dr.
  D only.   *Moderate*
Smoked salmon clam chowder can accompany all entrees
including pan-fried local oysters in two modish dining rooms with
an adjoining bar. Live piano music happens most nights.

Cannery Cafe (Gunderson's)   *(503)325-8642*
  downtown at 1 6th St.
  cannerycafe.com
  B-L-D.   *Moderate*
For breakfast with a view, the Cannery Cafe is the place. A short
menu of scrambles and pancakes is served over the water with an
outlook to the Columbia River bridge. At other meals, regional
Northwestern seafoods are featured in a century-old cannery
transformed into casual wood-toned dining areas with a
waterfront view.

★ **Columbian Cafe**   *(503)325-2233*
  downtown at 1114 Marine Dr.
  B-L-D. No D Sun.-Tues.   *Moderate*
Astoria's most surprising dining adventure is at Columbian Cafe.
Fresh seasonal Northwestern ingredients are prepared before
your eyes at a truly tiny kitchen at the end of a counter with nine
stools and three solid wood booths. Designer housemade jellies
(sold here by the jar) and salsa and desserts like key lime cake or
chipotle espresso brownie all make this cozy cramped cafe a
culinary gem worth finding. A small spillover room adjoins.

★ **Lindstrom's Danish Maid Bakery**   *(503)325-3657*
   downtown at 1132 Commercial St.
   B-L. Closed Sun.   *Low*
A remarkably diverse selection of pastries, donuts, cookies, bars
and desserts includes some notable specialties like "apple sand
dollar." There are a few booths to enjoy your treats with coffee
here, or to go.

Pier 11 Feed Store Restaurant & Lounge   *(503)325-0279*
   downtown at 77 11th St.
   L-D.   *Moderate*
A broad selection of traditional Northwestern seafoods is featured
and served as a complement to the outstanding window-wall
panorama of the Columbia River. Cecil the 18-foot Wood-Carved
Sea Serpent oversees casual dining rooms and a big wood-trim
lounge built on pilings over the water.

★ **The Schooner 12th Street Bistro**   *(503)325-7882*
   downtown at 360 12th St.
   B-L-D.   *Moderate*
This classy bistro opened in 2003 with an orientation toward
upscale Northwestern fare ranging from cornflake-encrusted
french toast with strawberries or hazelnut waffle with blueberry
sauce to buffalo meatloaf. Polished wood decor in the spiffy dining
areas and bar are complemented by an intimate view of the
landmark Hotel Elliott.

Ship Inn   *(503)325-0033*
   just W at 1 2nd St.
   L-D.   *Moderate*
English-style specialties like cod fish and chips, bangers and
mash, and shepherd's pie are served amid casual surroundings
with a picture-window view of the Columbia River.

★ **Silver Salmon Grille**   *(503)338-6640*
   downtown at 1105 Commercial St.
   silversalmongrille.com
   L-D.   *Moderate*
The Silver Salmon Grille presents the premier special-occasion
dining experience in Astoria. Northwestern gourmet specialties
from sea and land are showcased in a wealth of traditional and
creative dishes like smoked salmon crepes with lobster sauce
finished with swiss cheese; Dungeness crab and provolone cakes;
five salmon specialties plus salmon filet your way–baked, broiled,
blackened or poached. Housemade desserts are similarly expertly
prepared and delicious–like the flamboyant, authentic bananas
foster! The dining rooms and lounge reflect easygoing sophistication with dramatic whimsical wall murals and hangings in
dining areas and a spectacular hardwood backbar in the lounge.

★ **T. Paul's Urban Cafe**   *(503)338-5133*
  downtown at 1119 Commercial St.
  tpaulsurbancafe.com
  L-D. No D Sun.   *Moderate*
Fun food for adults is featured at T. Paul's Urban Cafe. Whether
you select one of the many kinds of quesadillas or gourmet salads,
designer pastas or sandwiches, you are assured of carefully
prepared distinctive dishes. This is also true of housemade
desserts like Shaker whole lemon pie. A cozy congestion of tables
around a little bar/service area and a room in back with
aquariums and furniture are as appealingly eclectic as the meals.

The Wet Dog Cafe   *(503)325-6975*
  downtown at 144 11th St.
  L-D.   *Moderate*
Handcrafted brews made in kettles on display are served in
samplers or support for assorted pub grub in a big, casual dining
room. There is occasional live entertainment and a game room.

LODGINGS

Accommodations in one of the West's great town sites with
spectacular views of the Columbia River, its mouth, and high
forested hills range from a luxurious restored landmark hotel
through upscale riverfront motels to delightful bed-and-breakfast
inns in transformed Victorian mansions. Rates are reduced 20%
or more from fall through spring in many places.

Astoria Dunes   *(503)325-7111*
  1 mi. W at 288 W. Marine Dr. - 97103
  58 units   *(800)441-3319*   *Moderate-Expensive*
This small modern motel has an indoor pool and whirlpool. Some
rooms have a fine view of the bridge and Columbia River. All of
the rooms are comfortably furnished and have either a queen or
king bed. Request king bed with river/bridge view.

★ **Benjamin Young Inn**   *(503)325-6172*
  2 mi. E at 3652 Duane St. - 97103
  benjaminyounginn.com
  5 units   *(800)201-1286*   *Moderate-Expensive*
High on a hill overlooking Astoria and the river, the Benjamin
Young Inn is a living history museum in one of Astoria's most
spectacular mansions. The handsome 1888 residence was
skillfully transformed into a charming bed-and-breakfast. Full
gourmet breakfast is served in an elegant dining room with a
town/mountain view. Each beautifully furnished room has all
contemporary amenities plus a private bath and queen or king bed.

  "Honeymoon Suite"–spacious, second floor, five-sided cupola
with fine views of Columbia River, canopy queen bed.

Clementine's Bed & Breakfast   *(503)325-2005*
downtown at 847 Exchange St. - 97103
clementines-bb.com
7 units   *(800)521-6801*   Moderate-Expensive
An 1888 home has been converted in a bed-and-breakfast.
Breakfast is complimentary. Rooms are nicely furnished with
antiques and one or two queen beds.
    "Clementine's Suite," "Room at the Top"–second
       floor, view over town to Columbia River, two queen beds.
    "Balcony Room"–second floor, private balcony with
       town/Columbia River view, queen bed.
★ **Comfort Suites Columbia River**   *(503)325-2000*
2 mi. E at 3420 Lief Erikson Dr. - 97103
75 units   *(800)424-6423*   *Expensive*
This post-millennium motor lodge has a choice location by the
Columbia River. Amenities include an indoor pool, whirlpool,
sauna and exercise room, plus an expanded Continental
breakfast. All of the well-furnished units have a microwave and
refrigerator and queen, two queens or a king bed. Many have
outstanding views of the river.
Crest Motel   *(503)325-3141*
3 mi. E at 5366 Lief Erikson Dr. - 97103
crest-motel.com
40 units   *(800)421-3141*   Moderate-Expensive
Crowning a bluff hundreds of feet above the Columbia is a
handsome little motel with a hot tub in a gazebo with a grand
river panorama. Each well-furnished room has a refrigerator and
microwave, one or two queens or a king bed, and many have a fine
river view.
    #23,#24–spacious, semi-private balcony with
       superb town and river views, king bed.
★ **Holiday Inn Express Hotel & Suites - Astoria** *(503)898-6222*
1 mi. W at 204 W. Marine Dr. - 97103
astoriahie.com
78 units   *(888)898-6222*   *Expensive*
One of Holiday Inn Express's best of this chain opened in 2004 by
the Columbia River in the shadow of the four-mile suspension
bridge. Amenities of the four-story complex include an indoor
pool, whirlpool, exercise room, game room and gift shop, plus
expanded Continental breakfast. Each of the well-furnished
rooms has a refrigerator and microwave, and one or two queens
or a king bed.
    #412,#414,#420,#312,#314,#320,#212,#214,#220–two-
       person whirlpool by picture window overlooking bridge/
       river, corner gas fireplace, fine river view from king bed.

★ **Hotel Elliott** *(503)325-2222*
   downtown at 357 12th St. - 97103
   hotelelliott.com
   32 units   *(877)378-1924*   *Expensive-Very Expensive*
The Hotel Elliott is one of America's most delightful hotel landmarks. The 1924 five-story building was thoroughly renovated and upgraded recently. Guests have access to the Roof Garden–with panoramic views of downtown, hillside neighborhoods, the bridge and river. The interior is full of special embellishments that showcase the historic significance of Astoria's foremost lodging and the best of contemporary amenities. Each room is luxuriously furnished, including handcrafted cabinetry, fixtures and art objects by notable Northwestern artists and craftsmen. Each queen or king featherbed uses 440-count Egyptian sheets and goose down pillows. Heated polished stone floors in the bathroom further distinguish each guest room. Some also have spun-glass wet bar sinks. An expanded Continental breakfast at **The Schooner** (see listing) is included. Many of the rooms have fine views of the bridge across the Columbia River.
   #504,#502–large room with raised gas fireplace,
      spectacular town/bridge/river view, large bathroom
      with polished marble heated floor, two-head walk-in
      shower, raised two-person whirlpool with grand river and
      bridge view and remote-control window shade, king bed.

Lincoln Inn - Best Western   *(503)325-2205*
   2 mi. W (on Hwy. 101) at 555 Hamburg Av. - 97103
   bestwestern.com
   75 units   *(800)621-0641*   *Expensive*
This contemporary four-story motel overlooking the Columbia River has an indoor pool, whirlpool and sauna, plus a full hot breakfast bar. Each well-furnished room has a microwave and refrigerator and one or two queen or king bed. Most have a good river view.
   #336,#236–spacious, fine river view, in-room
      two-person whirlpool, king bed.

Red Lion Inn   *(503)325-7373*
   2 mi. W at 400 Industry St. - 97103
   redlion.com/astoria
   124 units   *(800)733-5466*   *Expensive*
The marina and Columbia River adjoin this contemporary two-story motor hotel in the shadow of the big bridge. The complex includes a newly refurbished restaurant and lounge. Each well-furnished room has a microwave and refrigerator among extra amenities, and a choice of two queens or a king bed.

★ **Rose River Inn Bed & Breakfast**   *(503)325-7175*
  downtown at 1510 Franklin Av. - 97103
  roseriverinn.com
  4 units   *(888)876-0028*   *Moderate-Expensive*
The Rose River Inn is the most romantic bed-and-breakfast in
Astoria. It is on a gentle slope an easy stroll above downtown.
Surrounded by lovely gardens, the skillfully transformed 1912
home has rooms ideally suited for adult getaways. Full gourmet
breakfast is complimentary. Most of the beautifully furnished
rooms have a queen bed.
  "River Suite"–clawfoot tub, Finnish sauna, gas fireplace,
    fine Columbia River view from sun porch and queen bed.
  "Inspiration Suite"–two bedrooms, gas fireplace,
    in-bath clawfoot slipper tub with Columbia River
    view, double and king beds.
  "Rose Room"–cozy, gas fireplace, clawfoot
    slipper tub, canopy queen bed.

★ **Rosebriar Hotel**   *(503)325-7427*
  downtown at 636 14th St. - 97103
  rosebriar.net
  11 units   *(800)487-0224*   *Moderate-Very Expensive*
The Rosebriar Hotel is in a quiet upslope location affording views
of the Columbia and easy walking access to the heart of town. The
century-old hotel, once a convent, now has the ambiance of a bed-
and-breakfast with a light breakfast served in the dining room
each morning to guests, plus afternoon gourmet cookies. All of the
well-furnished rooms have contemporary conveniences including
private baths and double or queen bed. Several have special
features like fine river views, fireplace and spa.
  "Columbia"–two-person whirlpool in bath, corner gas
    fireplace, fine town/river view from queen bed.
  "Captain's Suite"–extra-large, in-room two-person
    whirlpool with river view, gas fireplace, microwave,
    refrigerator, queen bed.
  "Lewis & Clark"–good river view from queen bed.

Uppertown Bed & Breakfast   *(503)325-8306*
  2 mi. E at 3738 Franklin St. - 97103
  uppertownbandb.com
  2 units   *Moderate-Expensive*
A house on a hill overlooking the Columbia River now serves as
a bed-and-breakfast. Full breakfast is complimentary. Each
comfortably furnished unit has a private bath, a view of the town
and river, and a queen bed.
  "Columbia River Suite"–river view from full kitchen and deck.

Baker City

Baker City is a latter-day bonanza of "Old West" history and scenery. Situated along the Oregon Trail, it is a testament to why the cross-country trek was worth the walk. The idyllically situated townsite lies in a broad valley near pine-shrouded mountains. A relatively mild four-season climate supports ranching, farming, and abundant year-round recreation.

Intrepid transcontinental pioneers between 1841 and 1869, lured by the beauty and the bounty of the promised land, walked right past the townsite on the Oregon Trail as they neared their intended destination in the Willamette Valley. In 1861, gold was discovered in a nearby gulch. Thanks to water for a millsite, Baker City became the queen of the mines, and diversified its economy with trade, lumber, and cattle. The town prospered through the 19th century in spite of major fires. But, by the 1970s, "modernization" attempts plastered over much original architecture, and genteel decay had set in.

Baker City once again embraces its historic past, and venerable buildings have regained their luster, many restored to their glory days. Renovation and enhancement of the Geiser Grand Hotel, the region's most distinguished landmark, is the capstone. The town's evolving role as a major travel destination is further enhanced by a bonanza of recreation opportunities in the mountains and lakes around town. Today, Baker City's place on the Oregon Trail is celebrated by the National Historic Oregon Trail Interpretive Center–one of the most soul-stirring museums in America.

WEATHER PROFILE

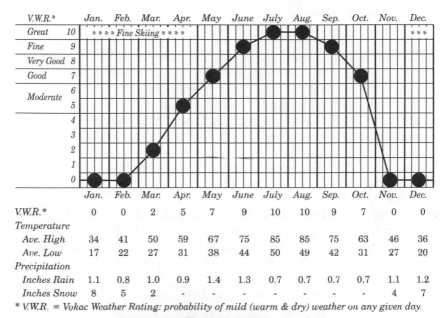

V.W.R.*	Jan.	Feb.	Mar.	Apr.	May	June	July	Aug.	Sep.	Oct.	Nov.	Dec.
V.W.R.*	0	0	2	5	7	9	10	10	9	7	0	0
Temperature												
Ave. High	34	41	50	59	67	75	85	85	75	63	46	36
Ave. Low	17	22	27	31	38	44	50	49	42	31	27	20
Precipitation												
Inches Rain	1.1	0.8	1.0	0.9	1.4	1.3	0.7	0.7	0.7	0.7	1.1	1.2
Inches Snow	8	5	2	-	-	-	-	-	-	-	4	7

* V.W.R. = Vokac Weather Rating: probability of mild (warm & dry) weather on any given day.

BASIC INFORMATION

Population: 9,860
Elevation: 3,449 feet
Location: 304 miles East of Portland
Airport (regularly scheduled flights): Pendleton - 97 miles

Baker City, Oregon Chamber of Commerce   (541)523-5855
   downtown at 490 Campbell St. - 97814   (800)523-1235
   baker-chamber.com
Baker County Unlimited   (541)523-5855   (800)523-1235
   downtown at 490 Campbell St. - 97814
   visitbaker.com

ATTRACTIONS

★ **Anthony Lakes**
34 mi. NW via Elkhorn Scenic Byway
anthonylakes.com
One of the most picturesque spots in Oregon is the shoreline of
Anthony Lake backed by jagged rockbound peaks of the Elkhorn
range. A trail leads through a luxuriant pine forest surrounding
the lake, and other trails extend to the peaks beyond. A full-
service campground is in the pines near the lake and there are
both sunny and pine-shaded picnic sites overlooking the
spectacular backdrop. A boat ramp is available for small boats.
Anthony Lakes Ski area (see listing) is less than a mile away.

★ **Downtown**   *(541)523-5442*
downtown
One of the West's best collections of Victorian main street
buildings has been included on the National Register of Historic
Places since 1978. Many, like the landmark Geiser Grand Hotel,
still serve their original functions. In recent years the entire
central business district has been greatly enhanced by a wealth of
street trees, flowers, benches and distinctive lighting, and the
District is being integrated via improved pedestrian access with
the naturally picturesque little nearby Powder River.

Haines   *(541)856-3366*
10 mi. NW on US 30 - Haines
hainesoregon.com
Haines is a tiny historic village by a railroad that stopped serving
it in 1962. The tracks paralleled a linear park with restored
pioneer buildings and related artifacts backed by a panoramic
view of a spectacular mountain range. In town is a museum, and
the **Haines Steak House** (D only. Closed Tues.–Moderate,
(541)856-3639) is a long-established landmark for steak dinners
amid Old West decor. Some of the few remaining buildings house
specialty shops.

Crossroads Carnegie Arts & Cultural Center *(541)523-5369*
downtown at 1901 Main St.
crossroads-arts.org
The impressive Carnegie Library building is becoming the
permanent home for performance and visual arts of all kinds in
Baker City. Currently, the gallery showcases the work of local and
regional artists. A variety of events and classes are also part of the
evolving Center's schedule. Open Tues.-Sat. noon-4 p.m.

★ **National Hist. Oregon Trail Interpretive Ctr.** *(541)523-1843*
   7 mi. E at 22267 Hwy. 86
   http://oregontrail.blm.gov/
   If you have time for only one major stop in the Baker City area, it
   should be the National Historic Oregon Trail Interpretive Center.
   Cantilevered out over the brim of a sagebrush-covered hill
   hundreds of feet above the broad Baker Valley floor is an
   expansive multi-room showcase that thoroughly explains the
   significance of the Oregon Trail as America's most famous
   emigration route and as a source of near-mystic pride for all those
   living in the West today who had ancestors who made the journey
   during the epic treks between the 1830s and 1860s. Detailed
   exhibits highlight the vehicles, livestock, provisions, clothing and
   wildlife of that place and time. The dramatic building includes
   clerestory picture-window views linking the exhibits to the
   cultivated valley and spectacular unchanged mountains beyond.
   Gently etched into the sagebrush swales far below the museum
   are traces of the original trail as it came over a rise and began a
   gradual descent in the valley. Take extra time for the audiovisual
   presentations that, in song and narration, dramatize this
   monumental adventure. There is an excellent museum store with
   a wealth of books, maps and related materials. Open daily 9-4
   (until 6 p.m. April through October).
★ **Oregon Trail Regional Museum**   *(541)523-9308*
   just E at 2480 Grove St.
   An imposing brick building across from the town park that once
   served as the biggest and best natatorium in Eastern Oregon was
   transformed in 1979 into a museum. Collections include a stellar
   display of crystals, fossils and minerals from the region and
   beyond, and a wealth of artifacts depicting the cultural evolution
   of the Baker City area from earliest times. Open 9-5 daily from
   late March through October.
★ *River Running*
   Hells Canyon Adventures   *(541)785-3352*   *(800)422-3568*
   80 mi. E via Hwy. 86
   hellscanyonadventures.com
   The best way to experience the grandeur and solitude of Hells
   Canyon National Recreation Area is by whitewater rafting or jet
   boat. Both floating or jet boating down the rapids of the Snake
   River through the Wild and Scenic Hells Canyon (the deepest
   gorge in North America) can be arranged. Sightseeing day trips
   varying from two to six hours are available from April to October.
   Overnighters all the way to Lewiston, Idaho; fishing; and dinner
   cruises can also be reserved.

41

Sumpter Valley Railroad   *(541)894-2268   (866)894-2268*
23 mi. SW via Hwy. 7 & Hwy. 184 - McEwan
svry.com
In the heart of a broad valley surrounded by forested mountains is a cluster of buildings and a depot adjacent to a railroad line with a steam engine and several historic cars. Five-mile excursions through the scenic valley to the historic gold town of Sumpter are available on weekends from Memorial Day through September–and there are several night train and photo-opportunity specials.

U. S. Bank   *(541)523-7791*
downtown at 2000 Main St.
In the lobby of the modern U. S. Bank is a glittering exhibit of various kinds of gold nuggets from this region. The centerpiece is the "Armstrong" nugget found in 1913 weighing more than eighty ounces. The exhibit is a gleaming testimony to Baker City's original claim to fame.

★ **Wallowa-Whitman National Forest**   *(541)523-1205*
nearby W and NE of town
fs.fed.us/r6/w-w
One of the largest national forests in the West (2.3 million acres) includes all of the luxuriant mixed pine forests on the highest peaks and beyond visible from Baker City. Good access roads lead to trailheads and the bases of four wilderness areas characterized by jagged peaks, small lakes, clear streams and waterfalls surrounded by dense stands of tall pines. Hiking, rock climbing, fishing, hunting, trail rides and backpacking are popular activities, and there are numerous well-sited campgrounds as well as remote hike-in campsites. **Phillips Lake**, a five-mile-long narrow reservoir surrounded by a luxuriant forest of pines, is the nearest forest recreation site from Baker City. This is a popular location for boating, fishing, camping and picnicking, and there are hiking trails by the lake and stream below the dam.

Warm Water Feature
Sam-O Swim Center   *(541)523-7747*
1 mi. E at 580 Baker St.
A large lap pool and a small adjacent pool are filled with spring-fed warm mineral water that can be enjoyed by the public year-round. Closed Sun. A small skate park adjoins.

Winter Sports
★ **Ski Anthony Lakes**   *(541)856-3277   (800)856-3277*
35 mi. NW at 47500 Anthony Lakes Hwy.
anthonylakes.com
Anthony Lakes Ski Area, at 7,100 feet, has the highest base in the state and one of the prettiest outlooks including little Anthony

Lake and the ragged Elkhorn Mountains. There is a snack shop and rental facility at the base. The vertical drop is 900 feet; longest run is 1.5 miles; and there is one chairlift. For some, the most compelling feature is the best powder skiing in Oregon which can be enjoyed from the lifts or by reserving a half or full day on the snowcat that takes small groups up to endless acres of pristine powder amid the highest peaks in the range. There are also more than 25 miles of groomed Nordic tracks, mostly for expert cross country skiers. The Anthony Lakes Ski Resort's season is mid-November to late April.

RESTAURANTS

★ **Arceo's Family Mexican Restaurant**   *(541)523-9000*
  1 mi. E at 781 Campbell St.
  L-D. No L Sat. & Sun.   *Low*
A large selection of border Mexican dishes is enhanced by all sorts of fresh shrimp and crab dishes like a shrimp fajita burrito on a big twelve-inch flour tortilla or "tres amigos" (real crab, shrimp and chicken with onions, bell peppers, tomatoes covered with jack cheese and a touch of wine), and for a change, deep-fried ice cream for dessert. The cheerful dining room fashioned from railroad diners has a view of the mountains and well-done murals.

★ **Baker City Cafe**   *(541)523-6099*
  downtown at 1840 Main St.
  B-L. No B Sat. Closed Sun.   *Low*
New at this location in fall 2004, the Baker City Cafe is a warm, cheerful place for specialty coffee cake for breakfast and designer pizzas, assorted grinders on focaccia bread, and soup with homemade beer bread for lunch. Counter stools up front overlook main street and the mountains west of town.

★ **Barley Brown's Brew Pub**   *(541)523-4266*
  downtown at 2190 Main St.
  D only. Closed Sun.   *Moderate*
One of Baker City's best restaurants features contemporary Northwestern cuisine like grilled salmon salad, baby back ribs, Porterhouse steak and, for an unusual treat, shrimp and alligator (grown in Idaho!) pasta. Support dishes also easily transcend expected pub fare and are delicious accompaniments to the range of microbrew beers and ales produced here (don't miss the "Jubilee"). The warm, wood-trimmed bar and dining room wrap around showcased gleaming brew kettles.

★ **El Erradero Mexican Restaurant**   *(541)523-2327*
  downtown at 2100 Broadway
  L-D. No L Sat. & Sun.   *Low*
The first of a small local chain of Mexican restaurants is a fine

choice for traditional border Mexican dishes and some creative specialties. Shrimp is featured in many styles including a shrimp salad starring tiger prawns. The flavorful well-prepared dishes are served in a colorful little cantina with padded booths.

★ **Geiser Grand Hotel**   *(541)523-1889*
   downtown at 1996 Main St.
   geisergrand.com
   B-L-D.   *Moderate*
In the classic **Palm Court Dining Room**, creative Northwestern cuisine is skillfully prepared in delicious presentations like wild line-caught grilled salmon on spinach, and various specialty steaks and prime rib. Delicious meals are complemented by the most spectacular dining room in Eastern Oregon. A stained-glass ceiling high above casts soft warm light on hardwood walls and casually elegant tables surround the namesake palm.

★ **Inland Cafe**   *(541)523-9041*
   1 mi. NW at 2715 10th St.
   B-L-D. No D Sun.   *Low*
For down-home all-American country fare, the Inland Cafe is *the* place. Since 1941, this unassuming little landmark has been luring knowledgeable natives with fresh, carefully prepared omelets or peach-infused pancakes, and other breakfasts that can be enjoyed with homemade cinnamon rolls. With American classics for lunch or dinner, don't miss the homemade pies like lemon meringue or huckleberry. The shaped-up little cafe has a choice of booths, table and chairs, or counter service.

Janet's Cook Shack   *(541)524-9310*
   1 mi. N at 2915 10th St.
   B-L-D. No D Sat.-Mon.   *Low*
American standards are featured at all meals, along with housemade pies, in a casual roadside coffee shop.

Mad Matilda's   *(541)523-4588*
   downtown at 1917 Main St.
   B-L. Closed Sun.   *Low*
Fruit scones and cookies made here can be enjoyed with coffee, espresso, herbal teas and other drinks in a large coffeehouse/art gallery overlooking main street. An assortment of tables and chairs, reading material and internet access are surrounded by wall hangings for sale in a historic building with a stamped-tin ceiling, polished hardwood floor and brick walls.

Sumpter Junction   *(541)523-9437*
   1 mi. E (by I-84) at 2 Sunridge Lane
   B-L-D.   *Moderate*
Families enjoy American standards served in this large coffee shop distinguished by an operational multilevel miniature railroad.

LODGINGS

Lodgings, while not abundant, range from a historic landmark hotel through bed-and-breakfasts to full-service modern motels. High season is June through October. Rates are only slightly less at other times.

Always Welcome Inn   *(541)523-3431*
   1 mi. E (by I-84) at 175 Campbell St. - 97814
   alwayswelcomeinn.com
   40 units   *(800)307-5206*   *Moderate*
One of Baker City's newer lodgings is a motel with a hillside view of the Elkhorn Mountains beyond a walkway. Each comfortably furnished room has a refrigerator and microwave and one or two queen beds.

Baer House Bed & Breakfast   *(541)523-1055*
   just N at 2333 Main St. - 97814
   baerhouse.com
   3 units   *(800)709-7637*   *Moderate-Expensive*
Baker City's premier bed-and-breakfast lodging is in an 1882 Victorian home on the National Register of Historic Places that is an easy stroll from the heart of town. Full breakfast is complimentary. Each of the well-furnished rooms has some antiques and period reproductions and a queen bed. The suite has a private bath (not connected) while the other two rooms have a shared bath.

Bridge Street Inn   *(541)523-6571*
   just S at 134 Bridge St. - 97814
   40 units   *(800)932-9220*   *Low*
This single-level motel is within walking distance of the heart of town and offers simply furnished rooms with extras including a refrigerator and microwave and a queen bed.

Budget Inn on Broadway   *(541)523-6324*
   just W at 2205 Broadway - 97814
   36 units   *(800)547-5827*   *Low*
A small pool and an easy walk into the heart of town distinguish this older motel. Ask for one of the remodeled compact, comfortably furnished rooms with a queen bed. Refrigerators and microwaves are available.

Eldorado Inn   *(541)523-6494*
   1 mi. E (by I-84) at 695 Campbell St. - 97814
   eldoradoinn.net
   56 units   *(800)537-5756*   *Low*
A large indoor pool is the feature of this Spanish-Colonial style motel. Each room is comfortably furnished (including a refrigerator by request) and has a queen bed.

★ **Geiser Grand Hotel**   *(541)523-1889*
  downtown at 1996 Main St. - 97814
  geisergrand.com
  30 units   *(888)434-7374*   *Expensive-Very Expensive*
The Geiser Grand is the heart of Baker City. The classic three-story hotel built in 1889 dominates the main street with a five-sided corner turret topped by an elegant clock tower. The building was painstakingly restored to its original grandeur and beyond, with contemporary amenities like larger bedrooms and luxurious private bathrooms and more than one hundred crystal chandeliers to lend warmth to polished hardwoods and unique decorative flourishes. The **Palm Court Dining Room** (see listing) is once again one of the classics of Western style, complete with the largest stained-glass ceiling in the Northwest. Adjoining is a handsome bar room overseen by a lion sculpture with an interesting history (be sure to ask). Each of the beautifully furnished rooms and suites has antiques and complementary modern furnishings plus all contemporary amenities and some extras, and one or two queens or a king bed.
    #302,#202–large corner suite with five-sided turret window
      view of main street and mountains, large bath with deep
      one-person whirlpool and separate shower, king bed.
Oregon Trail Motel   *(541)523-5844*
  just S at 211 Bridge St. - 97814
  54 units   *Low*
This older motel is within walking distance of the heart of town and has a small outdoor pool, sauna and cafe. Each small, simply furnished room has a refrigerator, microwave and queen bed.
Sunridge Inn - Best Western   *(541)523-6444*
  1 mi. E (by I-84) at One Sunridge Lane - 97814
  bestwestern.com/sunridgeinn
  155 units   *(800)233-2368*   *Moderate-Expensive*
Baker City's biggest lodging is the Sunridge Inn with a garden court pool, whirlpool, restaurant and bar-and-grill. Each well-furnished room has a queen or king bed and some of the rooms have a private balcony with a view of the mountains.
    #316,#318–private mountain-view balcony,
      in-room two-person whirlpool, king bed.
Super 8 Motel   *(541)523-8282*
  1 mi. E (by I-84) at 250 Campbell St. - 97814
  super8.com
  72 units   *(888)726-2466*   *Moderate*
This contemporary motel has a small indoor pool and whirlpool. Each comfortably furnished room has a refrigerator and two queens or king bed.

Bandon

Bandon is a delightful blend of natural grandeur and urbane renewal. The compact town extends to Pacific Ocean promontories that fall away to a smooth sandy beach accented by the West's most fanciful array of natural seagirt monoliths. Just inland at the base of sheltering bluffs by a tiny harbor along the Coquille River lies Old Town. During normally sunny and dry summer days, all sorts of ocean and beach-oriented recreation is enjoyed. During winter and spring, however, almost continuous rainstorms have allowed village boosters to claim the title of "Storm Watching Capital of the World."

Settlers first arrived shortly before the Civil War. They may have been drawn by deposits of black sand gold, but they stayed because of abundant natural resources like lumber and salmon. Bandon survived devastating fires in 1914 and in 1936, but languished until the 1980s when improving travel-oriented facilities began to fulfill its destiny as a major leisure destination.

Today, the Coquille River waterfront and Old Town are more desirable than ever. Local cranberry bogs and fishing vessels provide ingredients for a first-rate cranberry candy factory and fresh seafood markets. A growing coterie of quality restaurants further attests to preoccupation with local gourmet foods. Sophisticated studios, galleries, myrtlewood factories, and specialty shops reflect burgeoning interest in Northwestern arts and crafts. Newer bed-and-breakfasts and oceanfront lodgings serve crowds attracted in summer by the recreation and leisure appeal of the picturesque beaches and river.

47

Bandon

WEATHER PROFILE

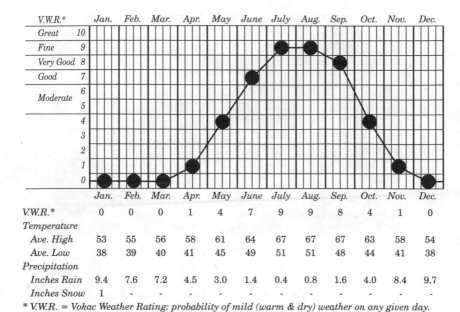

V.W.R.*		Jan.	Feb.	Mar.	Apr.	May	June	July	Aug.	Sep.	Oct.	Nov.	Dec.
Great	10												
Fine	9												
Very Good	8												
Good	7												
Moderate	6												
	5												
	4												
	3												
	2												
	1												
	0												

	Jan.	Feb.	Mar.	Apr.	May	June	July	Aug.	Sep.	Oct.	Nov.	Dec.
V.W.R.*	0	0	0	1	4	7	9	9	8	4	1	0
Temperature												
Ave. High	53	55	56	58	61	64	67	67	67	63	58	54
Ave. Low	38	39	40	41	45	49	51	51	48	44	41	38
Precipitation												
Inches Rain	9.4	7.6	7.2	4.5	3.0	1.4	0.4	0.8	1.6	4.0	8.4	9.7
Inches Snow	1	-	-	-	-	-	-	-	-	-	-	-

* V.W.R. = Vokac Weather Rating: probability of mild (warm & dry) weather on any given day.

BASIC INFORMATION

Population: 2,833
Elevation: 60 feet
Location: 230 miles Southwest of Portland
Airport (regularly scheduled flights): Coos Bay - 28 miles

Bandon Chamber of Commerce   (541)347-9616
   in Old Town at 300 SE 2nd St. (Box 1515) - 97411
   bandon.com

48

ATTRACTIONS

★ **Bandon State Natural Area**   *(800)551-6949*
   for parts of 6 mi. along Beach Loop Dr.
   oregonstateparks.org
Broad sandy beaches, Face Rock and a myriad other remarkably photogenic seagirt outcroppings, grassy headlands, and low sand dunes are enchanting attractions along this scenic byway. State park viewpoints, headlands hiking trails, beach accesses, and picnic sites abound.

Boat Rentals
★   **Adventure Kayak**   *(541)347-3480*
   downtown on the boardwalk in Old Town
   adventurekayak.com
This is a big shop where you can get instruction, tours, rentals and sales of kayaks and kites. For a great self-guided trip, they'll put you in upstream for leisurely paddling back toward the natural wildlife refuge and Lower Coquille River.

★ **Bullards Beach State Park**   *(541)347-2209   (800)551-6949*
   3 mi. N via US 101
   oregonstateparks.org
Miles of ocean beaches, low dunes, and a photogenic lighthouse on the tranquil north bank of the Coquille River by the ocean distinguish this park. Ocean and river fishing, beachcombing and dune hikes, and picnic facilities are all popular. The first-rate campground (for reservations, call (800)452-5687) in a sheltered locale near the river and ocean is the only full-service camping facility near the village.

★ **Cape Blanco State Park**   *(541)332-6774   (800)551-6949*
   25 mi. S on US 101
   oregonstateparks.org
Here is the most westerly park in the continental United States. It includes Oregon's highest lighthouse (250 feet above the sea), a campground, and a long section of near-wilderness beach.

★ *Cranberry Bog Tours*
   Faber Farms   *(541)347-1166   (866)347-1166*
   3 mi. SE at 54980 Morrison Rd.
   faberfarms.com
There are tours of cranberry bogs every day except Sunday. In October, you can watch the cranberry bogs being harvested with antique equipment. Enjoy tastes at their gift shop of cranberry salsa, chutney, candies and a wealth of related products. Closed December to February.

Fishing Charters
★   **Prowler Charters**   *(541)347-1901   (800)634-9080*
   downtown on the Boardwalk in Old Town

prowlercharters.com
You can reserve space aboard the "Mischief" or the "Barbara K" for trips across the Bandon Bar to nearby deep sea fishing for salmon or halibut with all tackle supplied.

Food Specialties

★ **Bandon Cheese**   *(541)347-2456   (800)548-8961*
   downtown at 680 E. 2nd St.
Some of the West's finest cheddar (from mild to extra sharp) and jack cheeses are produced under the Bandon label in Tillamook on the Northern Oregon coast. Samples are generously offered of each type of cheese. In the well-organized retail shop, visitors can taste, buy cheeses in various sizes, or buy other Oregon food specialties.

★ **Cranberry Sweets Co.**   *(541)347-9475   (800)527-5748*
   downtown at 1st St./Chicago Av.
One of Oregon's most distinctive and delicious regional specialties is the cranberry-flavored candy produced here. Samples of many flavors (including the original favorite–cranberry nut) are offered. Dozens of other kinds of white and dark mint and anise-flavored candies are also available for tastes and sale in a large handsome shop that also has an ongoing televised description of the process of harvesting cranberries.

★ **Port O'Call**   *(541)347-2875   (800)634-9080 in Oregon*
   downtown at 155 1st St.
Live Dungeness crab, the world's most delicious, is featured along with shrimp and oyster cocktails, steamer clams and smoked salmon for gourmet treats. There are outdoor tables, and a well-stocked bait and tackle shop by the boardwalk that also sells all sorts of maritime gifts plus crab rings (they will steam your catch) and fishing rod rentals.

Galleries

Bandon Glass Art Studio   *(541)347-4723*
downtown at 240 Hwy. 101
dutchschulze.com
This is a serious source for fine glass art in conjunction with a large studio where you can watch glass blowers at work through picture windows from the gallery.

★ **Second Street Gallery**   *(541)347-4133*
   downtown at 210 2nd St. SE
Three large rooms feature well-displayed, fine quality Northwestern art ranging from jewelry and pottery to massive metallic wall hangings, paintings and photographs, and furniture like myrtlewood rocking chairs. Whimsical and practical art objects in every price range also contribute to the gallery's appeal. Open 10-5:30 daily.

Woods of the West   *(541)347-9915*
  6 mi. S at 47611 Hwy. 101 S
All sorts of distinctive myrtlewood gifts are made and sold here, and tours are available.

Golf

★ **Bandon Dunes Golf Resort**   *(541)347-4380*
  5 mi. N at 57744 Round Lake Dr.
  bandondunesgolf.com
Two of Golf Magazine's top 75 courses in the world are here, and a third course opened in mid-2005. For purists, this is utopia, and they are public! Golfers walk (there are no power carts) among grass-and-heather-covered dunes by the ocean, or in a shore pine forest. All related facilities and services are available.

Horseback Riding

★ **Bandon Beach Riding Stables**   *(541)347-3423*
  3 mi. SW at 54629 Beach Loop Dr.
An exhilarating way to enjoy one of the most spectacularly scenic beaches in America is to take a one-hour guided horseback ride on a smooth sand beach overlooking the surf and wave-lashed hoodoo rocks and caves on the south side of town. Gentle horses and patient wranglers assure an unusual good time for every rider. Open 10-6 year-round. Reservations recommended.

★ **Old Town**   *(541)347-9616*
  downtown at 2nd St./Chicago Av.
The century-old heart of Bandon on a choice level site by the Coquille River near the ocean offers arts and crafts shops, restaurants, night spots, lodgings, and fishing charters in a compact walking district.

★ **Shore Acres State Park**   *(541)888-3732*   *(800)551-6949*
  24 mi. N via US 101 & Beaver Hill Rd. - Charleston
  oregonstateparks.org
One of the Northwest's most beautiful public gardens is meticulously maintained by the state on grounds of the once-grand estate of pioneer timber baron Louis Simpson. Flowers are in bloom almost year-round in the formal, Oriental, or rose gardens. Rarities like bamboo and fan palms attest to the Southern Oregon coast's "banana belt" micro-climate. Open daily year-round.

★ **Sunset Bay State Park**   *(541)888-4902*   *(800)551-6949*
  23 mi. N via US 101 & W. Beaver Hill Rd.
  oregonstateparks.org
A large cove with a curving fine-sand beach sheltered by forested bluffs, calm water ideal for swimming, and dramatic rock outcroppings offshore are elements of the quintessential Pacific Northwest scene. The shallow, protected bay is surprisingly

enjoyable for swimming in summer. Facilities include picnic tables, a campground, and bathhouse.

★ **West Coast Game Park**   *(541)347-3106*
    7 mi. S at 46914 Hwy. 101 S
    gameparksafari.com
For many years, hundreds of free-roaming animals and birds (over seventy species) have been meeting people face-to-face here. In America's largest wild animal petting park, you can enjoy the exciting experience of observing, walking among, and touching an extensive array of wild animals. It is also a fascinating place to note how people and animals can communicate. There is also a well-organized gift shop. Open daily year-round. Hours may vary.

RESTAURANTS

★ **Bandon Baking Company and Deli**   *(541)347-9440*
    downtown at 160 2nd St.
    bandonbakingco.com
    B-L.   *Moderate*
Cranberry creations like cranberry bars and cranberry-oatmeal cookies and cranberry bread highlight an assortment of baked goods made and displayed here. They are served with light fare and assorted beverages in a country-style coffeehouse, or to go.

Bandon Boatworks   *(541)347-2111*
    1 mi. W on S. Jetty Rd. at 275 Lincoln Av. SW
    L-D.   *Moderate*
Fresh seafoods are featured, along with a salad bar and fresh bread. The little wood-toned upstairs dining room is comfortable, and there are panoramic views of the lighthouse and river inlet.

★ **Bandon Dunes Golf Resort**   *(541)347-4380*
    5 mi. N (via Hwy. 101) at 57744 Round Lake Dr.
    bandondunesgolf.com
    B-L-D.   *Expensive*
The showcase dining room at the Lodge (**The Gallery**) has a picture-window view of fairways and the dunes. Creative and traditional Northwestern cuisine is offered on a menu that features seasonal fresh ingredients of the region and prime beef. The **Tufted Puffin Lounge** and the **Bunker Bar** offer light fare and warm casual surroundings. Nearby, **McKee's Pub** features local microbrews with Scottish-style pub fare and decor. The **Pacific Dunes Grill** offers breakfast and lunch amid a full bar by a patio overlooking the 18th green.

★ **Bandon Fish Market**   *(541)347-4282*
    downtown at 249 1st St. SE
    bandonfishmarket.com
    L-D.   *Moderate*

In this long-established little takeout market/cafe, their fresh seasonal fish and shellfish are all cooked to order. Locally caught, canned and smoked fish are also delicious. The thriving carryout features seafood cocktails or baskets, fish and chips, and chowder. There are picnic tables by the street.

★ **High Dock Bistro** *(541)347-5432*
  downtown at 315 1st St.
  L-D. No D Sun.-Mon.   *Moderate*
Northwestern cuisine is carefully prepared using fresh seasonal ingredients for dishes like pear, pine nuts and gorgonzola salad; local seafood; and desserts like housemade bourbon bread pudding. The wood-trimmed little upstairs dining room has a fine waterfront view.

Inn at Face Rock Resort - Best Western   *(541)347-7100*
  3 mi. SW at 3225 Beach Loop Dr.
  facerock.net
  B-D.   *Expensive*
The resort's **Rock Fire Grill** (opened in 2005) offers a breakfast buffet, and for dinner, seasonal regional ingredients with a Pacific Rim flair and grand atrium coastal views shared by the lounge.

★ **Korner Kafe**   *(541)347-3237*
  downtown at 92 2nd St.
  B-L.   *Moderate*
Big luscious sticky buns, cinnamon rolls and assorted fruit scones are displayed and served with omelets, scrambles and other light fare. Artisan breads for sandwiches, and pizzas, can be enjoyed later with eclairs, cakes, cookies or pies. There is a main street view from the casual upstairs dining area above the bakery.

★ **Lord Bennett's Restaurant & Lounge**   *(541)347-3663*
  2 mi. SW at 1695 Beach Loop Rd.
  sunsetmotel.com
  L-D. Sun. brunch.   *Moderate*
Fresh Northwestern seafood is featured–halibut, salmon and Dungeness crab. Housemade desserts like lemon-sour cream pie are also popular. The casually elegant upstairs dining room and a snazzy lounge offer gorgeous views of ocean surf and haystack rocks from a blufftop site.

★ **Minute Cafe**   *(541)347-2707*
  downtown at 145 N. 2nd St.
  B-L-D.   *Moderate*
At the Minute Cafe, breakfasts star with buttermilk or whole wheat pancakes with a choice of fruit in them, designer omelets, biscuits and gravy, and other fresh, flavorful American comfort foods. Generous portions are another hallmark of the cheerful little cafe with picnic-style dining in a garden patio.

Rayjen Coffee Company   *(541)347-1144*
downtown at 365 2nd St.
rayjencoffeeco.com
B-L.   *Moderate*
From a new roasting facility nearby comes fine blends served with
tasty light fare in the comfortable coffeehouse, or to go.
★ **Stan's Place**   *(541)347-9694*
downtown at 375 2nd St.
B only. Closed Mon.-Tues.   *Moderate*
Natives love Stan, whose credentials as a gourmet baker translate
each morning into enticing displays of fresh croissants, sticky
buns, and seasonal fruit pastry. Signatures–croissant french toast
plus stuffed croissants–can be complemented by scrambles and
other tasty fare in the warm little cafe by the Old Town arch.
The Tea Cosy   *(541)347-4171*
just S at 95 W. 11th St.
theteacosy.com
L-tea only. Closed Mon.-Tues. in winter.   *Moderate*
In this tranquil refuge for tea aficionados, assorted teas and
related gourmet treats are served at tables set with full linen in a
cozy cottage amid tea-related specialty gifts for sale.
The Wheelhouse   *(541)347-9331*
downtown at 125 Chicago St.
L-D.   *Moderate*
Northwestern oysters, Dungeness crab, salmon and halibut are
featured on a diverse menu, along with regional specialties like
hazelnuts and cranberries put to good use. Peanut butter pie tops
tempting desserts made here. Window walls give diners in the
split-level room and lounge a good harbor view.
★ **Wild Rose Bistro**   *(541)347-4428*
downtown at 130 Chicago St.
D only. Closed Tues.   *Expensive*
An eclectic selection of creative dishes is derived from around-the-
world specialties as diverse as Spanish paella, thyme-crusted rack
of lamb, or chicken breast with a chipotle cream sauce. Fresh
seasonal ingredients (many from their own garden) enhance
skillfully prepared meals served in the dining rooms of this popular
little bistro.

LODGINGS

Several distinctive lodgings have an ocean view. Summer is high
season. Prices at other times may be as much as 30% lower.
★ **Bandon Dunes Golf Resort**   *(541)347-5959*
5 mi. N at 57744 Round Lake Dr. - 97411
bandondunesgolf.com

174 units   *(888)345-6008*   *Expensive-Very Expensive*

World-class golfing arrived in Bandon in 1999 with the opening of Bandon Dunes tucked appropriately into expansive grass-covered dunes just inland from the ocean. Handsome wood-trim condos and lodge buildings sprawl across extensive grass-covered hillocks (strikingly similar to the Scottish coast) backed by a pine forest. While three (fee) 18-hole public golf courses are the challenging main event, the lodge also features gourmet dining (see listing) and a whirlpool and fitness center, plus two resort shops. Each beautifully furnished unit ranging from lodge rooms to four-bedroom suites is secluded in a forest or overlooking grassy dunes and has queen or king beds.

"Chrome Lake Rooms"–spacious, sitting area, lake or
    forest view, fireplace, two king beds.
"Northwest Room"–corner of lodge, private balcony,
    ocean and golf course view, queen bed.

★ **Bandon Ocean Guesthouse Bed & Breakfast** *(541)347-5124*
   3 mi. SW (via Beach Loop Dr.) at 87147 Beach Ln (Box 217) - 97411
   beach-street.com
   6 units   *(888)335-1076*   *Expensive*

One of the Oregon Coast's most romantic retreats is the Bandon Ocean Guesthouse Bed & Breakfast. It is a large contemporary building high atop a grass-covered sand dune overlooking nearby surf and haystack rocks by an unspoiled beach. Full gourmet breakfast and afternoon wine are complimentary. Each beautifully furnished room has a queen or king bed. Some also have a two-person whirlpool tub with a European shower, a gas fireplace and a romantic ocean view.

"Donegal Room"–spacious, windows on two sides with
    ocean and gorse-covered sand dunes views, large private
    balcony, gas fireplace, hot tub with ocean view, king bed.
"Kerry Room"–raised two-person whirlpool, gas
    fireplace, private ocean-view deck, queen bed.

Bandon Wayside Motel   *(541)347-3421*
   just E at 1175 2nd St. SE - 97411
   10 units   *Low*

This older single-level motel was recently shaped up, yet still is a bargain for small simply furnished rooms with all contemporary necessities and a queen bed. A full-service RV park adjoins.

★ **Gorman Motel at Coquille Point**   *(541)347-9451*
   1 mi. SW (on Beach Loop Dr.) at 1090 Portland Av. - 97411
   25 units   *Moderate*

Spectacular ocean views, access to a splendid beach, and a whirlpool distinguish this blufftop motel with comfortable rooms. Trailheads to Oregon Islands National Wildlife Refuge adjoin.

Many have refrigerator/microwave and semi-private view balcony,
and all have one or two queen beds.

> #206–awesome view, corner windows, refrigerator/micro-
> wave, private balcony, queen bed.

Harbor View Motel of Bandon   *(541)347-4417*
downtown at 355 Hwy. 101 (Box 1409) - 97411
57 units   *(800)526-0209*   *Expensive*
This contemporary blufftop motel lives up to its name with a
panoramic backdrop of the historic Old Town district just below,
and the harbor beyond. There is a whirlpool. Each room is well-
furnished and has a queen or king bed. Many have a small private
balcony and a big harbor view.

★ **Inn at Face Rock Resort - Best Western**   *(541)347-9441*
3 mi. SW at 3225 Beach Loop Rd. - 97411
facerock.net
74 units   *(800)638-3092*   *Expensive-Very Expensive*
Bandon's recently upgraded original seaside resort is on a bluff
across a highway from a superb ocean beach. A (fee) 9-hole golf
course adjoins, and there is an indoor swimming pool, whirlpool,
exercise room and sauna, an ocean-view restaurant (see listing),
and lounge. Each spacious room is attractively furnished and has
two queens or a king bed. Suites have a kitchenette, fireplace and
private view deck.

> "Spa Suite" (7 of these)–beautifully furnished,
> kitchenette, raised pressed-wood fireplace, in-room
> two-person whirlpool, private ocean view balcony,
> separate bedroom with king bed.

La Kris   *(541)347-3610*
just S (on US 101) at 940 Oregon Av. (Box 252) - 97411
lakrisinn.com
12 units   *(888)496-3610*   *Low*
In this highwayside one-story motel, each cozy, nicely furnished
unit has all contemporary amenities plus a microwave, refrigerator and a choice of twin and double, or queen bed.

★ **Lighthouse Bed & Breakfast**   *(541)347-9316*
just W at 650 Jetty Rd. SW (Box 24) - 97411
lighthouselodging.com
5 units   *Expensive-Very Expensive*
Lighthouse Bed & Breakfast is one of Oregon's great romantic
getaways. A contemporary residence on the river overlooking the
lighthouse and ocean is the premier bed-and-breakfast inn in
Bandon. It's a short walk to either the beach or Old Town after a
complimentary gourmet breakfast. Each of the luxuriously
furnished rooms has an ocean or river view, all contemporary
amenities, and a queen or king bed.

"Grey Whale Room"–spacious, spectacular view of ocean, river and lighthouse from whirlpool tub for two, wood-burning stove, king bed.

★ **Sunset Oceanfront Lodging**   *(541)347-2453*
2 mi. SW at 1865 Beach Loop Rd. (Box 373) - 97411
sunsetmotel.com
70 units   *(800)842-2407*   *Moderate-Expensive*
Some of the units in this motel/cabin/condo complex are built into a slope facing hauntingly beautiful rock monoliths along a sandy beach. Amenities include a beach access via stairs across little Beach Loop Drive, an indoor pool and whirlpool, and gift shop. **Lord Bennett's** (see listing) restaurant and lounge adjoin. Well-furnished units range from motel rooms to romantic suites with private view decks, kitchens and fireplaces. Each well-furnished room has one or two queen beds and some ocean view.

"ocean-view studios & Vern Brown Addition" (#350,#352, #354,#356,#359,#361,#363)–kitchenette, pressed-wood fireplace, private balcony with stunning ocean view, onc or two queen beds.

"ocean-view studios" (18 of these)–refrigerator, microwave, gas fireplace, patio or deck with some ocean view across road, one or two queen beds.

Table Rock Motel   *(541)347-2700*
1 mi. SW at 840 Beach Loop Dr. - 97411
tablerockmotel.com
24 units   *(800)457-9141*   *Low-Moderate*
This small single-level older motel has easy access to a spectacular beach. Some units without an ocean view are bargains. Guests can opt for a full kitchenette. Each nicely furnished unit has all contemporary amenities plus a refrigerator, microwave, and a queen bed. New in summer 2005 arc twelve well-furnished units with ocean views from private decks and patios and two queens or a king bed.

★ **Windermere on the Beach**   *(541)347-3710*
3 mi. SW at 3250 Beach Loop Dr. - 97411
windermerebythesea.com
25 units   *Moderate-Expensive*
Rustic and cozy oceanfront rooms are the forte of this long-established lodging by an exceptional beach. Each nicely furnished unit has two doubles, queen or king bed.

#18-25–newer, kitchenette, gas fireplace, fine dunes and ocean view from private balcony or deck, king bed.

Bend

Bend is the heart of one of America's finest year-round recreation wonderlands. Downtown's showcase attraction, Mirror Pond, suggests the tranquility and grandeur of this area. Nearby, majestic glacier-clad peaks of the central Cascade Range tower over an evergreen forest. A seemingly endless assortment of crystal-clear lakes and streams graces the sylvan landscape. Symmetrical cinder cones, lava tubes and flows, and other bizarre remnants of recent volcanism also punctuate the unspoiled countryside. Coupled with these dramatic surroundings is a surprisingly pleasant four season climate perfectly geared to year-round recreation. Winters, while relatively mild in town, provide heavy snowfall on nearby Mt. Bachelor with legendary downhill and cross-country skiing. Summer is the area's busiest season, when warm, sunny weather contributes to the fun of an unsurpassed diversity of outdoor recreation.

Bend was founded in 1900. A railroad arrived in 1911 and lumber milling became the dominant industry. As roads and recreation equipment improved, Bend was the logical locale for development of major resort complexes to take advantage of the skiing and outdoor recreation potential of this favored site.

Today, the center of town has a wealth of distinctive specialty shops and galleries, restaurants, lounges, and theaters in a strollable district with notable public improvements including one of America's most lavish town parks. Abundant lodgings in and around town, including several famous resorts, serve visitors enjoying Bend's world-class recreation facilities and leisure pursuits.

Bend

WEATHER PROFILE

V.W.R.*		Jan.	Feb.	Mar.	Apr.	May	June	July	Aug.	Sep.	Oct.	Nov.	Dec.

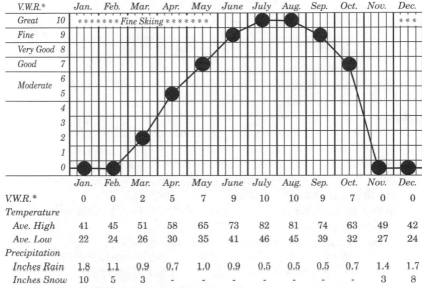

V.W.R.*	Jan.	Feb.	Mar.	Apr.	May	June	July	Aug.	Sep.	Oct.	Nov.	Dec.
	0	0	2	5	7	9	10	10	9	7	0	0
Temperature												
Ave. High	41	45	51	58	65	73	82	81	74	63	49	42
Ave. Low	22	24	26	30	35	41	46	45	39	32	27	24
Precipitation												
Inches Rain	1.8	1.1	0.9	0.7	1.0	0.9	0.5	0.5	0.5	0.7	1.4	1.7
Inches Snow	10	5	3	-	-	-	-	-	-	-	3	8

* V.W.R. = Vokac Weather Rating: probability of mild (warm & dry) weather on any given day.

BASIC INFORMATION

Population: 52,029
Elevation: 3,623 feet
Location: 160 miles Southeast of Portland
Airport (regularly scheduled flights): Redmond - 14 miles

Bend Visitor & Convention Bureau (541)382-8048 (800)949-6086
    downtown at 917 NW Harriman St. - 97701   visitbend.com
Bend Chamber of Commerce   (541)382-3221   (800)905-2363
    downtown at 777 NW Wall St. - 97701   bendchamber.org
Central Oregon Visitors Association   (800)800-8334
    visitcentraloregon.com

ATTRACTIONS

Ballooning

Bend's delightful "bend in the river" park and spectacular volcanic peaks in the background are memorably revealed in an early morning hot air balloon flight. This company has been flying passengers safely for many years.

Skydancer Balloon Company   *(541)593-4152*
balloonwithus.com

★ *Bicycling*

Scenic, relatively level terrain abounds in the pine forests around Bend. Many miles of designated bicycle paths are available in town and more than 30 miles of paved bikeways at Sunriver Resort. Bicycles can be rented by the half day or longer at:

Hutch's Rental Center   *(541)382-9253*
just E at 820 NE 3rd St. & just NW at 725 NW Columbia St.
hutchsbicycles.com

Pine Mountain Sports   *(541)385-8080*
1 mi. SW at 255 SW Century Dr.   pinemountainsports.com

Sunriver Resort Bike Shop   *(541)593-3721*
16 mi. SW (via Hwy. 97) at 1 Center Dr. - Sunriver

★ **Cascade Lakes**

starts 25 mi. SW via Century Drive Hwy.

An 87-mile paved loop (follow the signs) features dozens of small, clear lakes nestled in a vast pine forest near the base of glacier-shrouded volcanic peaks, including Mt. Bachelor and the Three Sisters. In addition to magnificent views, Cultis and Elk Lakes (among others) offer rustic resorts, sandy beaches, swimming areas for the hearty, boat launching ramps, picnic facilities and developed campgrounds.

★ **Cove Palisades State Park**   *(541)546-3412   (800)551-6949*

39 mi. N off Hwy. 97
oregonstateparks.org

One of central Oregon's most popular parks borders the southern shore of Lake Billy Chinook near the confluence of the Crooked, Metolius and Deschutes Rivers. Volcanic cliffs tower above narrow watery fingers that stretch back to shaded campgrounds, picnic, fishing, and swimming areas, and a marina with rental boats and houseboats.

★ **Deschutes National Forest**   *(541)388-5664*

S & W of town
www.fs.fed.us/r6/deschutes/

This giant pine forest includes Century Drive–a 100-mile paved scenic loop past some of the Northwest's finest glacier-shrouded peaks and dozens of small, clear lakes; several notable volcanic areas; parts of the Mt. Jefferson, Mt. Washington, Three Sisters, and the Diamond Peak wilderness areas; and the state's biggest winter sports facility–the Mt. Bachelor Ski Area. A good system of paved and dirt roads is backed by hundreds of miles of trails including part of the Pacific Crest National Scenic Trail. Hiking, backpacking, horseback and pack trips, boating, fishing, swimming, river running, and camping are popular. All kinds of snow sports are enjoyed in winter. Information and maps can be obtained at the Supervisor's office in town.

★ **Drake Park**   *(541)389-7275*
   downtown on Riverside Blvd.
Drake Park is one of the most photogenic of America's great town parks. Pine-shaded lawns slope to a placid stretch of the Deschutes River and frame splendid views of distant peaks. This is an enchanting place for a picnic near the heart of town. Canoeing is also popular. A half mile downstream is another picturesque haven, **Pioneer Park**, with shaded lawns, rock gardens, and flower beds by the river.

Food Specialties
★   **Newport Avenue Market**   *(541)382-3910*
   1 mi. NW at 1121 NW Newport Av.
   newportavemarket.com
The Newport Avenue Market is the most diverse source of traditional and gourmet grocery items in Central Oregon. Whether you're looking for smoked salmon, designer jams and condiments, or beers and wines, it's all skillfully displayed in this large, distinctively Northwestern grocery-plus store.

Golf
With more than a dozen public and private courses in and near Bend (including championship courses), it's not surprising that the Bend-Central Oregon area is ranked among the "Top 50 Golf Destinations in the World" by *Golf Digest*. Sylvan scenery backed by glistening peaks abounds. The two outstanding courses below also offer fine river views.

★   **Crosswater**   *(541)593-1000*   *(800)737-1034*
   16 mi. SW (via Hwy. 97) at 1 Center Dr. - Sunriver
   crosswater.com
At Sunriver is Crosswater, one of "America's 100 Greatest Golf Courses." The magnificent scenic course, threaded along the Deschutes River, is private, but can be reserved by both members and Resort guests.

★   **River's Edge**   *(541)389-2828*   *(866)453-4480*
   2 mi. N at 3075 N. Bus. 97   *riverhouse.com*
In town, *Golf Digest's* "Best Place to Play" near the Riverhouse Resort Hotel (see listing) is public. The course is as scenic as it is challenging.

★ **High Desert Museum** *(541)382-4754*
   7 mi. S at 59800 S. Hwy. 97
   highdesertmuseum.org
The High Desert Museum is one of Oregon's top destinations. The cultural and natural history of the arid region is the focus of this highly evolved "living museum" opened in 1982. Among interactive features are interpretive talks, and pioneer history demonstrations. The complex also houses a Desertarium with seldom-seen animals of the region. A Birds of Prey Center offers a chance to get close to eagles, owl and other regional raptors in naturalistic habitats. Major outdoor exhibits include an authentic century-old sawmill, and a dramatic fire trail. Nature trails meandering through a forest pass streams full of trout, and wildlife exhibits in natural habitats include an otter pond with underwater and den-view areas. **Silver Sage Trading** is a large well-stocked gift and bookstore, while the **Rimrock Cafe** offers a wide-ranging menu and indoor and outdoor seating. The complex is open year-round.

★ *Horseback Riding*
Several area stables rent horses for guided trips by the hour or longer. Some will also arrange extended pack trips into the national forest wilderness areas. For information and reservations, contact:
   Inn of the 7th Mountain River Ridge Stables *(541)389-9458*
   7 mi. SW on SW Century Dr.
   Sunriver Resort Saddleback Stables *593-6995 (800)547-3922*
   16 mi. SW (via Hwy. 97) - Sunriver

★ **Newberry National Volcanic Monument** *(541)593-2421*
   12 mi. S on Hwy. 97
   http:\\www.fs.fed.us/r6/centraloregon/newberrynvm/
The Lava Lands Visitor Center has automated displays, slide shows, and interpretive trails describing the remarkable geology of the area. Just north, a road winds to the top of Lava Butte, a cinder cone 500 feet high. At the top, an observation tower has panoramic views of the central Cascades. Across the highway, another paved road leads to lava river caves, where the highlight is a lava tunnel a mile long. Lanterns can be rented. There are also ice-filled caves. Two miles farther south on Highway 97 is the eerie lava-cast forest, a fascinating collection of tree molds–or casts–which were formed when flowing molten lava surrounded and destroyed living trees 6,000 years ago. It can be viewed from a mile-long paved interpretive trail. Twenty-seven miles beyond is Newberry Crater. Within the caldera (giant crater) of this enormous volcano that collapsed upon itself are waterfalls, streams, and two pretty little lakes. Boat ramps and rentals,

campgrounds, rustic resorts, and hiking trails have been provided. A winding grand road leads to a magnificent panoramic view from the summit of Paulina Peak. One of the world's largest obsidian (volcanic glass) flows is accessed by an interpretive trail.

★ **The Paulina Plunge**   *(541)389-0562   (800)296-0562*
   16 mi. SW (via Hwy. 97) - Sunriver
After a shuttle deep into the back country, you'll descend over 6 miles and 2,500 feet of vertical drop on a gentle winding forest trail via a (supplied) mountain bike. You'll explore six waterfalls and–as a highlight for any vacation–play in two delightful natural waterslides along the way.

Pilot Butte State Scenic Viewpoint   *(800)551-6949*
   2 mi. E via Hwy. 20
   oregonstateparks.org
A paved (free) road winds to the top of a classic lone cinder cone more than 500 feet above the city. The panorama of the high desert to the east, downtown Bend to the west, and glacier-shrouded volcanic peaks framing the far horizon is memorable.

★ *River Running*
   Several river guide services in and near town offer two hour, all day, or longer rafting trips on the Deschutes River near town, and on nearby streams during the summer. All equipment and meals are provided for scenic, and whitewater, trips. For information and reservations, contact:

   Alder Creek Kayak & Canoe   *(541)317-9407*
   aldercreek.com
   Ouzel Outfitters   *(800)788-7238*
   oregonrafting.com
   River Drifter   *(800)972-0430*
   riverdrifters.net
   Sun Country Tours   *(541)382-6277   (800)770-2161*
   suncountrytours.com

★ **Smith Rock State Park**   *(541)548-7501   (800)551-6949*
   26 mi. NE (via Hwy. 97) at 9241 NE Crooked River Dr.
   oregonstateparks.org
One of Oregon's most photographed spots features an uneven lineup of ragged reddish basalt pinnacles towering hundreds of feet above the aptly-named little Crooked River. It is a renowned destination for rock climbers, hikers, and mountain bikers, as well as shuttlebugs, movie and TV producers. Shaded picnic spots along the river, miles of hiking trails and numerous panoramic vista sites contribute to the appeal.

★ **Sunriver**   *(541)593-3740   (800)801-8765*
   16 mi. SW off Hwy. 97 - Sunriver
   http://sunriver-resort.com

Sunriver–the resort residential community–is the Northwest's premier destination for a recreation-oriented lifestyle. Since the master-planned development began in 1965, the natural environment was painstakingly integrated into the upscale village that grew up around the resort (see listing) and through golf courses in a broad meadow with a river (the Deschutes) running through it. A remarkable array of four-season recreation services and rentals (see listings) reinforce Sunriver's starring role as the Northwest's best resort community.

★ **Tumalo State Park**   *(541)388-6055   (800)551-6949*
  6 mi. NW on Highway 20
  oregonstateparks.org
This park of shade trees, lawns, and trails leading to (upstream) rock grottoes along the clear, gentle Deschutes River is an ideal locale for hiking, swimming, and fishing. Streamside picnic facilities and a complete campground are outstanding.

Warm Water Feature
★ **Juniper Swim & Fitness Center**   *(541)389-7665*
  just E at 800 NE 6th St.
  bendparksandrec.org
A twenty-five-meter warm multi-purpose pool and a forty-yard (cool water) fitness pool are the centerpieces of a complex that also offers waterslides, rope swings, diving boards, whirlpool, sauna, and a complete fitness center. In the surrounding park are tennis courts, trails, and scenic picnic tables.

★ **Sunriver Resort**   *(541)593-6752*
  16 mi. SW via Hwy. 97 - Sunriver
Sunriver's biggest pool is the Olympic-sized South Pool with a waterslide and beautifully furnished scenic deck.

Winter Sports
★ **Mt. Bachelor Ski Resort**   *(541)382-2607   (800)829-2442*
  22 mi. SW on Cascade Lakes Hwy.
  mtbachelor.com
With a chairlift to the mountain's 9,065-foot summit, the vertical drop in Oregon's biggest skiing complex is 3,365 feet and the longest run is nearly two miles. There are ten chairlifts. Or, take the "wonder carpet" or two tubing lifts at **Snowblast Tubing Park** to the top of an 800-foot tubing slide full of rollers that assure fun for the whole family. All services, facilities, and rentals are available at the base for downhill and cross-country skiing and snowboarding. Restaurant and lounge facilities ranging from posh to casual have been provided at the area, but no lodgings. The skiing season is one of the longest in the West–from late November to June. A chairlift operates through summer with scenic hiking and mountain biking and dining opportunities.

RESTAURANTS

★ **Alpenglow Cafe**   *(541)383-7676*
  downtown at 1040 NW Bond St.
  alpenglowcafe.com
  B-L.   *Moderate*
Freshness reigns (they post a "freshness pledge" and use no canned nor frozen foods) along with quality local ingredients like custom-smoked bacon. Their coffee cakes and thick fluffy pancakes are highlights on a menu ranging from a zesty breakfast burrito to apple-stuffed french toast. Fresh greenery, regional wall art, snazzy wood-trim tables and chairs, and a street view are part of the appeal.

★ **Ariana**   *(541)330-5539*
  1 mi. W at 1304 NW Galveston Av.
  arianarestaurantbend.com
  D only. Closed Sun.-Mon.   *Expensive*
Northwestern dishes with a Mediterranean touch are carefully prepared in entrees like paella de mariscos or wild salmon on lemon risotto served amid upscale decor in a charming cottage.

★ **Be-Bop Biscotti**   *(541)318-8675*   *(888)545-7487*
  just E at 1234 NE 1st St.
  be-bop.net
This tucked-away little bakery offers a delightfully sophisticated selection of their hand-crafted gourmet biscotti and delicious scones to be enjoyed with coffee at a few tables or to go.

Bend Brewing Company   *(541)383-1599*
  downtown at 1019 NW Brooks St.
  bendbrewingco.com
  L-D.   *Moderate*
Hand-crafted pilsners, ales, porters, and seasonal beers are brewed upstairs and piped down to the taps–they are a perfect accompaniment to a diverse selection of pub grub. The brew pub's outdoor patio is an especially appealing setting.

Big O Bagels   *(541)383-2446*
  1 mi. W at 1032 NW Galveston Av.
  B-L.   *Moderate*
Traditional and designer bagels (don't miss the cranberry-orange bagel) are expertly prepared with the big appearance and fluffy texture of fine big-city bagels, to enjoy at a few tables or to go.

★ **Blacksmith Restaurant**   *(541)318-0588*
  downtown at 211 NW Greenwood Av.
  theblacksmithrestaurant.com
  D only.   *Expensive*
The Blacksmith Restaurant's claim of "New Ranch cuisine" is just right. This is a great place for a big bone-in rib-eye steak or

a cider-brined maple-glazed pork rib chop among updated Old West classics. Desserts made here reinforce the theme in treats like a warm fudge brownie with chocolate sauce and a waffle cone tuile topped with coffee bean ice cream. The handsome polished-wood and candlelit dining room decorated with whimsical touches complements the "new" Old West dining adventure.

★ **Bluefish Bistro**   *(541)330-0663*
   downtown at 718 NW Franklin Av.
   D only. Closed Mon.   *Expensive*
Bluefish Bistro opened in late summer 2004 to instant success with dishes like pork tenderloin with hazelnut mustard or clay-pot roasted chicken in fennel and olive broth. The upscale eclectic bistro menu attracts crowds to several small, simply sophisticated dining areas that are in keeping with the cuisine.

★ **Cafe Rosemary**   *(541)317-0276*
   1 mi. NW at 1110 NW Newport Av.
   L-D. Sun. brunch. Closed Mon.-Tues.   *Expensive*
A limited, enticing selection of dishes that reflect the chef's classic background and creative spirit as well as the freshest seasonal ingredients is presented. For example, the chef game sampler includes rattlesnake sausage, boneless quail stuffed with mango chutney and Rocky Mountain elk with blackberry juniper sauce. Delicious housemade desserts are also displayed up front and served in several simply stylish dining areas in a handsome cottage.

★ **Coho Grill**   *(541)388-3909*   *(888)388-2646*
   3 mi. SE at 61535 Fargo Lane
   cohogrill.com
   L-D.   *Expensive*
Contemporary Northwestern cuisine gets creative touches in dishes like wild rice banana cakes with mango salsa or roast pork tenderloin with peach chipotle marmalade. The comfortably upscale dining room overlooks a golf course and mountains.

★ **Cork**   *(541)382-6881*
   downtown at 150 NW Oregon Av.
   D only. Closed Sun.   *Expensive*
Creative contemporary cuisine ranging from a hoisin pressed-duck salad through braised lamb shank with coconut milk demiglaze to cioppino is served at closely spaced tables in an intimate candlelit bistro with a cosmopolitan flair to match the cuisine. Desserts can be delicious too, like custard creme with Kentucky bourbon or chocolate hazelnut tart.

Dandy's   *(541)382-6141*
   1 mi. N at 1334 NE 3rd St.
   L-D. Closed Sun.   *Low*
Hamburgers, corn dogs and fishwiches, are served with soft drinks

and assorted milkshakes in a classic drive-in unchanged since 1968. Waitresses still use roller skates to serve patrons in cars.

★ **Deschutes Brewery & Public House**   *(541)382-9242*
  downtown at 1044 NW Bond St.
  deschutesbrewery.com
  L-D.   *Moderate*
One of the finest brew pubs in the Pacific Northwest is Deschutes Brewery & Public House. Bend's first brewery produces an array of handcrafted brews, plus hand-crafted root beer and ginger ale. Pub grub achieves gourmet status in fresh, housemade specialties like a salmon burger, barbecue-smoked pork loin sandwich, and brewery-made sausages, plus housemade desserts. Wooden armchairs, a wealth of greenery, an ever-popular bar, and a picture-window view of stainless-steel brew kettles distinguish the dining areas.

★ **Di Lusso Coffee Bakery Cafe** *(541)383-8155* *(866)345-8776*
  1 mi. W at 1135 NW Galveston Av.
  dilusso.com
  B-L.   *Moderate*
Di Lusso's is a fine Northwest baker with several stores in the area. Here at the original, their line of breads, including daily specials like apricot hazelnut, is superb. So are their breakfast baked goods like coffee cakes, and desserts like cherry cream cheese squares, to take out or enjoy at a few tables.

Goody's Soda Fountain   *(541)389-5185*
  downtown at 957 NW Wall St.
  L-D.   *Moderate*
One of the West's classic soda fountains features assorted homemade ice creams and toppings (and even cones made here) in all sorts of dairy delights. Their chocolates are also displayed and served in the corner parlor overlooking main street.

★ **Hans**   *(541)389-9700*
  downtown at 915 NW Wall St.
  hansrestaurant.com
  L-D. Closed Sun.-Mon.   *Moderate*
An eclectic international menu of dishes emphasizing seasonal Northwestern products ranges from hazelnut-crusted brie with cranberry-apple chutney through lime chipotle sautéed scallops on grilled spinach to St. Moritz schnitzel. The deservedly popular, casually elegant dining room also includes a display case lavishly outfitted with delicious pastries and desserts made here.

★ **High Tides Seafood Grill**   *(541)389-5244*
  downtown at 1045 NW Bond St.
  L-D. No L Sat. Closed Sun.   *Moderate*
A fine assortment of traditional and specialty seafoods is featured

in dishes ranging from Cajun popcorn shrimp to Dungeness crab and rock shrimp casserole in white wine sauce. Housemade desserts include hazelnut torte with peach sorbet. The snazzy little dining room keeps the focus on seafood.

★ **Jackalope Grill**   *(541)318-8435*
   2 mi. SE at 1245 SE 3rd St.
   D only. Closed Sun.-Mon.   *Moderate*
The Jackalope Grill lives up to its proclaimed "cowboy chic with a European drawl." Grilled cowboy steak or rack of lamb share a distinctive menu with grilled quail, wienerschnitzel, or jaeger (veal) schnitzel. Candles and full linen complement whimsical decor in this appealing young tucked-away dinner house.

La Rosa   *(541)318-7210*
   1 mi. NW at 1444 NW College Way #104
   L-D.   *Moderate*
Traditional border Mexican dishes are available, but the emphasis is on creative dishes like grilled salmon burrito, giant prawns with sweet onion poblano chiles and fresh mushrooms in a spicy glaze, and mango cheesecake for dessert in this contempo cantina.

★ **Marz - A Planetary Bistro**   *(541)389-2025*
   downtown at 163 NW Minnesota Av.
   D only. Closed Mon.   *Expensive*
An eclectic international menu ranges from Asian baby back ribs through green Thai curry to cherrywood-smoked pork tenderloin or rice-paper-wrapped fish. Housemade desserts are equally adventurous and flavorful. The small dining room is as flamboyant and casually fun as the food is seriously popular.

Mercury Diner   *(541)330-0037*
   1 mi. NW at 1444 NW College Way
   mercurydiner.net
   L-D, plus B on Sun.   *Moderate*
Traditional and innovative Northwestern diner dishes are featured here. Consider Dungeness crab and seafood hash cake for openers, or pecan and cornflake-crusted Southern fried chicken, and two-layer key lime pie for dessert, in a padded-booth dining room with a bar and outdoor deck.

★ **Merenda Restaurant & Wine Bar**   *(541)330-2304*
   downtown at 900 NW Wall St.
   L-D.   *Expensive*
Contemporary Northwestern cuisine with an Italian accent including homemade pasta and pizza is featured in a well-thought-out limited selection of dishes. The large two-level restaurant and bar have an easy sophistication that complements the fresh seasonal specialties and delicious housemade desserts.

★ **Nancy P's Baking Company**   *(541)322-8778*
  1 mi. NW at 1055 NW Milwaukee Av.
  B-L.   *Moderate*
Nancy P's, in a cottage in a garden since the millennium, is one
of Oregon's great bakeries. Multilayer cases display all kinds of
delicious cinnamon rolls, sticky buns, scones and other morning
delights, plus eclairs, cakes, cookies and squares for later meals
and assorted traditional and creative breads. For a whole meal, do
not miss the huge "pockets" like the ham and mustard cheese
that are a (really) full breakfast or lunch. Ten tables overlook the
displays and gardens. Hot and frosty drinks are special too.

★ **Newport Avenue Grill**   *(541)318-4768*
  1 mi. W at 1004 NW Newport Av.
  L-D. Sun. brunch. Closed Tues.   *Expensive*
Fresh seasonal ingredients are expertly prepared into classic
dishes from around the world. Breads and desserts are also made
in the trim cottage with several cozy dining areas.

Original Pantry   *(541)383-2697*
  1 mi. N at 62910 O.B. Riley Rd.
  B-L. Closed Mon.-Tues.   *Moderate*
A historic cottage has been transformed into a warm and cheerful
restaurant featuring traditional Western dishes (create-your-own
omelets, breakfast burritos, etc.) served amid comfortable country
decor. There is a raised river-stone fireplace in the main room.

★ **Pine Tavern Restaurant**   *(541)382-5581*
  downtown at 967 NW Brooks St.
  pinetavern.com
  L-D. No L Sun.   *Moderate*
Bend's oldest restaurant (built in 1936) is still one of Oregon's
finest. Splendid sourdough scones (a signature specialty) are a
unique introduction to Northwestern cuisine like Oregon flat iron
steak topped with caramelized onions, or cherry pork medallions.
Request the Garden Room where two giant living Ponderosa pines
highlight comfortably woodsy decor. Diners have an outstanding
view of Drake Park and the river from inside or on the garden patio.

Pizza Mondo   *(541)330-9093*
  downtown at 811 NW Wall St.
  L-D.   *Moderate*
New York-style pizza reigns in traditional and designer pies that
are hand-thrown and can be enjoyed by the slice or pie with tap
or bottled brews in the casual little parlor, or to go.

Sargent's Cafe   *(541)382-3916*
  1 mi. SE at 719 SE 3rd St.
  B-L.   *Moderate*
Traditional down-home American fare includes a wealth of

scrambles and omelets, biscuits and sausage gravy and specialties like fresh banana pancakes (bananas inside), plus homemade chili and cornbread and desserts like peach cobbler later. Padded booths and live greenery complement the comfort food.

★ **Scanlon's**   *(541)382-8769*
   3 mi. SW at 61615 Mt. Bachelor Dr. (in Athletic Club of Bend)
   athleticclubofbend.com
   L-D. No L Sat. & Sun.   *Moderate*
Northwestern cuisine is carefully prepared in an exhibition-style kitchen sporting a cheerful fire of local cherrywood. Creative contemporary specialties like giant prawns with tropical fruit salsa and coconut milk or cherrywood-roasted rack of lamb with an herb-horseradish crust are enjoyed with delicious white and whole wheat bread made here. So are all of the desserts including a stellar multi-fresh-fruit cobbler a la mode. Diners have a choice of padded booths or armchairs at tables set with full linen overlooking a luxuriant pine forest and the expo kitchen.

★ **Sunriver Resort**   *(541)593-3740*
   16 mi. SW via US 97 at Center Dr. - Sunriver
   sunriver-resort.com
   B-L-D.   *Expensive-Very Expensive*
Meadows at the Lodge (B-L-D–Expensive) features updated Northwestern cuisine in the lodge's big, casually posh dining room with a golf course view. At **The Grille at Crosswater** (L-D– Very Expensive) (open only to guests of Sunriver Resort), innovative Northwestern cuisine can be extraordinary. The dining room is the epitome of elegant rusticity, and the picture-window view is memorable. The **Merchant Trader Cafe** (B-L– Expensive) offers a wide selection of fresh, light fare.

★ **Toomie's Thai Cuisine**   *(541)388-5590*
   downtown at 119 NW Minnesota Av.
   L-D. No L Sat. & Sun.   *Moderate*
A wide range of authentic Thai dishes has made this restaurant a popular destination for out-of-the-ordinary fare. Live greenery enhances tasteful Thai decor including a large mural and expo wine cellar.

★ **Tumalo Feed Company**   *(541)382-2202*
   6 mi. NW at 64619 W. Hwy. 20
   tumalofeedcompany.com
   D only.   *Expensive*
Steaks are the specialty. New York, rib-eye, big T-bone and others are served with onion rings and salsa, salad, ranch fried potatoes, beans, bread and sherbet or liqueur dessert. Dining rooms are outfitted in Victorian rococo decor, and there is a comfortable Old West-style piano bar.

Bend

Victorian Cafe   *(541)382-6411*
1 mi. W at 1404 NW Galveston Av.
B-L.   *Moderate*
Creative contemporary American breakfasts like a salmon, blue
crab, and cheddar omelet with hollandaise sauce or a wild salmon
benedict contribute to the popularity of this warm wood-toned
coffee shop in a cottage.

Vino Mercato Deli   *(541)385-6979*
downtown at 916 NW Wall St.
L-D.   *Moderate*
Soups like creamy turkey and green chili stew and designer
panini sandwiches and salads like smoked salmon salad with
crumbled blue cheese are served amid gourmet displays in a
sophisticated little gallery/wine bar and at sidewalk tables.

★ **Westside Bakery & Cafe**   *(541)382-3426*
1 mi. W at 1005 NW Galveston Av.
B-L.   *Expensive*
The Westside is one of the biggest and best traditional
bakery/coffee shops in the West. A vast array of decadent delights
is displayed out front. Giant cinnamon rolls, pecan rolls and bear
claws are arrayed along with cinnamon-apple pullaparts and all
sorts of luscious scones, muffins, bagels, and fruit danishes. These
can be enjoyed with a selection of delicious egg scrambles,
omelets, pancakes, waffles and other American breakfast classics
in several casual dining areas decorated with a phantasmagoria
of whimsical toys.

LODGINGS

Lodgings are plentiful, including low and moderate cost motels
along Highway 97 through town. Most of the area's finest accommodations are by the Deschutes River in or near town. Summer
is high season. Many places reduce their rates 20% or more at
other times.

★ **Ameritel Inn**   *(541)617-6111*
1 mi. S at 425 SW Bluff Av. - 97702
ameritelinns.com
96 units   (800)600-6001   Expensive-Very Expensive
Ameritel Inn, one of Bend's newest (2004) and nicest lodgings,
crowns a gentle rise in the new "Old Mill District." Amenities
include a complimentary full buffet breakfast, pool, whirlpool, and
exercise room. Each well-furnished room has a refrigerator,
microwave and all contemporary conveniences plus high-tech
extras.
   "king spa with balcony" (3 of these)–two-person
      whirlpool with a mountain view shared by a
      large private balcony and king bed.

71

★ **Bend Riverside Motel Suites**   *(541)389-2363*
  just N at 1565 NW Hill St.- 97701
  bendriversidemotel.com
  128 units   *(800)284-2363*   *Moderate*
The Bend Riverside is the best-situated lodging in Bend. It is on
the quiet side, yet an easy stroll from downtown; and it is as close
as you can get (without getting wet) to the beautiful Deschutes
River. Lovely Pioneer Park adjoins. Landscaped grounds include a
large indoor pool, whirlpool, and sauna. Each spacious room is
attractively furnished and has a queen or king bed.
  #262,#263–large, studio, full kitchen, superb
    falls/rapids view, king bed.
  #258,#255-251–in one-level building, superb
    close-up falls/rapids view, king bed.
  #238,#242,#237,#241–balcony, overlooks falls,
    kitchen, gas fireplace, Murphy queen bed.

Best Western Inn & Suites - Bend   *(541)382-1515*
  just E at 721 NE 3rd St. - 97701
  100 units   *(800)937-8376*   *Moderate-Expensive*
This newer motel has a large outdoor pool and a whirlpool. Each
attractively furnished room has a microwave, refrigerator and a
queen or king bed.
  #129,#130–in-room whirlpool, king bed.

Cascade Lodge   *(541)382-2612*
  1 mi. SE (on Hwy. 97) at 420 SE 3rd St. - 97702
  33 units   *(800)852-6031*   *Low*
An outdoor pool and whirlpool are features of this single-level
bargain motel. Each simply furnished room has a refrigerator,
microwave, and a queen bed.

Cimarron Motor Inn North   *(541)382-8282*
  1 mi. E (on Hwy. 97) at 201 NE 3rd St. - 97701
  60 units   *(800)304-4050*   *Low*
This contemporary motel has an outdoor pool. Each comfortably
furnished room has a refrigerator, microwave and queen or king bed.

★ **Cricketwood Country Bed & Breakfast**   *(541)330-0747*
  7 mi. NE at 63520 Cricketwood Rd. - 97701
  cricketwood.com
  4 units   *(877)330-0747*   *Moderate-Expensive*
Cricketwood is a delightful adult getaway on a quiet ten acre site
near Bend. The contemporary wood-trimmed complex has an
outdoor whirlpool. Gourmet breakfasts customized to each guest
are complimentary, as are fresh-baked chocolate chip cookies,
beverages and snacks. Each beautifully furnished room has all
contemporary   conveniences,   plus   refrigerator   and   extra
amenities, and a queen or king bed.

Bend

"Champagne Chalet" (new in 2005)–a big romantic hideaway cottage, private deck with mountain views, full kitchen, massage table (with oil), two-sided woodburning fireplace in view of two-person whirlpool and king bed.

"Secret Garden Suite"–spacious, windows on three sides, two-person whirlpool, massage table (with oil), king bed.

"Enchanted Forest Suite"–extra large, alcove with two beds, two-person whirlpool, massage table (with oil), king bed.

Entrada Lodge   *(541)382-4080*
4 mi. SW at 19221 Century Dr. (Box 975) - 97702
entradalodge.com
79 units   *(800)528-1234*   *Moderate-Expensive*
A pine forest surrounds this appealing motel with an outdoor pool, whirlpool and sauna. Expanded Continental breakfast is complimentary. Each well-furnished room has a refrigerator, microwave, and a queen bed.

★ **The Inn of the Seventh Mountain**   *(541)382-8711*
7 mi. SW at 18575 SW Century Dr. - 97702
http://seventhmountain.com
180 units   *(800)452-6810*   *Moderate-Very Expensive*
The Inn of the Seventh Mountain is evolving into one of Oregon's most complete contemporary resorts following a long, complete renovation. The wood-trimmed hotel/condominium complex in a pine forest near the Deschutes River has hiking and jogging trails, two large pools including three whirlpools, sauna, three tennis courts, and (for a fee) an adjacent 18-hole golf course, whitewater rafting, canoes, horseback riding, and mountain bicycles in summer, plus ice skating and sleigh rides in winter. There is also a fine dining room (reopened in mid-2005), a family restaurant, and resort store. Each unit (up to a three-bedroom condo) is attractively furnished including a refrigerator and has a queen or king bed.

"Bachelor Suite" (several of these)–spacious, one bedroom, full kitchen, pressed-wood fireplace, private deck with mountain view, king bed.

"studio"–kitchenette, pressed-wood fireplace, private deck, Murphy queen bed.

Lara House Bed & Breakfast   *(541)388-4064*
just W at 640 NW Congress St. - 97701
larahouse.com
5 units   *(800)766-4064*   *Moderate-Expensive*
Bend's first bed-and-breakfast is in a stately turn-of-the-twentieth-century home across a street from the lovely Drake riverfront park. There is a whirlpool. Full breakfast is complimentary. Each well-furnished room is individually decorated and has a private bath and queen or king bed.

★ **Mount Bachelor Village Resort**   *(541)389-5900*
  3 mi. SW at 19717 Mt. Bachelor Dr. - 97702
  mtbachelorvillage.com
  100 units   *(800)452-9846*   *Expensive-Very Expensive*
On a high bluff above the Deschutes River is a well-landscaped
condominium resort with a pool; whirlpool; six tennis courts;
walking, biking and jogging trails; complimentary admission to
the adjoining state-of-the-art Athletic Club of Bend; plus a fine
restaurant (see **Scanlon's**) and lounge. In addition to well-
furnished hotel rooms, each spacious, one- to three-bedroom condo is
beautifully furnished, including a gas fireplace and a private view
balcony, plus twin, double, queen or king bed(s). Some have a
romantic river view from a large whirlpool on a private deck.
  "River Ridge Suite" (several of these)–one-bedroom suite,
    full kitchen, private balcony with good river views,
    two-person whirlpool, queen bed.
★ **Phoenix Inn Suites**   *(541)317-9292*
  downtown at 300 NW Franklin Av. - 97701
  phoenixinnsuites.com
  117 units   *(888)291-4764*   *Expensive*
Bend's only major downtown lodging is the Phoenix Inn Suites.
Amenities of the post-millennium three-story complex include an
indoor pool, whirlpool, exercise room, and complimentary
expanded Continental buffet. Each well-furnished room has a
microwave, refrigerator and two queens or a king bed.
  "Deschutes Suites" (2 of these)–spacious, private
    balcony with town/mountain view, two-person
    in-room whirlpool, king bed.
★ **Pine Ridge Inn**   *(541)389-6137*
  2 mi. SW at 1200 SW Century Dr. - 97702
  pineridgeinn.com
  20 units   *(800)600-4095*   *Expensive-Very Expensive*
This quiet country inn has a choice setting on a bench above the
Deschutes River. A full buffet breakfast and afternoon regional
wines, beers and treats are complimentary. There is a gift shop.
Each beautifully furnished room has a gas fireplace and a large
private deck and a king bed. Many have an outstanding river
view.
  "Upper Floor Riverfront" (4 of these)–one bedroom,
    spacious, two-person in-bath whirlpool,
    river view balcony.
Plaza Motel   *(541)382-1621*
  just N at 1430 NW Hill St. - 97701
  27 units   *(800)300-1621*   *Low*
Across from Pioneer Park is an older single-level motel that was

completely refurbished for the millennium. Each simply furnished room has a queen or king bed. Kitchens are available.

Rainbow Motel   *(541)382-1821*
  just E at 154 NE Franklin Av. - 97701
  50 units   *(888)529-2877*   *Low*
This simply furnished motel is a bargain with some newer rooms, a refrigerator and microwave in each room and a queen bed.

Red Lion Inn North   *(541)382-8384*
  just E (on US 97) at 849 NE 3rd St. - 97701
  redlion.com
  75 units   *(800)733-5466*   *Moderate*
This modern two-level motel by the highway has an outdoor pool and a whirlpool. Each nicely furnished room has a queen or king bed. There is a refrigerator, and a microwave is available in some rooms.

★ **The Riverhouse Resort Hotel**   *(541)389-3111*
  1 mi. N at 3075 N. Hwy. 97 - 97701
  riverhouse.com
  220 units   *(800)547-3928*   *Moderate-Expensive*
The picturesque Deschutes River borders this contemporary three-story hotel. Amenities include scenic nature trails; two pools, one indoors; whirlpools; saunas; two tennis courts; exercise room; fishing; and a nearby (fee) acclaimed 18-hole golf course. **Crossings** (B-L-D–Expensive) features prime steaks with a fine river view, and there is a casual dining and live entertainment lounge and a poolside cafe/bar. Midwestern expanded Continental buffet breakfast is complimentary. Each well-furnished room is spacious and has a refrigerator, microwave and a queen or king bed.
  #322,#324–in-room two-person whirlpool,
    pressed-wood fireplace, river view, private
    balcony, king bed.
  #412,#414,#416–pressed-wood fireplace, fine
    river view from private deck, queen bed.

Sather House Bed & Breakfast   *(541)388-1065*
  just S at 7 NW Tumalo Av. - 97701
  satherhouse.com
  4 units   *(888)388-1065*   *Moderate-Expensive*
In a quiet historic district a short stroll from Drake Park and downtown is a three-story 1911 Craftsman-style home that has been lovingly transformed into a bed-and-breakfast. Full gourmet breakfast (on weekends) and afternoon tea are complimentary. Each room is well furnished with period decor and contemporary amenities including private baths and a queen or king bed.

★ **Shilo Inn Suites Hotel**   *(541)389-9600*
   1 mi. N at 3105 O.B. Riley Rd. - 97701
   shiloinns.com
   151 units   *(800)222-2244*   *Moderate-Expensive*
One of Bend's finest lodgings is a well-landscaped all-suites hotel
by the Deschutes River. Amenities include two pools (one
indoors), whirlpools, sauna, steam room, exercise room, fishing
access, restaurant and lounge. Each well-furnished room has a
mini-kitchen and a queen or king bed. Some units have a big in-
room whirlpool.
   "Spa King suites" (12 of these)–spacious, private
      river-view balcony, in-room two-person
      whirlpool, gas fireplace, king bed.

★ **Sunriver Resort**   *(541)593-1000*
   16 mi. SW (via Hwy. 97) at 1 Center Dr. (Box 3609) - Sunriver 97707
   sunriver-resort.com
   600 units   *(800)801-8765*   *Expensive-Very Expensive*
One of America's renowned resorts is in a broad meadow
surrounded by a vast pine forest. Units ranging from hotel rooms
to private homes have panoramic views of distant snow-capped
volcanic peaks. A remarkable array of facilities includes three
pools (one very large with a waterslide), whirlpools, saunas,
recreation rooms, hiking trails, marina and fishing on the
Deschutes River, and (a fee for) championship golf (54 holes),
miniature golf, tennis courts, racquetball courts, bicycles (more
than thirty miles of paved separated bikeways), horseback riding,
canoes, kayaks, the remarkable Paulina Plunge (see listing), and
a wide range of spa services. Gourmet dining (see listing) includes
grand views, and there are entertainment lounges and resort
shops. Each spacious, beautifully furnished lodge unit has a
private view deck and gas fireplace and two doubles, two queens
or a king bed. Some condos also have a kitchen and a whirlpool on
a private view deck.

Westward Ho Motel   *(541)382-2111*
   1 mi. SE (on Hwy. 97) at 904 SE 3rd St. - 97702
   westwardhomotel.com
   65 units   *(800)999-8143*   *Low*
A large enclosed swimming pool and whirlpool are features of this
modern motel. Each nicely furnished room has a microwave,
refrigerator and a queen or king bed.
   #166–impressive stonework pressed-wood
      fireplace in full view of king bed.

Brookings

Brookings is the self-proclaimed "Banana Belt" of Oregon. With its border location, this southern gateway to the splendid Oregon coast enjoys many geographic advantages of a California climate. While bananas are not actually grown outdoors in Oregon, Brookings can be proud of its orange and palm trees, daffodils blooming in January, and most of the world's Easter lilies, coupled with natural Northwestern delights like azaleas and rhododendrons. Unlike much of Oregon, Brookings typically experiences moderate weather year-round (even winter, between major rainstorms). The Port of Brookings Harbor shelters pleasure boats as well as commercial fishing vessels near the mouth of the picturesque Chetco River. Beaches are memorably punctuated by rock monoliths, mounds of driftwood and tidepools.

Settlement began in the 1850s with logging. Later, commercial fishing, agriculture and tourism added balance to the local economy. In a historic footnote, near Brookings was the only U. S. mainland bomb-site (by Japan in 1942).

While traditional industries continue, more and better restaurants and lodgings reflect the increasing importance of tourism. Hiking on scenic natural beaches, in Azalea Park, or in wilderness settings, plus ample fishing opportunities, attract visitors year-round. Brookings is also becoming a popular retirement destination (including many former Californians!). The profusion of early spring flowers, lush vegetation and natural grandeur of the adjoining coast and river, and great weather, suggest why people are visiting and moving to this favored locale.

WEATHER PROFILE

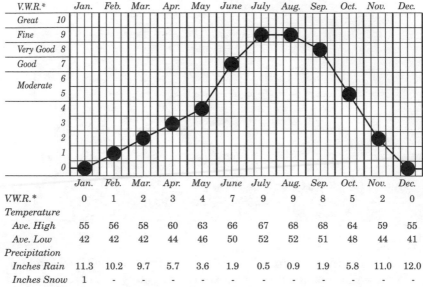

V.W.R.*		Jan.	Feb.	Mar.	Apr.	May	June	July	Aug.	Sep.	Oct.	Nov.	Dec.
Great	10												
Fine	9												
Very Good	8												
Good	7												
Moderate	6 5												
	4												
	3												
	2												
	1												
	0												

	Jan.	Feb.	Mar.	Apr.	May	June	July	Aug.	Sep.	Oct.	Nov.	Dec.
V.W.R.*	0	1	2	3	4	7	9	9	8	5	2	0
Temperature												
Ave. High	55	56	58	60	63	66	67	68	68	64	59	55
Ave. Low	42	42	42	44	46	50	52	52	51	48	44	41
Precipitation												
Inches Rain	11.3	10.2	9.7	5.7	3.6	1.9	0.5	0.9	1.9	5.8	11.0	12.0
Inches Snow	1	-	-	-	-	-	-	-	-	-	-	-

* V.W.R. = Vokac Weather Rating: probability of mild (warm & dry) weather on any given day.

BASIC INFORMATION

Population: 5,447
Elevation: 100 feet
Location: 315 miles South of Portland
Airport (regularly scheduled flights): Crescent City, CA - 25 miles

Brookings-Harbor Chamber of Commerce (541)469-3181 (800)535-9469
1 mi. S at 16330 Lower Harbor Rd. (Box 940) - 97415
brookingsor.com

ATTRACTIONS

★ **Alfred A. Loeb State Park**   *(541)469-2021   (800)551-6949*
8 mi. E on N. Chetco River Rd.
oregonstateparks.org
Deep in a lush forest of broadleafs and pines is a beautifully tended small day-use park with well-spaced picnic tables, maintained riverside trails, and fine rafting, swimming, and fishing sites. The key feature of the park the fact that it includes a protected stand of rare old growth myrtlewood and some of the most northerly redwoods on the continent.

★ **Azalea Park**
just E (via Hwy. 101) on Azalea Park Rd.
A few great towns have a world-class botanical attraction. Brookings has Azalea Park, a little gem high on a hill where giant rhododendrons and exquisite azalea collections of many varieties perfume the air and color the scene. Spectacular masses of flowers trim hiking trails winding among fountains and sculptures backed by a lush pine forest and sweeping greenswards.

Brandy Peak Distillery   *(541)469-0194*
6 mi. N at 18526 Tetley Rd.
brandypeak.com
On a ridge high above the ocean is a well-established award-winning brandy distillery. Premium aged pear brandy is the forte, and blackberries and wine grapes are put to good use. Tours can be arranged. (Fee) tasting and sales 1-5 Tues.-Sat.

★ **Brookings Harbor**   *(541)469-2218*
1 mi. S off Hwy. 101
port-brookings-harbor.org
Where the Chetco River empties into the ocean has been transformed to include commercial and recreational marinas, a popular public fishing and crabbing pier, an ocean-view campground, an expanding selection of shops and restaurants along the boardwalk, two of the region's best lodgings, and a driftwood-strewn sandy beach extending southward from the bar.

Flora Pacifica   *(541)469-9741   (800)877-9741*
7 mi. S (via Hwy. 101) at 15447 Oceanview Dr.
florapacifica.com
The shop displays all kinds of beautiful wreaths and seasonal lilies, proteas, lilacs and other flowers that suggest a truly special microclimate. In fact, selected citrus can survive here, along with some plants (like date palms) that grow nowhere else in the Pacific Northwest. Closed Mon. in winter. Open 10-5.

★ *Fishing Charters*
Deep-sea fishing beyond the Chetco River Harbor is deservedly popular. Several professional guides have boats and all equipment

for salmon and other sportfishing trips. Two of the best are:
Early Fishing   *(541)469-0525*
earlyfishing.com
Tidewind Sportfishing Ocean Charter   *(541)469-0337*
1 mi. S at 16368 Lower Harbor Rd.   *(800)799-0337*
tidewindsportfishing.com

Food Specialties

★ **Dick & Casey's Gourmet Seafood** *(541)469-9494 (800)662-9494*
   1 mi. S at 16372-A Lower Harbor Rd.
   gourmetseafood.com
For years, Dick & Casey's has been a destination for gourmet products of the sea. Their shaped-up store features all kinds of hand-packed salmon and albacore canned and smoked premium fish along with an assortment of related gourmet sauces, jams and jellies and more. They also have shrimp and crab cocktails in season to enjoy at nearby picnic tables overlooking the harbor. If you catch salmon or albacore on a fishing trip, they will custom can, smoke, and/or vacuum-pack your meat.

★ **The Great American Smokehouse**   *(541)469-6903*
   3 mi. S at 15657 Hwy. 101 South   *(800)828-3474*
   smokehouse-salmon.com
Long after winning a major contest for the world's best smoked albacore, the Great American Smokehouse continues as a key source for smoked and canned regional seafood. The smoked wild chinook salmon available in either vacuum-sealed packs or cans is a true gourmet highlight of the Northwest. Albacore, Dungeness crab and other regional specialties are seasonally available fresh, smoked and/or canned. Tastes are generously available in the big well-organized shop full of related products. They will also smoke or can your fish. Their seafood restaurant adjoins (see listing).

   Harbor Meat & Sausage Works   *(541)469-5279*
   1 mi. S at 16395 Lower Harbor Rd.
For assembling a picnic, possibilities made here include fine landjager sausage and various beef and buffalo jerky. Closed Sun.

★ **Harris Beach State Park**   *(800)551-6949*
   3 mi. N on Hwy. 101
   oregonstateparks.org
One of the crown jewels of the Oregon State Park System occupies a shoreline distinguished by a wealth of weird rock monoliths just offshore, fine sand beaches backed by a system of trails through lush forests and meadows leading to blufftop overlooks with unforgettable panoramic views of the Pacific Ocean. There are many well-positioned sea-view picnic tables. A large, deservedly popular full-service campground is in the pines within an easy stroll of the beaches.

Oregon's Largest Monterey Cypress
4 mi. S (via Hwy. 101) on Museum Dr.
The self-proclaimed "world's" largest Monterey Cypress tree has prospered here for more than 150 years and is now a genuine landmark easily visible from the nearby highway just inside the Oregon border with California. Take a picnic to enjoy at the single table in the shade of this splendid patriarch. The small **Chetco Museum of Local History** adjoins.

★ **Rogue River-Siskiyou National Forest**   *(541)858-2200*
13 mi. E on Chetco River Rd.
www.fs.fed.us/r6/rogue-siskiyou
Southern Oregon's largest wilderness area covers the summit of this large national forest. The lush vegetation, subjected to as much as 200 inches of rain annually, is some of the most diverse in North America. The Chetco River Road provides scenic access.

★ **Whalehead Beach**
8 mi. N on Hwy. 101
Visitors can enjoy a picnic in the pines or meadows overlooking a wild beach with gigantic Whalehead Rock just offshore. Hiking trails and walks on a soft sand beach are rewarded with awesome views of rain forests and nearshore sea stacks.

RESTAURANTS

Chetco Seafood Company   *(541)469-9251   (888)826-3495*
1 mi. S at 16182 Lower Harbor Rd.
chetcoseafood.com
L D.   *Low*
The Chetco Seafood Company (fisherman-owned) has a market displaying local and regional canned, smoked and fresh fish. Traditional and creative seafood dishes are offered in the cafe, or get it to go to eat at a nearby harbor-view picnic table.

Delaney's Bakery   *(541)469-5904*
just W at 1107 Chetco Av.
B-L. Closed Sun.-Mon.   *Low*
Tucked away in a strip mall is a cheerful full-service bakery. A wide range of breakfast pastries, several breads and assorted pies, cakes and eclairs are available to go or at several tables.

★ **The Great American Smokehouse**   *(541)469-6903*
3 mi. S at 15657 Hwy. 101 South
smokehouse-salmon.com
L-D. No D Tues. & Wed.   *Moderate*
Ocean fish and crustaceans star in a wealth of traditional American presentations. The split-level dining room amidst nautical memorabilia adjoins an excellent fish market (see listing) and a large nautically-oriented gift shop.

Home Port Bagels   *(541)469-6611*
just W at 1011 Chetco Av.
B-L. Closed Sat.-Sun.   Low
Among a good selection of bagels are two specialties–cranberry
and sweet nut. They also feature "dinghy rolls" (big fresh bagel
dough rolls) used for sandwiches, plus soups and salads that you
can enjoy in the large coffee shop or to go.
★ **Mattie's Pancake House**   *(541)469-7211*
2 mi. S at 15975 Hwy. 101 South
B-L. Closed Sun.   Moderate
Mattie's is one of the best bets for breakfast on the Oregon Coast.
All-American dishes range from assorted omelets through various
pancakes, including buckwheat, waffles, and freedom toast.
Sandwiches, soups and salads are served later. The warm and
cheerful little dining room includes a peek-a-boo view of the ocean
past a remarkable collection of antique model cars.
Oceanside Diner   *(541)469-7971*
1 mi. S at 16403 Lower Harbor Rd.
B-L.   Moderate
Fishermen and other early birds can appreciate the hearty all-
American selections that also include some seafoods for breakfast
in this cozy diner near a marina.
Rancho Viejo   *(541)412-0184*
just N at 1025 Chetco Av.
L-D.   Moderate
Mexican seafood specialties highlight a diverse selection of
traditional and creative Mexican dishes. The large colorful
restaurant includes several dining areas with padded booths and
a wealth of hanging greenery.
Smugglers Cove   *(541)469-6006*
1 mi. S at 16011 Boat Basin Rd.
B-L-D.   Moderate
The only dining room with any ocean view on the harbor serves
a wide range of Northwestern dishes including Angus beef as well
as all kinds of seafood with a picture-window view across a road
to the surf. A big gift shop adjoins.
★ **The Tea Room Cafe**   *(541)469-7240*
downtown at 424 Redland St. in Abbey Mall
B-L. Closed Sat.-Sun.   Moderate
The Tea Room Cafe has for twenty years been one of the best
destinations for breakfast or lunch in Oregon. Carefully prepared
omelets and other egg dishes can be enjoyed with delicious
housemade biscuits, cinnamon rolls, or sticky buns; while for
lunch, outstanding soups or chili complement a wealth of
sandwiches and salads. Mile-high kahlua or lemon meringue and

other pies displayed at the entrance are as luscious as they look. Big casual dining areas are surrounded by a diverse and colorful collection of tea pots.

Whaleshead Beach Resort   *(541)469-7446   (800)943-4325*
8 mi. N (on Hwy. 101) at 19921 Whaleshead Rd.
whalesheadresort.com
B-L-D. Closed Mon.-Tues.   *Moderate*
Natives flock here on Friday and Saturday nights for the prime rib, but their Northwestern classics are also good. Picture windows give diners in the large firelit room a panorama of surf pounding giant Whalehead Rock far below. Trophy game animals are on display. A general store, lodging, and RV park adjoin.

Wild River Brewing & Pizza Co. *(541)469-7454 (877)720-9453*
just S at 16279 Hwy. 101
wildriverbrewing.com
L-D.   *Moderate*
All sorts of specialty or do-your-own-combination pizzas from mini to large are served with beers and ales brewed in their Grants Pass and Cave Junction branches of this regional chain. Extra-long communal tables fill the expansive parlor.

LODGINGS

Several bed-and-breakfasts and the largest lodging in town provide ocean views. There are several moderately priced non-view motels on Highway 101 through town. High season is mid-May through September. Rates may be reduced as much as 20% at other times.

★ **Beachfront Inn - Best Western**   *(541)469-7779*
1 mi. S at 16008 Boat Basin Rd. (Box 2729) - 97415
bestwestern.com
102 units   (800)468-4081   Expensive-Very Expensive
Brookings' only major beachfront lodging is one of the best on the Oregon coast. Amenities include an outdoor pool and whirlpool with an intimate view of a wild beach and surf, and the mouth of the Chetco River is within easy strolling distance. Each beautifully furnished room has a microwave, refrigerator, and all contemporary amenities plus a private balcony with an unobstructed surf view and two queen or king bed.
"Executive Two-Room Jacuzzi Suite"
   (#325,#225,#125)–spacious, surf-view
   windows on two sides, two-person raised
   whirlpool tub with a breathtaking ocean
   view, full kitchen, king bed.
"Jacuzzi Room with two-person ocean-view
   whirlpool tub" (12 of these)–king bed.

Bonn Motel　　*(541)469-2161*
　just W (on Hwy. 101) at 1216 Chetco Av. (Box 6577) - 97415
　37 units　　　　　　　　　　　　　　　　*Moderate*
A large indoor pool is the feature of this single-level motel. Each
room is simply furnished and has a queen or king bed. You can
request a microwave or refrigerator.

★ **By the Sea Bed & Breakfast**　　*(541)469-4692*
　2 mi. N at 1545 Beach - 97415
　brookingsbythesea.com
　3 units　　　　　*(877)469-4692*　　　　　*Expensive*
Flower gardens surround a house lovingly transformed into a
romantic bed-and-breakfast on a rise overlooking the ocean.
Guests enjoy a sitting room filled with museum-quality jukeboxes
(some fully operational). A hearty full breakfast is complimentary. Each well-furnished unit has all contemporary
amenities, a private bath and double, queen or king bed.
　ocean-facing rooms (2 of these)–semi-private
　　balcony overlooking spectacular rock-studded
　　shoreline, gas or electric fireplace, queen bed.
　lodge–spacious, full kitchen, private deck,
　　hunting-lodge decor, king and double beds.

★ **Casa Rubio**　　*(707)487-4313*
　6 mi. S at 17285 Crissey Rd. - Smith River CA (Box 877 - 97415)
　casarubio.com
　4 units　　　　　*(800)357-6199*　　　　*Moderate-Expensive*
Casa Rubio is the area's most beautifully landscaped lodging. It is
also one of the most memorably sited with a grand outlook on a
driftwood-strewn beach and pounding surf. All of the units have
a lovely garden and ocean view, a refrigerator stocked daily with
a complimentary Continental breakfast, and double, queen or two
queen beds.
　"The Cabin"–spacious, expansive deck with grand ocean
　　panorama, small gas fireplace, full kitchen available,
　　double bed in separate room, ocean view from queen bed.
　"The Suite"–spacious, upstairs, big private deck,
　　kitchenette, woodburning stove, queen bed in
　　separate room with superb ocean panorama.

★ **Chetco River Inn**　　*(541)251-0087*
　18 mi. E at 21202 High Prairie Rd. - 97415
　chetcoriverinn.com
　6 units　　　　　*(800)327-2688*　　　　　*Expensive*
Far upstream in a near-wilderness setting by the Chetco River is
an expansive bed-and-breakfast inn with beautiful views of the
river, a meadow, surrounding luxuriant lavender and other flower
gardens, and forests. Fishing, swimming, hiking and boating all

compete for each guest's attention, particularly in summer when the gentle river runs clear and relatively warm. Drive in before dark, and take time to sit on a rocker on the front porch overlooking the river and as many as a dozen hummingbirds at porchside feeders. Full country-style breakfast is complimentary. (Dinners by advance arrangement.) Each of the rooms in the lodge and a cabin is cozy and comfortable with a kind of tailored rusticity appropriate for this special remote setting, and has private bath and twins or a king bed.

★ **Portside Suites**   *(541)469-7100*
    1 mi. S at 16220 Lower Harbor Rd. - 97415
    destinationbrookings.com
    12 units   *(866)767-8111*   *Expensive*
The Portside Suites are a newer lodging within walking distance of the mouth of the Chetco River and the Pacific Ocean. Each spacious, well-furnished suite has a living room and kitchenette, a large private deck with a nautical view, and a separate bedroom with a king bed.
    "spa rooms" (4 of these)–harbor view from
        large private balcony, two-person whirlpool
        in view of king bed.

★ **South Coast Inn Bed & Breakfast**   *(541)469-5557*
    downtown at 516 Redwood St. - 97415
    southcoastinn.com
    5 units   *(800)525-9273*   *Expensive*
On a rise above the heart of town near Azalea Park is a handsome Craftsman-style home circa 1917 that has been lovingly transformed into a handsome bed-and-breakfast inn. Full Scandinavian-style breakfast featuring organically-grown berries, vegies, and herbs from their garden is complimentary. Each well-furnished room has some nostalgic antique furnishings, a private bath, and a queen or king bed.
    "Maybeck Room"–spacious, gas fireplace/stove,
        private garden patio, king bed.
    "Rose Room"–Victorian furnishings, some distant
        ocean view, clawfoot tub, queen bed.
    "Garden Cottage"–lodgepole furnishings, garden deck,
        kitchenette, Continental breakfast in room, queen bed.

Spindrift Motor Inn   *(541)469-5345*
    just W (on Hwy. 101) at 1215 Chetco Av. (Box 6026) - 97415
    35 units   *(800)292-1171*   *Moderate*
This contemporary two-level motel has nicely furnished rooms with all contemporary amenities including a microwave, refrigerator and a queen bed.

Cannon Beach

Cannon Beach is an artistic haven in an enchanting coastal setting. Whitewashed and weathered-wood cottages and quaint specialty shops border three miles of broad "singing sands" beaches backed by low dunes and Haystack Rock, one of the world's largest coastal monoliths. Inland, a natural amphi-theater of wooded hills extends in a graceful curve to a massive seaward headland. State parks and forests that encircle the village assure preservation of the wealth of scenic attractions in the area, while providing an impressive variety of recreation opportunities. Summer attracts capacity crowds enjoying all sorts of beach-oriented recreation. Winters are a compelling spectacle of almost continuous rainstorms and wind-whipped storm surf.

Although the setting was admired by Lewis and Clark during the expedition of 1805, settlement was slow, appealing primarily to vacationers seeking coastal recreation and sylvan tranquility. Since the 1960s, improved auto access quickened the pace of visitor-oriented developments by merchants (mostly artisans and dreamers) inspired by the grand location.

Cannon Beach is still a village in which the artistry of residents is apparent everywhere–in subtleties of human-scaled architecture; abundant flowers and meticulous gardens; memorable public sculptures; and an acclaimed playhouse offering year-round live entertainment. Numerous studios and galleries display first-rate local handicrafts and artwork. Restaurants are plentiful. Lodgings include many posh oceanfront rooms in facilities loaded with romantic amenities.

WEATHER PROFILE

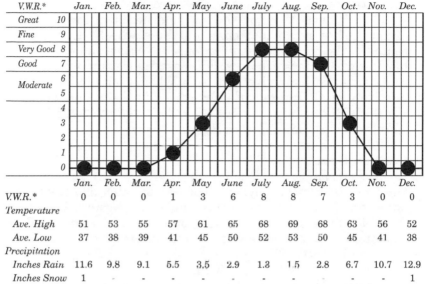

V.W.R.*		Jan.	Feb.	Mar.	Apr.	May	June	July	Aug.	Sep.	Oct.	Nov.	Dec.
V.W.R.*		0	0	0	1	3	6	8	8	7	3	0	0
Temperature													
Ave. High		51	53	55	57	61	65	68	69	68	63	56	52
Ave. Low		37	38	39	41	45	50	52	53	50	45	41	38
Precipitation													
Inches Rain		11.6	9.8	9.1	5.5	3.5	2.9	1.3	1.5	2.8	6.7	10.7	12.9
Inches Snow		1	-	-	-	-	-	-	-	-	-	-	1

* V.W.R. = *Vokac Weather Rating: probability of mild (warm & dry) weather on any given day.*

BASIC INFORMATION

Population: 1,588
Elevation: 20 feet
Location: 80 miles Northwest of Portland
Airport (regularly scheduled flights): Portland - 88 miles

Cannon Beach Chamber of Commerce   (503)436-2623
  downtown at 2nd & Spruce (Box 64) - 97110
  cannonbeach.org

ATTRACTIONS

★ *Bicycling*
A delightful way to enjoy the splendid beach in town is on a "Funcycle" (a recumbent chair on three wheels) that can be rented by the hour-and-a-half or longer to cruise on four miles of hard sand past Haystack Rock. For coastal byways, mountain bike rentals by the hour give access to sylvan countryside that is relatively gentle and remarkably scenic. Both kinds are at:

Mike's Bike Shop   *(503)436-1266*   *(800)492-1266*
downtown at 248 N. Spruce St.
mikesbikes.com

★ **Cannon Beach**
borders downtown on W side
One of the most idyllic beaches in the Northwest–or anywhere–forms the town's three-mile-long western boundary. Above the broad hard-sand beach, low dunes of dry and powdery "singing sands" provide a picturesque backdrop.

★ **Coaster Theatre Playhouse**   *(503)436-1242*
downtown at 108 N. Hemlock St.
coastertheatre.com

For more than a third of a century, the Coaster Theatre Playhouse has entertained audiences with stage plays, concerts and art shows year-round. The rustic wood-trim building in the heart of town that is now an intimate multipurpose theater was built in the 1920s and once housed a roller skating rink.

★ **Ecola State Park**   *(503)436-2844*   *(800)551-6949*
1 mi. N via Ecola Park Rd.
oregonstateparks.org

This large park occupies most of the southern slopes of Tillamook Head–the massive promontory between Cannon Beach and Seaside. Several well-spaced picnic tables overlook magnificent coastline views from a pine-bordered highland meadow. Nearly six miles of protected coastline include two picturesque sandy beaches. Rock fishing, tide pool exploring, sunbathing, surfing, and kayaking are popular. Hiking trails lead through dense rain forests to secluded coves, and to overlooks of sea lion and bird rookeries on offshore rocks. Or, on the Clatsop Loop Interpretive Trail, you can walk in the 1806 footsteps of Capt. William Clark. Tillamook Rock Lighthouse (circa 1889), one mile offshore, served for 77 years.

Food Specialties
★   **Blue Heron French Cheese Factory**   *(503)842-8281*
blueheronoregon.com   *(800)275-0639*
39 mi. S (via Hwy. 101) at 2001 Blue Heron Dr. - Tillamook
French-style brie cheese is produced, sold, and available for

sampling here daily. A fine assortment of international cheeses is also featured, and samples are generously offered. Premium Oregon wines, jams, and other regional gourmet specialties are displayed, sampled and sold. Locally raised and cured meats and smoked salmon from nearby **D's Sausage Factory** are also notable.

★ **Tillamook Cheese Factory**   *(503)815-1300   (800)542-7290*
    38 mi. S at 4175 Hwy. 101 North - Tillamook
    tillamookcheese.com
One of the world's largest cheese-processing plants produces the West's most renowned cheddar cheese. The farmer-owned co-op has used the same great cheese recipe for over a century. Visitors can watch through picture windows, and take a free self-guided tour of the whole process. Samples of all of their cheeses are offered. An excellent regional food and gift shop, and a cafe featuring other delicious Tillamook dairy products, adjoin. Don't miss the award-winning ice creams in all sorts of luscious flavors and styles.

★ **Haystack Rock**
    1 mi. S - just offshore
The third largest coastal monolith in the world rises 235 feet from the surf adjacent to Cannon Beach. Its natural scenic beauty is a major source of local pride. While the rookery and tidepools around the base of the rock are protected, observing the small marine life that abounds there is a favorite pastime. High on the grassy north face is the most visible nesting site (of only four in Oregon) of the colorful Tufted Puffin with its bright orange bill.
Horseback Riding
★   **Sea Ranch Stables**   *(503)436-2815*
    just N at 415 Fir St.
Guided rides along the beach or into the mountains are offered daily from mid-May to mid-September. The hour-long ride along the beach to Haystack Rock is especially memorable.

★ **Manzanita-Nehalem Area**
    15 mi. S on Hwy. 101 - Manzanita
Where a broad sandy beach several miles long abuts picturesque 1,800-foot Neahkahnie Mountain, the tiny village of Manzanita is developing as an artisan and recreation center. The main street includes restaurants and some distinctive galleries, shops, and lodgings. Inland two miles, where Highway 101 crosses the tranquil Nehalem River, another appealing village caters to sportfishing. Nehalem Bay State Park, on a large sandspit between the river and the ocean, attracts fishermen and campers.

★ **Oswald West State Park**   *(800)551-6949*
    10 mi. S on Hwy. 101

oregonstateparks.org

This state park memorializes the farsighted governor who, in 1912, preserved all of Oregon's coastal beaches for the people. An outstanding walk-in campground one-quarter mile from the parking lot provides tent sites set in an old-growth coastal rain forest. A sheltered cove (popular with windsurfers, boogie boarders, and picnickers), intimate sandy beach, and tidepools are a short walk beyond.

RESTAURANTS

Bill's Tavern & Brewhouse   *(503)436-2202*
  downtown at 188 N. Hemlock St.
  L-D.   *Moderate*
The village's favorite tavern is bigger and better than ever. You can see the kettles between the two dining areas and there are several raised tables overlooking the picturesque main street. They serve their own premium brews with an expanded selection of Northwestern pub grub in a warm, fun setting.

★ **Cannon Beach Bakery**   *(503)436-0399*
  downtown at 240 N. Hemlock St.
  cannonbeachbakery.com
  B-L. Closed Tues.   *Moderate*
One of the best bakeries along the Northwest coast is famous for its bread loaf in the shape of Haystack Rock. Outstanding cinnamon rolls and other pastries, plus light fare and desserts, are all made from scratch. It's all available with coffee at a few tables overlooking main street, or to go.

★ **Dooger's Seafood & Grill**   *(503)436-2225*
  just S at 1371 S. Hemlock St.
  doogersseafoodandgrill.com
  B-L-D.   *Moderate*
This branch of a local chain is also deservedly popular (see listing in Seaside). For a different breakfast, consider petrale sole and eggs. Later, try the award-winning clam chowder followed by sautéed Dungeness crab legs (in season) for dinner. Top it off with delicious peanut butter pie in their warm wood-trimmed dining rooms.

★ **Gower Street Bistro**   *(503)436-2729*
  just S at 1116 S. Hemlock St.
  gowerbistro.com
  B-L-D.   *Expensive*
An eclectic menu of international specialties is served amid a cozy congestion of casual contempo tables backed by desserts, deli cases and an expo kitchen. The popular little charcuterie, opened in 2004, also has a small dining porch by the main street.

★ **JP's at Cannon Beach**   *(503)436-0908*
  downtown at 240 N. Hemlock St.
  L-D. Closed Sun.   *Expensive*
JP's at Cannon Beach is one of the best sources of Northwestern cuisine on the Oregon coast. Expert consistent attention is paid to traditional and innovative Northwestern dishes featuring fresh quality seasonal ingredients. Consider clam and salmon chowder topped with chopped hazelnuts; wild salmon topped with olives baked with white wine, herbs and lemon; and for dessert, a "lemon thing." The comfortable candlelit dining room overlooks an expo kitchen and the flower-bedecked main street.

★ **Lazy Susan Cafe**   *(503)436-2816*
  downtown at 126 N. Hemlock St.
  B-L. Closed Tues.   *Moderate*
The area's best breakfasts have been served here for years. Omelets featuring Tillamook cheese are expertly prepared, and there are specialties like oatmeal waffles and fresh seasonal fruit. Seating is on two levels in a handcrafted wood-toned dining room enhanced by soft music and fresh bouquets of flowers. Out front, **Lazy Susan Grill & Scoop** (B-L-D–Moderate) offers more traditional fare.

Morris' Fireside Restaurant   *(503)436-2917*
  downtown at 207 N. Hemlock St.
  B-L-D.   *Moderate*
Traditional and innovative Northwestern dishes like pan-fried razor clams with eggs, hash browns and biscuits have been served here for years. Warm wood tones contribute to the charm of a hand-hewn log dining room with a giant river-rock two-sided fireplace, lots of art and greenery, and intimate village views.

Pizza à fetta   *(503)436-0333*
  downtown at 231 N. Hemlock St.
  pizza-a-fetta.com
  L-D.   *Moderate*
Hand-tossed designer pizzas with homemade sauces and fresh quality toppings are featured, along with create-your-own gourmet pizza. Several tables fill tiny rooms in this pizzeria.

★ **Stephanie Inn**   *(503)436-2221*
  2 mi. S at 2740 S. Pacific St.
  stephanie-inn.com
  D only.   *Very Expensive*
By reservation, you can join guests at the luxurious inn for fixed-price four-course dinners that showcase fresh seasonal foods with an emphasis on the Northwest. The gourmet fare is presented in a room that artistically conveys the nostalgic refinement of a New England country inn.

Wayfarer Restaurant & Lounge   *(503)436-1108*
   just S at 1190 Pacific Dr.
   wayfarer-restaurant.com
   B-L-D.   *Expensive*
Contemporary American fare with an appropriate emphasis on
Northwestern dishes is served at all meals in the village's best
oceanfront restaurant. Try to get a table near the large picture
windows for a soul-stirring view of Haystock Rock.

LODGINGS

Many romantic small resorts, inns and motels feature
Northwestern artistry and ocean views. There are also a few
moderately priced non-view motels on Hemlock Street. High
season is June through September. Prices may be reduced 25% or
more at other times.

Blue Gull Inn   *(503)436-2714*
   just S at 632 S. Hemlock St. (Box 660) - 97110
   bluegullinn.net
   8 units   *(800)507-2714*   *Moderate-Expensive*
This historic cottage complex (circa 1939) has been thoroughly
upgraded around a rose-filled courtyard a short walk from the
beach. Each well-furnished unit (studios to two-bedroom cottage)
has all contemporary amenities including a refrigerator and twins
and a double or queen bed.
   "Spa Cottage"–large private cottage, kitchen,
      two-person whirlpool in bath, gas fireplace,
      queen bed.
   "Garden Cottage"–one bedroom, full kitchen,
      gas fireplace, in-loft queen bed.

★ **Hallmark Resort**   *(503)436-1566*
   just S at 1400 S. Hemlock St. (Box 547) - 97110
   www.hallmarkinns.com
   142 units   *(888)448-4449*   *Expensive-Very Expensive*
Hallmark Resort at Cannon Beach is one of the finest resort
motels in the Northwest. The contemporary wood-crafted
complex (a perfect example of the "Cannon Beach Style") crowns
a beachfront bluff overlooking Haystack Rock, and has a big
indoor pool, whirlpool, sauna, and exercise room. Stairs provide
access to the adjoining "singing sands" beach and monolith.
Each unit (up to two bedrooms with choice of bed size) has
beautiful contemporary furnishings, plus a refrigerator, gas
fireplace, and a private balcony overlooking the ocean and
Haystack Rock. Some suites also have a large in-room whirlpool
and/or a full kitchen.

#340,#333,#324,#322,#240,#233,#224,#222–
spacious, refrigerator, microwave, raised gas
fireplace, in-room two-person whirlpool, private
balcony and floor-to-ceiling window wall share
romantic Haystack/surf and sand view, king bed.

Hidden Villa Motel   *(503)436-2237*
just S at 188 E. Van Buren St. (Box 426) - 97110
hiddenvillamotel.com
6 units   *Moderate*
A verdant garden enhances this tiny cottage colony. Built in the
1930s, it is the last of the cabin courts that were the lodgings in
Cannon Beach before the 1960s. A major renovation project
beginning in mid-2005 will update the facilities. Each small,
simply comfortable unit has a kitchen and one or two double beds.

Inn at Cannon Beach   *(503)436-9085*
2 mi. S at 3215 S. Hemlock St. (Box 1037) - 97110
atcannonbeach.com
40 units   *(800)321-6304*   *Expensive-Very Expensive*
This contemporary garden-style motel is an easy stroll from the
beach. An expanded Continental breakfast in their art gallery and
a pass to the Cannon Beach Athletic Club are complimentary.
Each well-furnished unit has a gas fireplace, refrigerator, microwave, and queens or a king bed.

★ **The Inn at Manzanita**   *(503)368-6754*
15 mi. S (via Hwy. 101) at 67 Laneda (Box 243) - Manzanita 97130
innatmanzanita.com
13 units   *Expensive*
One of the Oregon coast's most romantic inns is tucked away in
a peaceful village by the sea (see listing). The modern shingled
inn in a pine forest is a short stroll from miles of sandy beach.
Each beautifully furnished room has a refrigerator/wet bar and
both a gas fireplace and a large in-room whirlpool, and a queen
bed. Some also have a skylight and deck with a distant ocean
view.

Lands End Motel   *(503)436-2264*
downtown at 263 W. 2nd St. (Box 475) - 97110
landsendmotel.com
14 units   *(800)793-1477*   *Expensive*
This newly remodeled (in 2005) contemporary beachfront motel
has an outdoor whirlpool. Each well-furnished unit has a (pressed
wood) fireplace, refrigerator, microwave, an ocean view, and a
queen bed.

#6–1 BR, newly remodeled unit, fine ocean
view from living room and dining room.

★ **Ocean Lodge**   *(503)436-2241*
   2 mi. S at 2864 S. Pacific St. (Box 1037) - 97110
   theoceanlodge.com
   45 units   *(888)777-4047*   *Very Expensive*
The Ocean Lodge opened in 2002 with a delightful blend of upscale comforts and beachfront rusticity. An expanded Continental breakfast is complimentary. Each beautifully furnished unit in the three-story complex has a wet bar, refrigerator and microwave, a gas fireplace, a shared or semi-private deck or balcony (many with a full oceanfront view), an in-bath two-person whirlpool, and a queen or king bed.
   #214,#114–corner window view of beach/surf
      and rock, king bed.
   #201,#101–one bedroom, corner windows view
      of beach and surf, queen bed.

★ **St. Bernards Bed & Breakfast**   *(503)436-2800*
   4 mi. S(on Hwy. 101)at 31970 E. Ocean Rd.(Box 102)-Arch Cape 97102
   www.st-bernards.com
   7 units   *(800)436-2848*   *Expensive-Very Expensive*
St. Bernard's combines Old World storybook charm with upscale contemporary comforts. The big wood-trimmed chateau is a stroll from the beach. A multi-course breakfast and afternoon social hour are complimentary. Each room is individually beautifully furnished including antiques, and has a private bathroom, refrigerator, gas fireplace and queen or king bed. Some have ocean views.
   "Tapestry"–spacious, nook with stained-glass ceiling,
      oversize in-bath soaking tub, ornate king bed.
   "Provence"–private patio, in-room
      large whirlpool, queen bed.

★ **Schooner's Cove**   *(503)436-2300*
   downtown at 188 N. Larch St. (Box 86) - 97110
   schoonerscove.com
   30 units   *(800)843-0128*   *Expensive-Very Expensive*
One of Oregon's most handsome oceanfront lodgings is Schooner's Cove by the shore in the heart of Cannon Beach. Cannon Beach-style architecture is surrounded by natural landscaping that extends to a memorable "singing sands" beach. There is a large surf-view whirlpool. All of the well-furnished studios and one-bedroom units have a kitchenette, gas fireplace, a private deck with a grand beach-and-surf view, and a queen bed.
   #45,#53–romantic studio, kitchenette,
      large private surf-view deck and gas
      fireplace in view of queen bed.

Sea Sprite Guest Lodgings   *(503)436-2266*
2 mi. S at 280 S. Nebesna St. (Box 66) - Tolovana Park 97145
seasprite.com
7 units   *(866)828-1050*   *Expensive-Very Expensive*
The beach adjoins this small inn overlooking Haystack Rock. Each
unit has a fully equipped kitchen and one or two queen beds.
   Suite #3–1 BR, gas Franklin fireplace in living room,
      rocking chair, full kitchen, big private balcony with
      superb ocean/Haystack view, twin and queen bed.

★ **Stephanie Inn**   *(503)436-2221*
   2 mi. S at 2740 S. Pacific St. (Box 219) - 97110
   stephanie-inn.com
   50 units   *(800)633-3466*   *Very Expensive*
Stephanie Inn is one of the Northwest's most elegant country
inns. A fine sandy beach stretches for miles in front of the
"Cannon Beach-style" wood-trimmed three-story building that
opened in 1993 in a tranquil oceanfront site near Haystack Rock.
A gourmet breakfast buffet and an afternoon wine gathering are
complimentary. The plush dining room (see listing) offers four
course dinners by reservation. There is also a gift shop. Each
spacious, luxuriously furnished room is newly renovated and has
a gas fireplace, wet bar/refrigerator with complimentary refreshments, large in-bath whirlpool, large private mountain- or ocean-
view deck, and queen or king bed.
   "oceanfront dormer rooms" (#303,#304,#305,
      #308,#309,#310)–romantic, beach/ocean view
      from semi-private balcony and king bed.
   "Janice Kay" Room (#211)–grand
      panoramic ocean view, queen bed.

★ **Surfsand Resort**   *(503)436-2274*
   just S at 148 W. Gower St. (Box 219) - 97110
   surfsand.com
   84 units   *(800)547-6100*   *Expensive-Very Expensive*
Amenities in this contemporary three-story oceanfront motor
hotel, in addition to direct access to a fine-sand beach near
Haystack Rock, include a large indoor pool and whirlpool,
complimentary use of an athletic club, an ocean-view restaurant
and lounge (see **Wayfarer** listing) and a new gift shop. Each room
is beautifully furnished. Units on the top floor have a gas
fireplace, private ocean-view deck, two-person in-bath whirlpool,
and a queen or king bed.
   #402,#403,#404,#408,#409,#410–spacious,
      gas fireplace, in-bath two-person whirlpool,
      refrigerator, microwave, private balcony with
      oceanfront view, king bed.

★ **Tolovana Inn**   *(503)436-2211*
  2 mi. S at 3400 S. Hemlock St. (Box 165) - Tolovana Park 97145
  tolovanainn.com
  177 units   *(800)333-8890*   *Moderate-Very Expensive*
Wood-trim and shingles distinguish this large oceanfront condo-style motor hotel. Amenities include a choice location on the beach, a big indoor pool, whirlpool, saunas, exercise room, and a game room with table tennis and pool tables, plus an adjoining view restaurant and lounge. Each room was recently attractively refurbished, including all contemporary amenities and a queen bed. Studios to two-bedroom units have a kitchen, gas fireplace, and a private deck (many with an ocean view). There are also non-ocean-view motel-style rooms.
  #326,#226,#126–one bedroom, kitchen, glass-front
    fireplace, private balcony, great beach/ocean/
    Haystack Rock view, Murphy queen bed in living
    room and queen bed in bedroom.
  #325,#225,#125–as above, but can't see Haystack Rock.

★ **The Waves Motel**   *(503)436-2205*
  downtown at 188 W. 2nd St. (Box 3) - 97110
  thewavesmotel.com
  36 units   *(800)822-2468*   *Moderate-Very Expensive*
Artistically handcrafted units are especially memorable in the Waves, an intimate Cannon-Beach-style enclave on the beach next to the heart of town. There is a large surf-view whirlpool. Each room ranging from studio to two bedrooms is beautifully furnished. Most have a kitchen, gas fireplace, private ocean-view deck, and a queen or king bed.
  "Flagship"(10 of these)–studio, gas fireplace,
    kitchenette, private oceanfront deck, queen bed.

Webb's Scenic Surf   *(503)436-2706*
  downtown at 255 N. Larch St. (Box 67) - 97110
  webbsscenicsurf.com
  14 units   *(800)374-9322*   *Expensive-Very Expensive*
Near the heart of town on the beach is a small motel with some fine ocean views. Each simply furnished unit has a refrigerator and twins, queen or king bed.
  #6–brick fireplace, kitchenette, private beachview
    deck, queen bed.
  #11–gas fireplace, refrigerator, microwave, private
    beach-view balcony, king bed.

Florence

Florence is the center of the most diverse coastal recreation wonderland in the Pacific Northwest. To the north, lush pine forests cover mountain slopes that rise precipitously from the sea. The lovely little Siuslaw River estuary adjoins the heart of town. Mammoth sand dunes along the far side of the river extend to the ocean a mile to the west. Southward along the coast for more than forty miles are some of the world's most spectacular sand formations. Numerous small freshwater lakes with sandy or pine-forested shorelines are tucked into the surrounding countryside. Temperatures are moderate year-round. Wild rhododendron bushes bloom throughout the area in late spring following long, very wet winters.

The village grew slowly after settlement began during the 1870s. A bridge was completed in 1936 as one of the final links in the Oregon coast highway. Businesses gradually relocated along the busy thoroughfare and nearly abandoned the original heart of town. The beguiling old business district was happily rediscovered and brought back to life during the 1970s, and the estuary was reopened to navigation.

Today, Oregon Dunes National Recreation Area, Siuslaw National Forest, and state parks protect an extraordinary range of natural attractions with unlimited recreation opportunities. Highway-fronting uptown, while lacking in charm, provides for basic needs and ample lodgings, while Old Town burgeons as the rediscovered soul of Florence with many of the region's best specialty shops, restaurants, and lodging choices.

Florence

WEATHER PROFILE

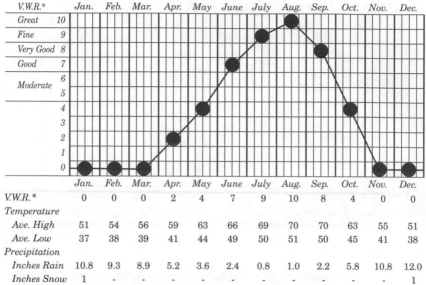

V.W.R.*		Jan.	Feb.	Mar.	Apr.	May	June	July	Aug.	Sep.	Oct.	Nov.	Dec.
Great	10												
Fine	9												
Very Good	8												
Good	7												
Moderate	6												
	5												
	4												
	3												
	2												
	1												
	0												

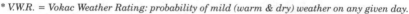

	Jan.	Feb.	Mar.	Apr.	May	June	July	Aug.	Sep.	Oct.	Nov.	Dec.
V.W.R.*	0	0	0	2	4	7	9	10	8	4	0	0
Temperature												
Ave. High	51	54	56	59	63	66	69	70	70	63	55	51
Ave. Low	37	38	39	41	44	49	50	51	50	45	41	38
Precipitation												
Inches Rain	10.8	9.3	8.9	5.2	3.6	2.4	0.8	1.0	2.2	5.8	10.8	12.0
Inches Snow	1	-	-	-	-	-	-	-	-	-	-	1

* V.W.R. = Vokac Weather Rating: probability of mild (warm & dry) weather on any given day.

BASIC INFORMATION

Population: 7,263
Elevation: 25 feet
Location: 160 miles Southwest of Portland
Airport (regularly scheduled flights): Eugene - 62 miles

Florence Area Chamber of Commerce   (541)997-3128
   downtown at 270 Hwy. 101 (Box 26000) - 97439
   florencechamber.com   (800)524-4864

ATTRACTIONS

★ **Boat Rentals**
Boat rentals can be arranged for freshwater fishing near town on Siltcoos and Woahink Lakes. (Highway signs identify where the lakefront facilities are located.) For salmon and trout fishermen, there are recreational marinas with boat launch and moorage, plus boats, motors and tackle for rent or sale year-round. Full-service RV parks adjoin.

Port of Siuslaw Marina   *(541)997-3040*
downtown at 100 Harbor St.
Siuslaw Marina   *(541)997-3254*
3 mi. E at 6516 Hwy. 126

★ **Cape Perpetua Scenic Area**   *(541)547-3289*
22 mi. N on Hwy. 101
fs.fed.us/r6/siuslaw
The Cape Perpetua Interpretive Center features great views, movies and "touch" exhibits explaining the geography and marine highlights of this section of the Oregon coast. Well-marked hiking trails fan out from the Center to tidepools, blowholes, churning surf and sandy coves bordering the dramatic shore. Inland, trails extend along a heavily forested creek (don't miss the mile-long Giant Spruce Trail to an enormous 500-year-old evergreen amid colossal sword fern deep in a rain forest); and up to the summit of Cape Perpetua–the highest point along the Oregon coast. The easiest way to get to the top is via a paved road that winds and climbs 1.8 miles to a parking area, from which a short trail leads to a magnificent panoramic view of the coast far below. There is also a full-service campground.

Cook's Chasm
22 mi. N on Hwy. 101
The chasm is a deep cleft in the coastal volcanic basalt rock next to the highway. When tidal and wind conditions are right, a blowhole (spouting horn) sends flumes of sea water forty feet into the air.

Darlingtonia Botanical Wayside
6 mi. N on Hwy. 101
A paved hiking trail offers a short stroll to a bog filled with Darlingtonia, commonly known as cobra lilies. This rare, carnivorous plant native to southwestern Oregon and north-western California traps and eats bugs.

★ **Dune Buggy Rentals**
The most exhilarating way to explore the vast rolling seas of sand that border the ocean south of Florence is on a dune buggy. Rent a two-seater to do your own motorized exploration by the hour or longer at:

Sand Dunes Frontier   *4 mi. S on Hwy. 101   (541)997-5363*
sanddunesfrontier.com
Dune Tours
★ **Sand Dunes Frontier**   *(541)997-3544*
  4 mi. S at 83960 Hwy. 101
  sanddunesfrontier.com
Balloon-tired open-air buses, or little sand rails for thrill seekers, are used for approximately half-hour guided tours into some of the world's highest sand dunes at the heart of a vast sandy "frontier" that begins just south of Florence and continues for forty-five miles along the coast. The tours are a unique experience. Longer private tours can be arranged, or rent your own dune buggy (see listing). There is also a miniature golf course, trout fishing pond, game room and souvenir shop at this deservedly popular roadside attraction by the dunes.

★ **Sandland Adventures**   *(541)997-8087*
  1 mi. S at 85366 Hwy. 101
  sandland.com
Dune buggies seating up to five passengers are featured for half hour or hour guided tours with a professional driver, while groups up to forty can be accommodated in their giant dune buggies. There is also a fun center at the base with bumper boats, a go-cart track, miniature golf, and a mile-long mini-railroad plus a gift shop. There is also "Balloon Busters" where you can launch water balloons fifty feet at your friends and family with a giant slingshot.

★ **Florence Events Center**   *(541)997-1994   (888)968-4086*
  downtown at 715 Quince St.
  eventcenter.org
Since 1996, the Florence Events Center has been providing rotating theatrical and musical performances in a 457-seat theater with good acoustics and comfortable seating, as well as rotating art exhibits, special community events, and more. Call or visit their website for a calendar of events.

★ **Heceta Head Lighthouse**   *(541)547-3696*
  12 mi. N on Hwy. 101
  hecetalighthouse.com
High on a precipitous slope of a massive headland, a lighthouse stands watch over a ruggedly beautiful section of the Oregon coast. Circa 1894, the picturesque landmark (on the National Register of Historic Places with the Lightkeeper's House) is one of the most photographed buildings in the West. The lighthouse and cabin are open for tours in summer. The cabin serves as an interpretive center by day and bed-and-breakfast at night.

★ **Honeyman State Park**   *(541)997-3851   (800)551-6949*
  3 mi. S at 84505 Hwy. 101
  oregonstateparks.org
Tiny Cleawox Lake is the gem-like centerpiece of a peerless
recreation wonderland within easy hiking distance of the ocean.
Picnic tables are well-spaced along a pine-shaded shoreline. In
sharp contrast, a few hundred feet away on the other side of the
small lake, enormous sand dunes plunge into crystal-clear waters.
The clean, soft-sand slopes and beaches are idyllic places for
sunbathing, and the fresh water lake is warm enough for an
invigorating swim in summer. A complete campground in a pine
forest amid the dunes is just south. A road and hiking trails lead
to nearby Woahink Lake–popular for boating, fishing, water-
skiing, and swimming.

★ *Horseback Riding*
  C & M Stables   *(541)997-7540*
  8 mi. N at 90241 Hwy. 101 N
  oregonhorsebackriding.com
This is one of a relatively few places where you can experience the
feeling of riding a horse across sand dunes, and through ocean
surf on hard sand beaches. Guided group rides ranging from one
hour to half-day are offered year-round.

★ **Old Town**   *(541)997-1646*
  oldtownflorence.com
In recent years, the waterfront business district has come back to
resemble the way it was in the raucous and rowdy good old days.
Numerous restaurants and bars line the main street including
some that are in buildings that had served earlier uses like the
Old Waterfront Depot. With the historic bridge at one end and a
much-improved major marina with a scenic promenade at the
other, this has become one of the Oregon coast's most appealing
walking areas. In addition to good dining and drinking venues,
there are numerous shops that now feature arts and crafts by
Northwestern artisans.

★ **Oregon Dunes National Recreation Area**   *(541)271-3611*
  starts 1 mi. S on Hwy. 101
  fs.fed.us/r6/siuslaw/recreation/tripplanning
A remarkable mixture of sandy beaches, clear freshwater lakes
and streams, and islands of pine forests mingle with some of the
biggest sand dunes in the world. Fishing, beachcombing, hiking,
dune buggy riding, swimming, and camping are popular activities
in this unique recreation area which extends along the coast for
more than forty miles.

★ **Sand Master Park** *(541)997-6006*
  1 mi. N at 87542 Hwy. 101
  sandboard.com/locations/usa/oregon/smp.htm
Here is the world's first sandboard park, complete with jumps (including a cliff jump), rail slides, chutes, and bowls in a terrain park built into many acres of private sculpted dunes. At the base is a pro shop with sandboard sales and rentals, related gear, a gift shop, and a game room.

★ **Sea Lion Caves** *(541)547-3111*
  11 mi. N at 91560 Hwy. 101
  sealioncaves.com
Here is the only year-round natural habitat for wild sea lions on the American mainland. A scenic walkway and an elevator take visitors down to the world's largest sea cave. The wave-carved grotto, more than 300 feet long and 100 feet high, is in the base of a massive cliff. Hundreds of sea lions can usually be seen from the viewing area. The bulls are especially notable, with some weighing more than a ton. There is also a large gift shop and a dramatic life-sized bronze sculpture of "Steller Sea Lion Family."

Siltcoos Park *(541)682-2000*
  8 mi. S via Hwy. 101 and park access road
This large coastal park provides trailheads for hikers, staging areas for ORVers, miles of dunes from the park northward, several campgrounds, and picnic areas in the dunes. Inland, there is fine fishing at Siltcoos Lake.

★ **Siuslaw National Forest** *(541)547-3289*
  E, N and S of town
  fs.fed.us/r6/siuslaw/
This is the only coastal national forest in the Northwest. Cape Perpetua Visitor Center (on Highway 101) offers a movie and exhibits about the Oregon Coast. Ten miles of scenic hiking trails branch out from the center into a lush rain forest, driftwood-strewn beaches, and rock-bound tidepool formations. The view from the top of Cape Perpetua (the highest point on the Oregon coast) is magnificent and accessible by car. Nearby are some fascinating rock and sea attractions–including Cook's Chasm where a natural blowhole in volcanic rock can send seawater forty feet in the air. Inland, luxuriant forests blanket Coast Range mountains that top out at nearly 4,000 feet above sea level.

South Jetty Dune and Beach *(541)997-3426*
  1 mi. S on Hwy. 101
ORV staging areas, hiking trailheads into sand dunes, and beach access parking lots are positioned along a six-mile paved road to the south jetty where the Siuslaw River empties into the ocean. There are also shore fishing sites and a crabbing pier.

RESTAURANTS

BJ's Ice Cream   *(541)997-7286*
in Old Town at 1441 Bay St.
L-D.   *Low*
Dozens of delicious flavors of ice creams (made in their original
roadside parlor at 2930 Highway 101 North) can be enjoyed in
assorted fountain treats in this cheerful shop, or to go.

Benny's International Cafe   *(541)997-4549*
1 mi. N at 1517 Hwy. 101
B-L.   *Moderate*
Contemporary American breakfasts are featured, along with some
international specialties like lumpia, in a bright and cheerful little
coffee shop by the highway that attracts both locals and visitors.

Bliss' Route 101 Restaurant   *(541)997-6769*
1 mi. N at 1179 Hwy. 101
B-L-D.   *Moderate*
Here is a blast from the past. The Route 101 theme is delightfully
carried off with all-American road food served at padded booths.
Better yet, get a table in one of the vintage cherry convertibles
where you can enjoy your retro meal while listening to 1950s hits
on a Wurlitzer.

Bridgewater Restaurant   *(541)997-9405*
in Old Town at 1297 Bay St.
L-D.   *Moderate*
Seafoods star among contemporary American fare served in a
restored historic building with nostalgic decor and bric-a-brac.

Cheri's Bakery & Donut Shop   *(541)997-7100*
2 mi. N at 2107 Hwy. 101
B-L. Closed Sun.   *Moderate*
A short list of donuts and other morning delights like cinnamon
rolls are displayed and sold to go, or to be enjoyed here with coffee
and espresso in a cheerful little coffee shop.

Driftwood Shores   *(541)997-8263*
6 mi. NW (via Rhododendron Dr.) at 88416 First Av.
driftwoodshores.com
B-L-D.   *Moderate*
In Florence's only oceanfront lodging, the **Surfside Restaurant**
offers contemporary American fare like crab-stuffed mushrooms,
potato-wrapped salmon filet, or beer-battered prawns. But, the
real draw is the area's only surfside view from the comfortable
split-level dining room outfitted with wicker armchairs.

★ **Grand Occasions Cafe**   *(541)547-4409*
24 mi. N at 84 Beach St. - Yachats
L only.   *Moderate*
A short, well-thought-out selection of fresh flavorful sandwiches

and salads is served, along with soup, but the main event is pie–made here fresh daily and delicious. Everything is available to go or at one of a half-dozen casual tables in a little cafe/gift shop with an ocean view.

★ **Grape Leaf**   *(541)997-1646*
   in Old Town at 1269 Bay St.
   L-D. Call for hours.   *Low*
Florence's best wine shop is now also an appealing destination for good complementary cuisine. When the owner/chef does dinner (by reservation only), guests can enjoy the choice ambiance of half-a-dozen candlelit tables surrounded by all kinds of wine-related decor. Out front are a few sidewalk tables with a view of the bridge across the Siuslaw in the backdrop.

★ **Hickory's BBQ Grill**   *(541)997-9739*
   1 mi. N (near Hwy. 101) at 1565 9th St.
   B-L-D. Closed Sun.   *Moderate*
Hickory's BBQ Grill is one of the post-millennium-best additions to flavorful dining on the Oregon coast. It is the region's serious source for hickory and alderwood-grilled barbecue pork, beef, and chicken. Tasty regional nods include smoked salmon burger. In tribute to the Northwest, when wild salmon is in season, it is featured broiled with chipotle-lime sauce. All desserts are home-made, and Hickory's peanut butter pie is the best on the Oregon coast. Wood-trim chairs and booths with red-checkered tablecloths and whimsical wall hangings and art objects lend the right flavor to the delicious down-home cuisine.

ICM International C-Food Market   *(541)997-7978*
   in Old Town at 1498 Bay St.
   icminternationalcfoodmarket.com
   L-D.   *Moderate*
Fresh regional seafoods are transformed into a wealth of dishes like popcorn shrimp, crab sandwich, pan-fried oysters, seafood pot pie or classic seafood newburg. The big casual dining room and sunny deck adjoin their riverside fish-receiving station and the fishing fleet.

★ **La Serre Restaurant**   *(541)547-3420*
   24 mi. N (on Hwy. 101) at 160 W. 2nd St. - Yachats
   D only. Closed Tues.   *Moderate*
First-rate fresh local seafood like clams baked in puff pastry, a house salad of mixed field greens with hazelnut vinaigrette dressing, and a creative spirit with herbs and sauces are the hallmarks of La Serre, one of the Oregon coast's foremost dinner houses since 1977. In the capacious atrium dining room, a skylit jungle of healthy greenery surrounds diners at stylish tables. A tranquil firelit lounge adjoins.

Florence

Mo's Restaurant   *(541)997-2185*
in Old Town at 1436 Bay St.
moschowder.com
L-D.   *Low*
Simply prepared seafood is served at wood picnic-bench-style chairs in a big dining room with a cannery-like setting especially appealing to families. The bridge-and-river view is notable.

Morgan's Country Kitchen   *(541)997-6991*
2 mi. S at 85020 Hwy. 101 S
B-L.   *Moderate*
Morgan's features down-home American dishes like assorted omelets with biscuits and gravy, along with cinnamon rolls and various fruit and berry pies. The long-established cafe offers a choice of a counter or small cheerful dining areas.

★ **Siuslaw River Coffee Roasters**   *(541)997-3443*
in Old Town at 1240 Bay St.
B-L.   *Moderate*
Here is the most delightful coffeehouse for many miles. They roast their own beans and vacuum-seal them for sale. Some of the best baked goods in town range from cinnamon rolls to cookies. Several cozy dining niches are in the store, and a little deck out back is perfect for viewing the adjoining river and bridge.

Traveler's Cove   *(541)997-6845*
in Old Town at 1362 Bay St.
B-L-D.   *Moderate*
Mexican dishes include a wide assortment of traditional and some appealing creative nods using Northwestern ingredients. The seafood burrito or enchilada are good choices while enjoying the little deck on the river beyond the casual little dining room.

★ **Waterfront Depot**   *(541)902-0502*
in Old Town at 1252 Bay St.
L-D.   *Moderate*
The Waterfront Depot is a delightful destination for lively adult dining. A short eclectic list of small plate appetizers and entrees that reflect seasonal fresh ingredients from the Northwest are described on a big blackboard. In the high-ceilinged historic building, a snazzy bar with padded chrome stools shares the fine riverfront view with a roomful of wood-toned tables and chairs.

Weber's Fish House Restaurant & Market   *(541)997-8886*
downtown at 820 Hwy. 101
L-D.   *Moderate*
For years, Weber's has been a highwayside landmark fish market and restaurant. Northwestern seafood like wild salmon, crab, shrimp and oysters are displayed in extensive cases in the market and featured in the adjoining casual coffee shop.

LODGINGS

There are several distinctive river-view accommodations and an oceanfront hotel, plus standard motels along the highway in town, plus several special oceanfront lodgings near Yachats. Apart from summer high season, rates may be reduced 30% or more.

★ **The Adobe**   *(541)547-3141*
   25 mi. N at 1555 Hwy. 101 (Box 219) - Yachats 97498
   adoberesort.com
   94 units   *(800)522-3623*   *Moderate-Very Expensive*
The Adobe features some of the most remarkably close coastal seascapes in Oregon. A basalt coastline borders an expansive park-like setting and spacious lawns of this contemporary hotel. Facilities, in addition to access to a spectacular shore with tiny sandy coves amid rocky outcroppings, include a large indoor pool, whirlpool, sauna, exercise room, plus a large restaurant and lounge that share the romantic ocean view, and a gift shop. Most of the beautifully furnished rooms have fine surf views. All have a refrigerator, microwave, and doubles, queens or king bed. Many have a high-tech electric fireplace and/or a double whirlpool.
   #317,#319–spacious, corner, living room with high-tech
      electric fireplace, raised two-person whirlpool that
      shares awesome ocean view with king bed.
   #375–spacious, high-tech electric fireplace, raised
      two-person whirlpool by front corner window
      that shares splendid view with king bed.
   #377,#379,#381,#383,#385,#387,#389–as above,
      but no corner window.

★ **The Blue Heron Inn**   *(541)997-4091*
   3 mi. E at 6563 Hwy. 126 (Box 1122) - 97439
   blue-heroninn.com
   5 units   *(800)997-7780*   *Moderate-Expensive*
The Siuslaw River is across the highway from this large bed-and-breakfast in a garden. Features include a video entertainment room with a wealth of showtime possibilities. Gourmet breakfast is complimentary. Each cozy, well-furnished room has a private bath and a queen or king bed.
   "Bridal Suite"–river-view windows, dual-head
      shower, large in-bath whirlpool, king bed.
   "Raspberry Cream Room"–two-person in-bath
      whirlpool, queen bed.

★ **Driftwood Shores**   *(541)997-8263*
   6 mi. NW (via Rhododendron Dr.) at 88416 First Av. - 97439
   driftwoodshores.com
   128 units   *(800)422-5091*   *Moderate-Very Expensive*
Florence's only oceanfront lodging is also its largest. The four-

story motor hotel includes a long sandy beach, large indoor pool, whirlpool, and an ocean-view restaurant and lounge (see listing). Each well-furnished room has a large private balcony or deck with a fine surf-and-sand view, refrigerator, microwave, and one or two queen or a king bed. Many also have a kitchen.

Economy Inn   *(541)997-7115*
   3 mi. N at 3829 Hwy. 101 - 97439
   economyinnflorence.com
   29 units   *(800)630-2689*   *Low*

This contemporary motel has a small indoor pool and whirlpool. Each comfortably furnished room has a queen or king bed.

★ **Edwin K Bed & Breakfast**   *(541)997-8360*
   in Old Town at 1155 Bay St. (Box 2687) - 97439
   edwink.com
   7 units   *(800)833-9465*   *Moderate-Expensive*

Edwin K is the most romantic lodging in Florence. An artistically transformed 1914 mansion is surrounded by intimate luxuriant gardens and a soothing waterfall. Old Town is a short stroll away and sand dunes rise dramatically above the far side of the Siuslaw River a hundred yards to the south. Formal five-course breakfast is complimentary as are tea, sherry and cookies in the evening. Each spacious, beautifully furnished room blends antiques and contemporary conveniences including a small refrigerator, and has a queen or king bed. Several also have a sensual bath (whirlpool, clawfoot tub, or double shower) and a view of the river and dunes, or an intimate waterfall.

   "Spring Room"–river and dunes view, double shower,
     two-person whirlpool in view of queen bed.
   "Indian Summer"–elegant glass-block wall by corner
     two-person whirlpool in view of king bed.
   "Autumn Room"–cozy, private deck to garden and
     waterfall, one-person whirlpool, sleigh queen bed.

★ **The Fireside**   *(541)547-3636*
   25 mi. N at 1881 Hwy. 101 N (Box 313) - Yachats 97498
   firesidemotel.com
   43 units   *(800)336-3573*   *Moderate-Expensive*

The Fireside is beautifully situated in a park-like setting where most of the rooms are only a few yards from a dramatic rocky beach. There is a well-stocked gift shop with Northwestern items. Each attractively furnished oceanfront unit has a refrigerator and microwave, and a queen or king bed.

   #19–private balcony, raised gas fireplace, in-room
     two-person whirlpool, king bed.
   "king fireplace"–large semi-private balcony with fine
     oceanfront view, raised gas fireplace, king bed.

Le Chateau Motel   *(541)997-3481*
  just N at 1084 Hwy. 101 - 97439
  lechateaumotel.com
  49 units   *(800)451-1688*   *Low-Moderate*
This modern two-level motel has several amenities–an outdoor pool, whirlpool, sauna, and an exercise room, plus a complimentary Continental breakfast. Each spacious, comfortably furnished room has refrigerator, microwave and queen or king bed.

Ocean Haven   *(541)547-3583*
  18 mi. N at 94770 Hwy. 101 - 97498
  oceanhaven.com
  5 units   *Moderate-Expensive*
Perched by the highway in a meadow high above a rugged shoreline is a nature-friendly old lodge with a lot of character. Artistically refurbished wood-crafted rooms are well furnished, including a kitchen, romantic ocean view, and queen bed(s).
  "Shag's Nest"–rustic studio cabin for lovers, private
    bath, kitchenette, woodburning fireplace, glorious
    coastal views from three sides, queen bed.
  "South View"–picture-window surf view panorama
    from overstuffed rockers, two queen beds.

Old Town Inn   *(541)997-7131*
  in Old Town at 170 Highway 101 - 97439
  old-town-inn.com
  40 units   *(800)587-5591*   *Low-Moderate*
This modern motel a stroll from Old Town offers spacious, comfortably furnished rooms with one or two queen or a king bed.

★ **Overleaf Lodge**   *(541)547-4880*
  25 mi. N at 280 Overleaf Lodge Lane (Box 291) - Yachats 97498
  overleaflodge.com
  55 units   *(800)338-0507*   *Expensive-Very Expensive*
One of the most sybaritic lodgings on the Oregon coast is Overleaf Lodge. It opened in 1997 and underwent major expansion in 2005 on a volcanic headland above the surf with convenient access to beaches, and there is a large exercise room. A (fee) complete spa (new in 2005) features ocean-view whirlpools, men's and women's steam and sauna rooms, and massage rooms. A full breakfast is complimentary. All rooms are beautifully furnished in contemporary Northwestern style, and have a romantic close-up surf view, refrigerator, microwave, and queen or king bed. Many suites also have a gas fireplace, plus a large in-room whirlpool and private deck with an ocean view.
  #312,#212,#305,#205–spacious, living room area,
    raised gas fireplace, private balcony with ocean
    view shared by raised two-person whirlpool, king bed.

Pier Point Inn - Best Western   *(541)997-7191*
   just S at 85625 Hwy. 101 S (Box 2235) - 97439
   bestwestern.com/pierpointinn
   56 units   *(800)435-6736*   *Expensive*
This contemporary three-story motel on a bluff has a bird's-eye
view across the river to Old Town. Amenities include an indoor
pool with a river/town view, two whirlpools, sauna, and expanded
Continental breakfast. Each spacious, well-furnished room has a
private balcony and a river/town view and queens or a king bed.
   #347 thru #353–large private balcony shares
      fine Old Town/river view with king bed.

★ **River House**   *(541)997-3933*
   in Old Town at 1202 Bay St. - 97439
   riverhousemotel.com
   40 units   *(888)824-2829*   *Moderate*
River House has one of Oregon's most memorable settings. A
historic Highway 101 bridge and the Siuslaw River with a
tranquil pine forest and enormous sand dunes looming abruptly
from the far shore frame the view from many of the rooms in a
modern building that juts into the river. There is also a large
river-view whirlpool. Each spacious room is well furnished with
Northwestern decor touches, and has a queen or king bed.
   #230,#108–large private riverfront balcony with dunes view,
      two-person in-room whirlpool, king bed.

★ **Sea Quest Bed & Breakfast**   *(541)547-3782*
   18 mi. N at 95354 Hwy. 101 (Box 448) - Yachats 97498
   seaq.com
   5 units   *(800)341-4878*   *Expensive-Very Expensive*
Sea Quest is one of the West Coast's most romantic oceanfront
hideaways. The big comfortable bed-and-breakfast is sequestered
on a low bluff above a wild sandy beach. A gourmet breakfast
buffet with an unforgettable view is complimentary. Each room has
a private view deck, in-bath whirlpool tub, and a queen or king bed.
   "The Suite"–extra-large, big raised woodburning
      fireplace, raised two-person whirlpool with close-up
      surf view, private wraparound balcony with romantic
      ocean view shared by king bed.
   #3–ocean view from private deck and two-
      person whirlpool, queen bed.

Silver Sands Motel   *(541)997-3459*
   1 mi. N at 1449 Hwy. 101 (Box 1516) - 97439
   50 units   *Low*
A small outdoor pool with a slide is a feature of this modern two-
story motel. Each comfortably furnished unit has a microwave,
refrigerator, and queen or king bed.

Gold Beach

Gold Beach is the Northwest's best source for freshwater and saltwater adventures in one place. It is located on the flat little delta at the mouth of the famed Rogue River. The Coast Range rises abruptly to the east, while a fine black-sand beach borders the Pacific Ocean to the west. With a warm winter climate, freezes and snow are so scarce that Gold Beach has the distinction of having the biggest palm tree in all of the Pacific Northwest. It's just a few miles inland by the Rogue, one of America's first designated National Wild and Scenic Rivers.

Gold in the dark sand first attracted miners to this site during the 1870s (which is why the town was named "gold beach.") However, it was the river that brought permanence to the remote settlement. In 1895, mail boats began to provide postal service to isolated up-river settlers. Freight was soon added, and it wasn't long before home-cooked meals were being served to river passengers who tagged along to Agness to view the great scenery along the way. Happily, this tradition continues, with skilled operators of hydro-jet boats offering swift, thrilling whitewater trips deep into the beautiful Rogue River canyon.

Gold Beach manages to retain a relentless rusticity that goes back to the days when this town was oriented around fishing camps. Shops (with a few notable exceptions) are still relatively modest. Lodgings range from humble to gracious, many with ocean views. Salmon and steelhead fishing remain the area's passion, providing great opportunities for sportfishers, and restaurants do fine work with fresh local seafoods.

WEATHER PROFILE

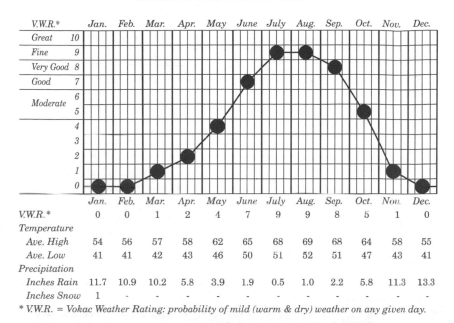

V.W.R.*	Jan.	Feb.	Mar.	Apr.	May	June	July	Aug.	Sep.	Oct.	Nov.	Dec.
V.W.R.*	0	0	1	2	4	7	9	9	8	5	1	0
Temperature												
Ave. High	54	56	57	58	62	65	68	69	68	64	58	55
Ave. Low	41	41	42	43	46	50	51	52	51	47	43	41
Precipitation												
Inches Rain	11.7	10.9	10.2	5.8	3.9	1.9	0.5	1.0	2.2	5.8	11.3	13.3
Inches Snow	1	-	-	-	-	-	-	-	-	-	-	-

* V.W.R. = Vokac Weather Rating: probability of mild (warm & dry) weather on any given day.

BASIC INFORMATION

Population: 1,897
Elevation: 50 feet
Location: 290 miles Southwest of Portland
Airport (regularly scheduled flights): North Bend - 80 miles

Gold Beach Visitor Center   (541)247-7526   (800)525-2334
   just S at 94080 Shirley Lane (off Hwy. 101) (Box 375) - 97444
   goldbeach.org
Gold Beach Chamber of Commerce   (541)247-0923
   1 mi. S at 29795 Ellensburg Av. (Box 489) - 97444
   goldbeachchamber.com

ATTRACTIONS

Boat Rentals
 Jot's Resort   *(541)247-6676   (800)367-5687*
 1 mi. N at 94360 Wedderburn Loop Rd.
Fishing boats with motors can be rented at the resort's marina near the mouth of the Rogue River, along with all related tackle and equipment.

★ ***Boat Rides***
Whitewater jet boat rides are Gold Beach's most famous attraction. The Northwest's most exhilarating narrated cruises are offered by two companies with a choice of 64, 80, or 104-mile round trips up the magnificent Rogue River canyon daily from May through October. The scenery is enhanced by sightings of black bear, deer, river otter, eagles and osprey. Shorter trips (approximately six hours) explore a scenic section of the lower Rogue and includes a meal break. Longer excursions go beyond to some thrilling whitewater in the "Wild and Scenic" portion. It's an all day (approximately eight hours) trip with a meal break at a wilderness lodge. Each company charges the same amount, provides optional (fee) meals (lunch or dinner) at the same up-river lodges, and leaves from near the bridge in town (their docks are well-marked). Reservations are recommended for both outfitters.

★ **Jerry's Rogue River Jet Boats** *(541)247-4571 (800)451-3645*
 roguejets.com
Jerry's, under family management since 1958, offered the first jet boat tour in America. Their complex includes a large shop full of Northwestern gifts, and a worthwhile museum of Rogue River history.

★ **Mail Boat Hydro Jet Trips**   *(541)247-7033 (800)458-3511*
 mailboat.com   *(Box 1165)*
Mailboats still deliver the U. S. Mail as they have since 1895. Their fleet includes a glass-enclosed excursion boat (perfect for rainy days), and there is a large shop featuring Northwest-oriented gifts.

★ **Cape Sebastian State Park**   *(541)469-2021*
 6 mi. S on Hwy. 101
A steep paved road winds up to the crest of a precipitous headland more than 700 feet above the sea. From the parking lot, visitors have a panoramic view of the coast to the Rogue River and beyond. Well-marked trails lead to other inspiring overlooks along the crest of the cape. To the south is a "perfect" Northwestern scene–forested mountains tumbling down to broad sandy ocean beaches. Offshore, oddly shaped rocks and tiny islands are constantly battered by the pounding surf.

Curry Historical Society Museum   *(541)247-6113*
  just S at 29419 Ellensburg Av. (Hwy. 101)
  curryhistory.com
More than 150 years of local history are showcased in extensive exhibits of artifacts and photos, and there is a bookstore. Closed Sun.-Mon.

★ *Fishing*
Salmon and steelhead lure visitors to the renowned Rogue River in droves to try their luck at catching "the big one." While most fishermen reserve guides with charter boats, many rent boats (from Jot's) or fish from the river bank with success. You can get licenses, rental gear, and information on current "hot spots" for bank fishing at:
  Jot's Resort   *(541)247-6676   (800)367-5687*
  1 mi. N at 94360 Wedderburn Loop Rd.
  Rogue Outdoor Store   *(541)247-7142*
  downtown at 29865 Ellensburg Av. (Hwy. 101)

★ *Fishing Charters*
  just N at Gold Beach Marina
Many charter boats operate daily for river and ocean salmon and steelhead fishing during summer and fall seasons. Guides are also readily available at other times for river fishing trips. You can get details on who's available, and what's being caught, by calling the Gold Beach Chamber of Commerce. The best outfitters and guides (all with many years of experience) using both drift and power-boats to fish for salmon or steelhead on the Rogue River include:
  Fish Oregon   *(541)247-4138   (800)348-4138*
  fishoregon.com
  Fishboss Guide Service   *(541)247-2051   (800)263-4351*
  fishchinook.com
  Five Star Charters   *(541)247-0217   (888)301-6480*
  goldbeachadventures.com
  Rogue River Outfitters   *(541)451-4498   (888)235-8963*
  rogueriveroutfitters.com
  Sport Fishing Oregon   *(541)247-6046   (800)501-6391*
  sportfishingoregon.com

Food Specialties
★ **Fishermen Direct Seafood**   *(541)247-9494   (888)523-9494*
  downtown in the Cannery Building
  fishermendirect.com
Award-winning smoked and regular albacore tuna are excellent, as are alder-smoked salmon in cans, fresh, frozen or as jerky, plus related condiments suitable for a picnic to go or to ship back home. They will smoke, vacuum-seal and freeze your fish after you catch it.

Wedderburn Store   *(541)247-7604*
1 mi. N at 94219 N. Bank Rogue Rd. - Wedderburn
The historic Wedderburn Store is a good place to assemble a
gourmet picnic to enjoy by the river. Big luscious cinnamon rolls
are made here several times a week, and there are all kinds of
hearty sandwich possibilities, plus tasty treats like onion rings,
cold salads, and gourmet and regular grocery items, all to go.

Horseback Riding

★ **Hawk's Rest Ranch**   *(541)247-6423*   *(800)525-2161*
10 mi. S on Hwy. 101 at 94667 N. Bank Pistol River Rd.
siskiyouwest.com
Some delightfully remote beaches are near Hawk's Rest Ranch
stables. Guided rides may include galloping through the surf past
massive rock seamounts, exploring sand dunes, and/or passing
through a primeval rainforest. Horseback rides range from one
hour to a full day. Reservations can be made at **Siskiyou West
Day Lodge** with a gift store, pioneer museum, and art gallery.

★ **Humbug Mountain State Park**   *(541)332-6774*
23 mi. N on Hwy. 101
oregonstateparks.org
The centerpiece of this sylvan park is a mountain towering 1,756
feet directly above the sea. Well-marked trails lead to the top of
Humbug Mountain (three miles); along a scenic (two-plus miles)
stretch of no-longer-used coastal highway; and for miles along a
remote beach. Creek swimming and stream and ocean fishing are
also popular, and there are excellent full-service camping facilities
in a sheltered little valley.

★ **Prehistoric Gardens**   *(541)332-4463*
15 mi. N at 36848 Hwy. 101 - Port Orford
Here is an unusual tourist attraction that's surprisingly well done
(and dates back to 1953). Life-sized technically-realistic replicas
of prehistoric dinosaurs are situated along meandering paths in
a luxuriant coastal rain forest that looks and feels prehistoric with
gigantic ferns and hanging moss. The gift shop is also notable.

★ **Rogue River**
The ruggedly beautiful Wild Rogue Wilderness lies in deep
canyons upstream beyond roads and jet boats from Gold Beach.
Access is only by raft from the Grants Pass side (see listing) or on
foot. The Rogue River Trail is a well-marked pathway along the
entire forty-three-mile wilderness stretch through an enchanting
canyon. Tranquil drifts punctuated by famous whitewater rapids
like Graves Creek Falls and Blossom Bar are unforgettable.
Spring is the quietest time–the weather is mild and wildflowers
are at peak bloom. Summer is the most popular season–days are
often hot, and the crystal-clear river is perfect for rafting,

swimming, and fishing. As an unusual added feature, rustic riverside lodges are an easy hike a day apart along the entire trail. You can travel for days in the wilderness carrying only a light pack and enjoy hot showers, clean beds, and hearty meals by reserving these places well in advance. Contact:

Half Moon Bar Lodge   *Box 455 (541)247-6968*
Lucas Pioneer Ranch   *Box 37   (541)247-7443*
Paradise Lodge   *Box 456 (541)247-6022 (800)525-2161*
Singing Springs Resort   *Box 68   (541)247-2782*

RESTAURANTS

★ **Chives Oceanfront Dining**   *(541)247-4121*
1 mi. S at 29212 Ellensburg Av. (Hwy. 101)
D only. Closed Mon.-Tues.   *Expensive*
Creative Northwestern cuisine featuring fresh top-quality seasonal ingredients is expertly prepared for dishes like crisp salmon cakes with lemon-caper beurre blanc or shrimp bisque, or roast breast of pheasant with soft polenta and creamed demiglaze, or half-duck with wild mushroom risotto. Delicious desserts like sabayon or bananas foster are also served. The stylish dining room has a raised stone fireplace and a picture-window panoramic view of nearby surf beyond some foredunes. The fine view is also available from a comfortable patio.

★ **Gold Beach Books**   *(541)247-2495*
downtown at 29707 Ellensburg Av. (Hwy. 101)
oregoncoastbooks.com
B-L-D.   *Moderate*
Gold Beach Books is one of the largest bookstores on the Oregon coast. It is also a destination for stellar housemade pastries ranging from cinnamon rolls and sticky buns, scones and coffee cake in the morning to shortbread and cookies later. They have light fare to go with it, along with bright, cheerful atmosphere amidst quality local art for sale. The store overlooks the main street and includes good collections of new and used books .

Grants Pancake & Omelette House   *(541)247-7208*
downtown at 29790 Ellensburg Av. (Hwy. 101)
B-L.   *Moderate*
All-American breakfasts are featured including build-your-own omelets and pancakes. The big contemporary coffee shop houses dining areas with many padded booths. Along the back is a distant panoramic view of the ocean.

★ **Honey Bear Campground**   *(541)247-2765   (800)822-4444*
9 mi. N (via Hwy. 101) at 34161 Ophir Rd. - Ophir
honeybearrv.com
D only. Closed Mon.-Tues. or more off-season.   *Low*

Authentic German fare including German sausage and honey-cured ham from the in-house Black Forest Sausage Kitchen, potato pancakes, sauerkraut, and more are generously served along with some American dishes. The big friendly dining room in a campground achieves the warm appeal of a classic German beer hall when the talented owner, Gary Saks, provides the musical entertainment as he has since 1980.

Indian Creek Cafe   *(541)247-0680*
   1 mi. NE at 94682 Jerry's Flat Rd.
   B-L.   *Moderate*
Pancakes, waffles and choose-your-own-combination omelets are served in hearty portions in a plain roadside cafe with a view of forest out back.

★ **Nor'Wester Seafood Restaurant**   *(541)247-2333*
   just N at Port of Gold Beach
   D only.   *Moderate*
Fresh regional seafood (like line-caught wild Rogue River salmon) stars–broiled, baked or sautéed, as well as grilled or fried–in Gold Beach's longest-established dinner house. Located upstairs, the warmly contemporary split-level dining room includes a massive raised-relief wood mural of two whales, a freestanding fireplace, and a fine picture-window view of the mouth of the Rogue near the ocean.

Playa Del Sol   *(541)247-0314*
   just S at 29455 Ellensburg Av. (Hwy. 101)
   L-D. Closed Mon.   *Moderate*
Traditional Mexican specialties including some seafood dishes like shrimp fajitas or seafood burrito are served in a colorful little cafe filled with south-of-the-border knickknacks.

Port Hole Cafe   *(541)247-7411*
   downtown at 29975 Harbor Way
   portholecafe.com
   B-L-D.   *Moderate*
Port Hole Cafe offers hearty homestyle dishes at all meals with a picture-window view of an adjoining marina near the mouth of the Rogue River. An added attraction is a large selection of homemade fruit and cream pies on display near the entrance.

Riverview Restaurant   *(541)247-7321*
   1 mi. NE at 94749 Jerry's Flat Rd.
   D only.   *Moderate*
Contemporary Northwestern fare from salmon several ways to designer pizzas and calzones is offered in a long-established riverside roadhouse. The big, recently improved dining room shares the area's best window-wall view of the lower Rogue River with an adjoining lounge.

Rod 'n Reel   *(541)247-6823*
  1 mi. N at 94321 Wedderburn Loop
  D only.   *Expensive*
A wide range of contemporary American dishes is presented. A
dining area with a lovely view of landscaping and a lounge have
a comfortable rusticity appropriate to Jot's Resort (see listing).

★ **Rollin 'N Dough**   *(541)247-4438*
  1 mi. NE at 94257 N. Bank Rogue Rd. - Wedderburn
  L-D. Only brunch on Sun. Closed Mon. No D Tues.   *Moderate*
Rollin 'N Dough is one of Oregon's most delightful surprises
among culinary hideaways. Natives know that the delicious
creative Northwestern cuisine and assorted designer breads made
fresh daily are some of the best on the Oregon coast. Fresh
seasonal ingredients are given skilled, careful attention for light,
bright lunches and flavorful dinners that are worth driving long
distances for. The few tables in the tiny cottage overlook display
cases with their superb breads, delectable desserts (like lemon
curd cheesecake) and sophisticated deli items.

★ **Spinner's**   *(541)247-5160*
  downtown at 29430 Ellensburg Av. (Hwy. 101)
  D only.   *Expensive*
Spinner's is a deservedly popular destination for some of the best
seafoods on the Southern Oregon coast. The cedar-planked fresh
wild Oregon salmon is a deservedly popular entree. But, don't
miss the fresh Dungeness Oregon crabcake sautéed golden brown
served over fresh spinach with a lemon beurre blanc–it is a
perfectly executed Northwestern specialty. Intimate candlelit
tables set with a fresh flower and full linen distinguish romantic
dining areas with walls displaying regional art. All share a
window-wall view of the distant ocean beyond a picturesque vine-
covered rock wall.

LODGINGS

Most of the area's best lodgings are an easy stroll from the ocean
or river. High season is from June through September. Prices are
often reduced 30% or more at other times.

Azalea Lodge   *(541)247-6635*
  1 mi. S at 29481 Ellensburg Av. (Hwy. 101) (Box 1167) - 97444
  azalealodge.biz
  17 units   *(800)381-6635*   *Low-Moderate*
This single-level motel offers modern, comfortably furnished
rooms with a refrigerator and queen bed.

Breakers Gold Beach   *(541)247-6606*
  1 mi. S at 29171 Ellensburg Av. (Hwy. 101) - 97444
  breakersgoldbeach.com

38 units   *(800)503-0833*   *Moderate-Expensive*
This motel is on a high rise across the highway from a superb
dark sand beach. Each compact, nicely furnished room has some
ocean view and a queen or king bed.
   #226 thru #222–larger, refrigerator, microwave, private
      balcony with distant panoramic ocean view, king bed.

Gold Beach Inn   *(541)247-7091*
1 mi. S at 29346 Ellensburg Av. (Hwy. 101) - 97444
goldbeachinn.com
   41 units   *(888)663-0608*   *Moderate*
This contemporary motel is situated on a rise above the nearby
ocean so all of the well-furnished rooms on the third and fourth
floors have good ocean views beyond the foredunes, and two
queens or a king bed.

★ **Gold Beach Resort**   *(541)247-7066*
1 mi. S at 29232 Ellensburg Av. (Hwy. 101) - 97444
gbresort.com
   45 units   *(800)541-0947*   *Expensive*
Gold Beach Resort is the area's most elaborate oceanfront
lodging. Less than 200 yards away is a spectacular dark sand
beach that extends for miles from the jetty at the mouth of the
Rogue River to some picturesque rock monoliths to the south.
Amenities of the contemporary motel/condo complex include a
large indoor pool and whirlpool, and a complimentary expanded
Continental breakfast buffet. Each spacious, well-furnished room
has a private ocean-view balcony, a microwave, refrigerator, and
two queens or a king bed. Condos also have a kitchen and a gas
fireplace in the living room.
   #329 thru #338–top floor, spectacular view
      beyond grassy foredunes, king bed.
   Condo #7–raised corner gas fireplace, extra-large
      balcony off of living room, in-bath whirlpool tub,
      separate bedroom with king bed.

Inn of the Beachcomber   *(541)247-6691*
1 mi. S at 29266 Ellensburg Av. (Hwy. 101) - 97444
beachcomber-inn.com
   50 units   *(888)690-2378*   *Moderate-Expensive*
This contemporary motel has a paved path to a fine sandy beach,
a large indoor pool, and whirlpool. An expanded breakfast bar is
complimentary. Many recently renovated well-furnished rooms
have an ocean view beyond the foredunes, and two queens or a
king bed.
   #239,#212–end rooms, private balcony, woodburning
      fireplace, refrigerator, microwave, good ocean view
      from king bed.

★ **Ireland's Rustic Lodges**   *(541)247-7718*
  1 mi. S at 29330 Ellensburg Av. (Hwy. 101) (Box 774) - 97444
  irelandsrusticlodges.com
  40 units   *(877)447-3526*   *Low-Moderate*
Over many years, Ireland's has been upgraded, but remains a major destination for everyone yearning for romantic rusticity on the Oregon coast. Lovely pine-shaded lawns and colorful gardens surround individual log cabins and modern motel rooms, and a trail extends to the adjacent picturesque black-sand beach. Each room is comfortably furnished in Northwestern knotty-pine decor and has a microwave, refrigerator or kitchen, and double, queen or king bed. Most have a gas or woodburning fireplace. Several also have a kitchenette and/or a private ocean-view balcony.
  #22,#23–upstairs, vaulted ceiling, raised stone wood-
    burning fireplace, windows on two sides, large private
    balcony, private ocean view from queen bed.
  #14,#15–raised corner gas fireplace, large private
    balcony shares outstanding ocean view with king bed.

★ **Jot's Resort**   *(541)247-6676*
  1 mi. N at 94360 Wedderburn Loop (Box 1200) - 97444
  jotsresort.com
  140 units   *(800)367-5687*   *Moderate-Expensive*
Jot's Resort is the South Coast's largest and most complete motor hotel. The long-established complex sprawls along a choice site by the Rogue River near the ocean. Amenities include two pools (one indoors), whirlpool, sauna, dock and gift/tackle shop, restaurant (see **Rod 'n Reel**) and lounge, plus rental boats and fishing equipment, and reservations for (fee) river excursions and fishing charters. Each well-furnished room has a river view and two doubles, queen or king bed. Spacious one- or two-bedroom condos also have a kitchen, woodburning fireplace, and a private deck.
  one-bedroom condo (approximately 10 of these)–spacious,
    queen or king bed in back, full kitchen, woodburning fire-
    place, picture-window view of Rogue beyond private deck.
  #316,#317–spacious, river view, in-room
    two-person whirlpool, king bed.

Motel 6   *(541)247-4533*
  just E at 94433 Jerry's Flat Rd. - 97444
  motel6.com
  50 units   *(800)759-4533*   *Moderate*
The local Motel 6 is on a hill near the beautiful bridge across the Rogue River behind their extra-large, intrusive neon billboard at the south end of the bridge. Each larger-than-expected room has either two queens or a king bed. Some have a view of the bridge and river beyond a common walkway and parking lot.

Oregon Trail Lodge   *(541)247-6030*
downtown at 29855 Ellensburg Av. (Hwy. 101) - 97444
17 units   *Low*
One of Gold Beach's oldest motels is a single-level bargain near
the jet boat dock. Recently refurbished, simply furnished rooms
have a microwave, refrigerator, and a queen or king bed.

Sand Dollar Inn   *(541)247-6611*
just S at 29399 Ellensburg Av. (Hwy. 101) - 97444
sanddollar-inn.com
24 units   *(866)726-3657*   *Low-Moderate*
This single-level older motel has a nearby access across a highway
to foredunes and the beach. Each compact, comfortable room has
a refrigerator, microwave and one or two queen or a king bed.

Sand 'n Sea Motel   *(541)247-6658*
1 mi. S at 29362 Ellensburg Av. (Hwy. 101) - 97444
sandnseamotel.com
45 units   *(800)808-7263*   *Moderate-Expensive*
Sand 'n Sea is a contemporary oceanfront motel with an indoor
whirlpool and easy access to a spectacular sandy beach. Expanded
Continental breakfast is complimentary. Each well-furnished unit
has a microwave and refrigerator. Many also have an ocean view
from a private balcony and two queens or a king bed.
   #220,#224,#229,#230–panoramic ocean view beyond
      foredunes from large private balcony, king bed.

★ **Tu Tu Tun Lodge**   *(541)247-6664*
7 mi. NE at 96550 North Bank Rogue Hwy. - 97444
tututun.com
20 units   *(800)864-6357*   *Expensive*
Tu Tu Tun is the most inspiring sanctuary on the Rogue River.
Luxuriant grounds surrounding the posh wood-trimmed complex
include a lap pool with a view, pitch-and-putt course, boat dock
and ramp with complimentary kayaks available, scenic hiking
trails, fishing holes, and a gift shop; plus (fee) massage, guided
salmon fishing and boat trips. A gourmet river-view restaurant,
bar, and terrace for appetizers are available to guests from May
through Oct. (non-guests for breakfast and dinner by reservation).
Each room is a study in understated elegance, with fresh flowers,
a private patio or balcony overlooking the tranquil river valley,
and two queens or king bed. There are also two deluxe houses.
   "Chinook Suite"–spacious, one bedroom, romantic
      panorama of the Rogue, galley kitchen, cast-iron
      woodburning fireplace, large deck shares view with king bed.
   "Hawkins Riffle" (4 others like this)–outdoor soaking tub
      on private corner balcony, fine river view, raised wood-
      burning fireplace in view of king bed.

Grants Pass

Grants Pass is the West's ultimate river town. The Rogue River is calm and clear as it flows past the heart of town. A few miles upstream, several small dams have created scenic lakes. Downstream, the river dashes wildly down breathtaking gorges and meanders through forested vales. Noted for one of the mildest climates in the Northwest, Grants Pass is further enhanced by the variety of broadleaf and pine trees and flowers including thriving rhododendrons and azaleas–as well as some of the continent's most northerly inland palm trees.

Tortuous mountain passes and unfriendly Indians discouraged early pioneers from coming to this area until the 1840s. Following the discovery of gold in nearby Jacksonville in 1851, and the last major Indian battle in 1854, homesteaders began to move here drawn by the area's fertile soil and mild climate. A diversified economy of lumber milling, dairying, and farming has continued to support the population to this day.

While traditional industries are still important, residents' pride in their river is the town's binding force today. Sharing the Rogue with visitors is becoming the major industry. Guide and rental services now offer jet boats, inflatable kayaks and sailboards, plus old favorites like fishing boats and whitewater rafts. One of the West's finest riverside parks is near an unpretentious downtown with a notable historic district. Many restaurants and lodgings serve crowds enjoying the peerless river and pleasant four-season climate. Continuing improvements to downtown's riverfront area will sustain the town's ascendancy.

WEATHER PROFILE

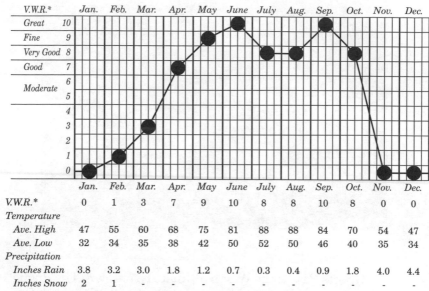

V.W.R.*		Jan.	Feb.	Mar.	Apr.	May	June	July	Aug.	Sep.	Oct.	Nov.	Dec.
V.W.R.*		0	1	3	7	9	10	8	8	10	8	0	0
Temperature													
Ave. High		47	55	60	68	75	81	88	88	84	70	54	47
Ave. Low		32	34	35	38	42	50	52	50	46	40	35	34
Precipitation													
Inches Rain		3.8	3.2	3.0	1.8	1.2	0.7	0.3	0.4	0.9	1.8	4.0	4.4
Inches Snow		2	1	-	-	-	-	-	-	-	-	-	-

* V.W.R. = Vokac Weather Rating: probability of mild (warm & dry) weather on any given day.

BASIC INFORMATION

Population: 23,003
Elevation: 950 feet
Location: 240 miles South of Portland
Airport (regularly scheduled flights): Medford - 28 miles

Grants Pass Visitors Bureau   (541)659-4279   (800)547-5927
   downtown at 198 SW 6th St. (Box 970) - 97528
   visitgrantspass.org
Grants Pass/Josephine County Chamber of Commerce (541)955-7144
   1 mi. N at 1995 NW Vine St. - 97528   (800)547-5927
   grantspasschamber.org

ATTRACTIONS

Boat Rides

★ **Hellgate Jetboat Excursions** *(541)479-7204(800)648-4874*
downtown at 966 SW 6th St.
hellgate.com
An exciting and popular way to enjoy the spectacular Rogue River in summer is via jet boat. Narrated excursions involve some whitewater and range from two hours for the round trip to Hellgate Canyon (see listing) to five hours for the 75-mile whitewater trip to Grave Creek (with a meal). Some trips include a lunch, champagne brunch or country dinner by the river.

★ **Club Northwest**   *(541)955-2582*
3 mi. N at 2160 NW Vine St.
clubnw.com
Club Northwest is Oregon's best "next generation" attraction dedicated to both recreation and fitness for the whole family. Features in this extra-large post-modern complex include two saltwater pools; three championship tennis courts, indoor courts for racquetball and handball; indoor and outdoor basketball; indoor golf; high-tech human-sized gyroscopic gym; indoor climbing wall, co-ed weight room, big cardio-devices and Nautilus centers, steam rooms, saunas, and whirlpools; plus a pro shop, gallery, day spa and one of America's largest staffed kid-zones.

★ **Crater Lake National Park**   *(541)594-2511*
80 mi. NE (via I-5 & Hwy. 234) on Hwy. 62
Oregon's only national park has as its centerpiece Crater Lake. The clear, brilliant blue waters of this magnificent mountain-rimmed lake are 1,932 feet deep–America's deepest. The renowned six-by-five-mile water body was formed when rain and snow filled what was left of volcanic Mount Mazama more than 6,000 years ago after violent eruptions collapsed the mountaintop. A paved scenic thirty-two-mile rim drive around the lake doesn't open until approximately the 4th of July except in years of light snowfall. The highway is kept open year-round to Rim Village (in spite of normal winter snowfall of fifty feet) where **Crater Lake Lodge** (Expensive–(541)830-8700), a 1915 landmark, has a dining room (B-L-D–Expensive) and bedrooms with views of the splendid lake. Boat tours leave daily to Wizard Island, a symmetrical cinder cone that rises about 760 feet above the lake's surface. Alpine panoramas and lush meadows of wildflowers line spur roads and trails that extend from many points along the rim drive.

★ *Fishing Charters*
on Rogue River
Several guides accept reservations year-round for salmon or

steelhead trips on the famed Rogue River. You can get details on what's being caught, and who's available, by calling the Grants Pass Visitors Bureau, or contact (in Grants Pass) the following, with many years of experience:

Malone's Guided Fishing   *(541)476-0567*
malonesfishing.com

★ **Hellgate Canyon**
14 mi. NW on Galice Rd.
The Rogue River's phenomenal entrance into the Coast Range is a narrow passage with sheer volcanic rock walls more than 250 feet high. It is an especially popular section for river trips. High above is a vertiginous viewpoint by the paved scenic road that parallels the river. On warm, calm days when the river is crystal-clear, there is a magical feeling–like flying–where boaters on deep, smooth water can watch salmon swimming far below.

★ **Indian Mary Park**   *(541)474-5285*
15 mi. NW via I-5 and Galice Rd.
www.co.josephine.or.us/parks
The crown jewel of Rogue River parks is one of the most complete. A beach, boat ramp, hiking trails, playground, picnic areas, and a full-service campground fill a tree-shaded large park with an orientation toward swimming, fishing, and rafting.

★ **Oregon Caves National Monument**   *(541)592-2100*
49 mi. SW (via Hwys. 199 & 46) at 20000 Caves Hwy. - Cave Jct.
nps.gov/orca/
Visitors can explore many dramatic and beautiful chambers in the "Marble Halls of Oregon." Massive columns, pillars, stalactites, stalagmites, flowstone and other calcite formations plus jaguar and bear fossils distinguish many galleries, including one room nearly as long as a football field. Guide service is required and available from March through October for strenuous hour-and-a-half cave tours. Visitors should have a jacket since the average temperature is only 41°F, and non-slip walking shoes. There are hiking loop trails and picnic and camping facilities nearby in the lush mountain forest. A few steps away, **Oregon Caves Chateau** ((541)592-3400) (circa 1934) is a charming five-story landmark with 22 rooms, a fine dining room (with a trout stream channeled through it!), diner, and major gift galleries.

★ **Riverside Park**   *(541)471-6435*
just S on E. Park St.
Well-maintained lawns sloping down to the Rogue River delight sunbathers, and swimmers enjoy clear pools just offshore. Above, noble trees provide shade for picnic tables. Imaginative play equipment, formal rose gardens, and playfields are other attractions of Southern Oregon's finest riverfront park.

★ **Rogue River - Downstream**
An eighty-four-mile portion of the Rogue River is designated as a "National Wild and Scenic River." The segment begins a few miles west of town at the junction of the Rogue and Applegate Rivers, and extends almost to the ocean. The stretch between Grave Creek and Illahe has been classified as "Wild River" and is inaccessible except by people-powered boat or a scenic forty-mile hiking trail along the north bank. Gentler sections are classified as "Scenic" or "Recreational," and are accessible by Galice Road which parallels the river for nearly twenty miles, and by jet boats which join rafts and other oar-powered craft on these stretches. An extraordinary diversity of river experiences is available. Guided scenic, whitewater, or fishing trips varying from a half day to several days can be arranged in crafts ranging from jet boats to individual inflatable kayaks. Do-it-yourself rental kayaks or rafts, and shuttle services, are also available. Visitors bringing their own raft can be left off and picked up at prearranged spots. Several rustic lodges and picturesque campgrounds are along the river. Excellent maps, books, and guide service info can be obtained at the Visitor's Center. The best local outfitters are:

Arrowhead River Adventures *(541)830-3388 (800)227-7741*
arrowheadadventures.com
Ferron's Fun Trips *(541)474-2201 (800)404-2201*
roguefuntrips.com
The Galice Resort *(541)476-3818*
galice.com
Noah's River Adventures *(541)488-2811 (800)858-2811*
noahsrafting.com
Orange Torpedo Trips *(541)479-5061 (800)635-2925*
orangetorpedo.com
Raft the Rogue *(800)797-7238*
rafttherogue.com
Rogue River Raft Trips *(541)476-3825 (800)826-1963*
www.rogueriverraft.com
Rogue Wilderness *(541)479-9554 (800)336-1647*
wildrogue.com
Sundance River Center *(541)479-8508 (888)777-7557*
sundanceriver.com

★ **Rogue River Hiking Trail**
starts 24 mi. NW on Galice Rd. at Grave Creek
The "Wild River" portion of the Rogue River is paralleled by a scenic hiking trail along the entire north bank. The 40-mile-long path begins at Grave Creek on the Galice Road and ends at tiny Illahe. It is closed to motorized vehicles, horses, and pack animals. Hikers (by permit) often take five days for the wilderness trip.

★ **Rogue River-Siskiyou National Forest**   *(541)471-6500*
   S & W of town
   www.fs.fed.us/r6/rogue-siskiyou
This vast forest includes most of the southwestern corner of
Oregon. The only redwood trees outside of California are an
unusual feature. The Kalmiopsis Wilderness Area is a botanist's
paradise of rare plants. Nearly half of the designated National
Wild and Scenic River portion of the Rogue River is in the forest,
as is Oregon Caves National Monument. A good system of paved
and graded dirt roads and hundreds of miles of designated trails
provide access for river running, swimming, fishing, hiking,
backpacking, horseback riding, and camping. Information,
permits and maps can be obtained at the Galice Ranger District
(in town at 200 NE Greenfield).

★ **Rogue River - Upstream**
   east of town
Several small scenic reservoirs in the sylvan canyon upstream
from Grants Pass are popular for speed boating, waterskiing and
enjoying most watercraft. Areas for picnicking, sunbathing,
swimming and fishing abound. Riverside full-service campgrounds, lodges, and motels are also numerous along the Rogue
River Highway which parallels the south side of the river east of
town.

★ **Rogue Theatre**   *(541)471-1316*
   downtown at 143 SE H St.
   roguetheatre.com
Downtown Grants Pass' historic movie theater (circa 1938) was
skillfully transformed into a handsome performing arts showcase
for national talent (like Pat Boone, Judy Collins and George
Winston in recent years) as well as local and regional entertainers
in various media.

★ *Wineries*
   sorwa.org
Southern Oregon is becoming an important grape-growing and
winemaking region. Peter Britt planted grapes in the Rogue
Valley more than a century ago, but serious modern production
didn't start until his vineyards at Valley View became the premier
source of Southern Oregon wine production in the 1970s. Micro-
climate in the Rogue drainage make it possible, now, to produce
the full range of Bordeaux and Burgundian varieties. The
wineries below all have tasting and sales facilities.
   Bear Creek Winery   *(541)592-3977*
   38 mi. SW (via Hwy. 199) at 6220 Caves Hwy. - Cave Junction
"Bear Creek" and "Siskiyou Vineyards" wines (cabernet,
chardonnay and pinot noir) are featured. Open daily in summer.

Bridgeview Vineyards   *(541)592-4688   (877)273-4843*
34 mi. SW (via Hwy. 199) at 4210 Holland Loop Rd. - Cave Junction
19 mi. SE at 16995 N. Applegate Rd.
bridgeviewwine.com
Some of the finest pinot noirs, pinot gris, chardonnay and merlot in the state can be sampled at Oregon's biggest winery in Cave Junction. Enjoy a picnic amid gardens, and consider a wine-themed room in their nearby Kirbyville Inn. Open daily 11-5.

Del Rio Vineyards   *(541)855-2062*
14 mi. E at 52 N. River Rd. - Gold Hill
delriovineyards.com
Diverse varietals are poured (fee after first taste) in the 1864 Rock Point Stage Hotel (partially restored). A picnic area adjoins. Open daily 11-5.

Foris Vineyards Winery   *(800)843-6747*
39 mi. SW (via Hwy. 199) at 654 Kendall Rd. - Cave Junction
foriswine.com
Alsatian and Burgundian varietals are produced here, and available for tastes daily 11-5.

Troon Vineyards   *(541)846-9900*
12 mi. SE at 1000 Upper Applegate Rd.
troonvineyard.com
Estate-bottled cabernets, chardonnays and zinfandels are featured in this evolving winery. Open weekends 11-6.

RESTAURANTS

Backroad Grill   *(541)476-4019*
9 mi. NW at 330 Galice Rd. - Merlin
L-D. Closed Mon.-Tues.   *Low*
After an exhilarating day on the river, this is an ideal stop for a hearty lunch or dinner. Traditional American dishes (bountiful but given light, bright, updates) range from chicken-fried steak to filet mignon or old-fashioned chicken pot pie. Housemade cobblers with fresh seasonal fruit are also served in a nifty little knotty-pine-accented dining room with some whimsical Northwest-oriented wall art.

★ **The Bistro**   *(541)479-3412*
1 mi. N at 1214 NW 6th St.
L-D. No L Sat. Closed Sun.   *Low*
For many years, the Bistro has been a fine regional source of deep-dish pizza ranging from individual to large, and from house specialties to all kinds of do-it-yourself. It is also popular for baked lasagne, beef ravioli, and a fine bistro supreme house calzone. Comfortable booths or chairs fill two dining rooms decorated with old movie star pictures.

Black Forest Family Restaurant   *(541)474-2353*
1 mi. E at 820 NE E St.
B-L-D.   *Low*
Here is a long-established source of hearty American comfort
food. Assorted berry and mile-high meringue pie on display can
top off any meal in the big, simply comfortable dining room.

★ **Blue Stone Bakery & Coffee Cafe**   *(541)471-1922*
downtown at 412 NW 6th St.
B-L.   *Moderate*
The Blue Stone Bakery & Coffee Cafe is the best source of
morning delights in Grants Pass. Assorted premium coffees can
be enjoyed with delicious fruit and berry muffins, cinnamon roll,
scones and bagels, plus selected egg dishes. Later, designer salads
and sandwiches are served, along with spectacular desserts like
orange hazelnut cream torte. The snazzy split-level cafe (backed
by wall art for sale) has a view of umbrella-shaded outdoor tables.

The Brewery   *(541)479-9850*
downtown at 509 SW G St.
L-D. No L Sat. & Sun. Closed Mon. Sun. brunch.   *Moderate*
Contemporary American fare can be accompanied by assorted
premium tap beers in the nostalgic brick-lined dining rooms and
saloon of a turn-of-the-century brewery.

Gaetano Ristorante Italiano   *(541)471-1554*
just E at 323 NE E St.
gaetanoristoranteitaliano.com
D only. Closed Mon.   *Expensive*
Italian dishes are given careful attention including desserts made
here and served in intimate dining rooms with an upscale
European flair enhanced by a wealth of crisp white linen.

The Galice Resort   *(541)476-3818*
21 mi. NW at 11744 Galice Rd. - Merlin
galice.com
B-L-D.   *Low*
Big housemade cinnamon rolls are a specialty among hearty
American dishes served in a rustic cafe with a fireplace. The cafe,
river-view dining/drinking deck, supplies and gifts store, and
lodgings are all perfectly geared for river-users.

Grants Pass Pharmacy   *(541)476-4262*
downtown at 414 SW 6th St.
L-D. Closed Sun.   *Low*
Since 1933, Grants Pass Pharmacy has been a delightful source
for enjoying ice cream treats. Centered among a wealth of gift
items are bentwood chairs at tables and padded stools at an old-
time hardwood fountain bar featuring banana splits; all kinds of
malts, sodas, and other ice cream treats; plus light fare.

Hog Wild BBQ   *(541)479-7633*
   2 mi. E at 1229 Rogue River Hwy.
   hogwildbbq.com
   L-D. Closed Sun.-Mon.   Low
Authentic Southern-style barbecue is featured in pork, beef and
chicken dishes with all of the usual fixin's in a casual comfortable
little dining room. The specialty–pork ribs slow-smoked over
hickory–are served dry, with spices, or wet (with a choice of
sauces).

★ **Jimmy's Classic Drive-In**   *(541)479-5313*
   1 mi. E at 515 NE E St.
   L-D. Closed Sun.   Low
The '50s live on in this spiffy little drive-in with dozens of
milkshakes and assorted ice cream flavors in support of
traditional and designer ¾ pound burgers (including turkey and
buffalo). Besides a drive-up window there are tables inside and on
a covered highway-front deck that evoke the era with pictures of
Elvis, Marlon, Marilyn and others.

Laughing Clam   *(541)479-1110*
   downtown at 121 SW G St.
   L-D. Closed Sun.   Moderate
Clams star (natch) in chowder, steamers, baskets and strips along
with beer-batter fish 'n chips among distinctive pub grub served
in a restored historic building with a well-worn wood floor and a
brick wall interior enhanced by a dramatic backbar. There is
occasional live entertainment.

★ **Matsukaze Japanese Restaurant**   *(541)479-2961*
   1 mi. N at 1675 NE 7th St.
   L-D. No L Sat. Closed Sun.   Low
Matsukaze is a long-established destination for flavorful Japanese
cuisine. All sorts of traditional dishes from sushi or tempura
appetizers to charbroiled favorites like beef teriyaki or spicy
barbecue chicken or rib-eye steak are served amid warm casual
Japanese decor at a choice of regular or traditional low tables in
three rooms.

★ **Powderhorn Cafe**   *(541)479-9403*
   downtown at 321 NE 6th St.
   B-L. Closed Sun.   Moderate
For hearty American-style home-cooked breakfasts, this is the
place. But, there is more. The really big cinnamon rolls are fine
and desserts on display like black bottom peanut butter or mile-
high lemon meringue pie can be outstanding. The cheerful, no-
frills cafe has earned a loyal local following.

★ **River's Edge**   *(541)479-3938*   *(888)511-3343*
   1 mi. SE at 1936 Rogue River Hwy.

riversedgerestaurant.net
L-D. Sun. brunch.   *Moderate*
The River's Edge opened in mid-2005 to early acclaim for food,
atmosphere and view. Pacific cuisine gets creative attention in
dishes like lobster quesadilla, baby blue pear salad, beer-battered
salmon and chips, and fried Tahitian banana for dessert. Their
orientation is "elegant dining in blue jeans" in a setting with a
fireplace, water-wall, a bar with handcrafted accents, and an
especially fine view of the Rogue River.

★ **Riverside Inn Resort**   *(541)476-6873*
   just S at 971 SE 6th St.
   raftersbarandgrill.com
The Resort's wood-trim restaurant, **Rafters Bar & Grill**,
features contemporary Northwest cuisine from Angus burgers to
Porterhouse pork chop, plus homemade seasonal pies inside, or
better yet, out on a deck by the Rogue River. A full-service bar
adjoins.

★ **Summer Jo's**   *(541)476-6882*
   1 mi. W at 2315 Upper River Road Loop
   www.summerjo.com
   Brunch-D. No D Sun. Closed Sun.-Tues. Closed Jan.   Expensive
Tucked away on a country lane is a tranquil hideaway restaurant
surrounded by farmlands and some of Southern Oregon's most
colorful gardens. Organic ingredients grown here are featured
seasonally, along with regional specialties like Oregon cheeses and
wines, in from-scratch innovative cuisine like smoked chicken
salad with field greens, toasted walnuts, Oregon blue cheese,
raspberries and walnut oil vinaigrette or a buffalo osso bucco
entree. Dine in a lovely garden room with a picture-window view
of the flowery scene adjoining a stylish lounge by an expo kitchen.

Tee Time Coffee Shop   *(541)476-3346*
   downtown at 117 SW H St.
   B-L.   *Moderate*
Breakfast served all day includes build-your-own omelets and
assorted scrambles, plus comfort foods like biscuits and gravy.
Locals also like all kinds of one-third or one-half pound
hamburgers and assorted wrap sandwiches served for lunch in a
laid-back two-level coffee shop.

★ **Wild River Brewing & Pizza**   *(541)471-7487*
   1 mi. E at 595 NE E St.
   wildriverbrewing.com
   L-D.   *Moderate*
Hand-tossed pizzas and calzone from hardwood-fired ovens star
in the flagship of a Southern Oregon chain. A wide selection of
carefully made pub grub features their fine Bohemian-style brew

in several dishes like beer-boiled shrimp or deep-fried beer-battered onion rings or beer salsa. Seasonal fruit cobbler and other luscious desserts and flavorful breads are also made here and served in several warm relaxed dining areas.

Wild River Pub   *(541)474-4456*
  1 mi. E at 533 NE F St.
  wildriverbrewing.com
  L-D. No L Sun.   *Moderate*
Hand-tossed wood-oven-fired pizza specialties or build-your-own are featured, along with assorted soups, salads and sandwiches. More elaborate dinners range from New York steak to coconut shrimp. The large casual pub includes a pool table.

★ **Wolf Creek Inn**   *(541)866-2474*
  20 mi. N (on I-5) at 100 Front St. (Box 6) - Wolf Creek
  thewolfcreekinn.com
  L-D. Closed Mon.-Tues. apart from summer.   *Moderate*
Traditional and creative Pacific Northwest fare like steak and wild mushroom soup with homemade breads is served in a large authentic stagecoach stop (circa 1883) that is the oldest continuous-use hotel in Oregon. It has been painstakingly restored and furnished with period pieces. Upstairs, nine antique-filled rooms provide novel overnight accommodations. A firelit barroom/lobby and exquisitely detailed parlor adjoin the nostalgic dining rooms. It is on the National Historic Register.

Yankee Pot Roast   *(541)476-0551*
  just N at 720 NW 6th St.
  D only. Plus L on Sun.   *Moderate*
Traditional American classics are all served with a giant biscuit freshly made out front. Waitresses costumed in granny gowns blend smoothly amidst nostalgic decor in several pleasant dining rooms of a turn-of-the-century landmark house.

LODGINGS

Happily, five of the best area lodgings are by the river. Moderately priced contemporary motels are plentiful on the main roads into town. May through September is high season. Rates may be at least 20% less at other times.

★ **Buckhorn Mountain Lodge**   *(541)471-9516*
  17 mi. W (via I-5) at 4880 Galice Rd. (Box 161) - Merlin 97532
  buckhornmountainlodge.com
  4 units   *Expensive*
Hellgate Canyon lies just beyond this unusual bed-and-breakfast on expansive landscaped grounds an easy hike from one of the best launch sites on the Rogue River. Big, hearty breakfasts, wine and appetizers in the evening and homemade cookies are complimentary. The Main Lodge, completed in 2005, will feature

an intimate fine dining restaurant showcasing local produce, wine, fruits and cheeses. Each individually well-furnished unit will also convey the host's spirit of "elegant rusticity" and have a private bath and double, queen or king bed.

"The Tree House"–in a hillside forest,wraparound private balcony, quaint gas stove, one-of-a-kind shower in the Bath House, double bed.

"The Bear Paw Cabin"–refrigerator, in-bath whirlpool tub, fine view deck, two queen beds.

Budget Inn   *(541)479-2952*
1 mi. N at 1253 NE 6th St. - 97526
21 units   *Low*
In this small single-level motel, each simply furnished room has a microwave, refrigerator and two doubles or a queen bed.

★ **Chateau LeBear Bed & Breakfast**   *(541)471-6269*
1 mi. SE at 2155 SE Portola Dr. (Box 98) - 97528
chateaulebear.com
3 units   *Expensive*
A handsome country home on landscaped riverfront property now serves (since 2003) as a peaceful bed-and-breakfast. Full gourmet breakfast, wine and other beverages, appetizers and dessert are complimentary. Each attractively furnished room has a romantic river view, gas fireplace, in-bath whirlpool or Roman tub, and queen feather bed.

"Suites" (2 in a separate building)–fine river view, two-person in-bath whirlpool with view through gas fireplace to queen bed.

Del Rogue Motel   *(541)479-2111*
3 mi. E at 2600 Rogue Valley Hwy. - 97526
moteldelrogue.com
16 units   *Low-Moderate*
Luxuriant rhododendrons and colorful gardens accent this homey, historic motel in a delightfully tree-shaded location with a lawn sloping down to the river. Each individually well-furnished unit was recently refurbished and upgraded, and has a large private screened porch, a refrigerator, microwave, and two doubles or a queen bed. Most overlook the tranquil Rogue. A kitchen can be added.

#8–fine river view from upstairs, queen bed.

Discovery Inn   *(541)476-7793*
downtown at 748 SE 7th St. - 97526
35 units   *(888)828-3886*   *Low*
The feature of this older motel with an outdoor pool is that it's close to the river and in the heart of town. Each simply furnished, compact room has a refrigerator, microwave and one or two queen beds.

★ **Flery Manor Bed & Breakfast**   *(541)476-3591*
  12 mi. N (via I-5 exit 66) at 2000 Jumpoff Joe Creek Rd. - 97526
  www.flerymanor.com
  5 units   *Moderate-Expensive*
Flery Manor Bed & Breakfast is one of the Northwest's quintessential romantic getaways. Pine-shrouded low mountains surround a genteel seven acre enclave amidst exquisite zen-like gardens with ponds, waterfalls, streams, overlooks and paths extending to views of the luxuriant surroundings. The contemporary mansion that was built to serve its current function complements the surroundings with architectural good taste and decor touches that reflect artistry of the owners. Three-course gourmet breakfasts served on heirloom linen in an elegant garden-and-mountain-view dining room is complimentary, as is port in the afternoon. There is a (new in 2005) separate art studio that serves as a tranquil, creative launching pad for guests to enjoy a hands-on experience with their choice of media–clay, paint, photography, music, writing, etc. Each luxuriously appointed room includes some exquisite antiques and complementary modern amenities including a private bath and extra touches, plus a queen or king bed.
  "Moonlight Suite"–private balcony with romantic
    garden/mountains view, two-person whirlpool,
    gas fireplace in view of canopied king bed.
  "Vintage Suite"–private mountain/garden view
    patio, gas fireplace, one-way garden-view window
    by two-person whirlpool, large glass shower,
    feather king bed.

★ **Half Moon Bar Lodge**   *(541)247-6968*
  49 mi. W on the Rogue River (Box 455) - Gold Beach 97444
  halfmoonbarlodge.com
  16 units   *(888)291-8268*   *Expensive*
The small lodge has no access road. It can only be reached by drift boat, plane, or on foot from the Grants Pass side (and by jet boat from Gold Beach). The rate includes gourmet home-cooked meals prepared from their own garden-fresh produce and served family-style to guests sharing the Rogue River wilderness. Rates include three family-style meals plus Oregon wines at dinner. (Additional nights are discounted.)

Holiday Inn Express   *(541)471-6144*
  2 mi. E (by I-5) at 105 NE Agness Av. - 97526
  hiexpress.com/grantspassor
  80 units   *(800)838-7666*   *Moderate-Expensive*
On a rise by the freeway overlooking the valley is a four-story contemporary motel with an outdoor pool. An expanded

Continental breakfast buffet is complimentary. Each well-furnished room has one or two queens or a king bed.

"Jacuzzi Suite" (8 of these)–spacious,
    separate sitting room, microwave, refrig-
    erator, in-bath whirlpool tub, king bed.

Inn at the Rogue - Best Western   *(541)582-2200*
8 mi. E at 8959 Rogue River Hwy. - 97527
bestwestern.com
53 units   *(800)238-0700*   *Expensive*
This contemporary motel near the Rogue has a pool, whirlpool, exercise room, and gift shop. Each unit is well furnished and has a queen or king bed. Microwaves and refrigerators are available. Some rooms have a river view.

"Jacuzzi Room" (4 of these)–spacious,
    microwave, refrigerator, in-room two-
    person whirlpool, king bed.

★ **The Lodge at Riverside**   *(541)955-0600*
just S at 955 SE 7th St. - 97526
thelodgeatriverside.com
32 units   *(877)955-0600*   *Expensive-Very Expensive*
The best riverfront location in town (across from the beautiful Riverside Park) is the site of the area's newest and finest lodging. Facilities include a lushly landscaped outdoor view pool and whirlpool, riverside access, and **Rafters Bar & Grill** in the adjacent Riverside Inn (see listing). Most of the beautifully furnished oversized rooms have an intimate view of the river, a mini-refrigerated cooler, private balcony or patio, and queens or a king bed.

#200,#100 ("Executive Suites")–raised gas
    river-rock fireplace, fine river view from
    large private deck, two-person in-room
    whirlpool, king bed.

★ **Morrison's Rogue River Lodge**   *(541)476-3825*
16 mi. NW at 8500 Galice Rd. - Merlin 97532
morrisonslodge.com
13 units   *(800)826-1963*   *Expensive*
A sylvan bend of the Rogue River is an ideal site for this ranch-style lodge-and-cabins complex that has been popular since 1946. There's boating, fishing, swimming, gold panning and rock hounding in the river, a pool, whirlpool, tennis court, putting green, gift shop and a family-style river-view dining room and deck. (Full breakfast and four-course dinner are included in lodging price.) Each lodge room and (one- or two-bedroom) cottage is comfortably furnished with all modern conveniences, a refrigerator, and queens or a king bed. Cottages also have a fireplace.

Motel 6   *(541)474-1331*
  2 mi. N at 1800 NE 7th St. - 97526
  motel6.com
  122 units   *(800)466-8356*   *Low*
The nationwide bargain chain is represented here by a large modern motel with an outdoor pool. Each compact, no-frills room has doubles or a queen bed.

Pine Meadow Inn   *(541)471-6277*
  11 mi. NW at 1000 Crow Rd. - Merlin 97532
  pinemeadowinn.com
  4 units   *(800)554-0806*   *Moderate-Expensive*
Tucked deep into a pine forest near the Rogue River is a handsome contemporary home that was built to serve as a bed-and-breakfast. A hearty healthy breakfast is complimentary, as is use of a hot tub on a deck overlooking a koi pond, lovely gardens, and sylvan tranquility. Each well-furnished room has some antiques, a private bath, forest view, and a queen bed.
  "Garden," "Willow"–spacious, fine garden and fountain view.

Redwood Motel   *(541)476-0878*
  1 mi. N at 815 NE 6th St. - 97521
  redwoodmotel.com
  31 units   *(888)535-8824*   *Moderate-Expensive*
Two towering redwoods and a colorful garden surround a large landscaped outdoor pool and whirlpool which are the focal points in this well-maintained single-level motel. Each well-furnished unit has a microwave, refrigerator, and queens or a king bed.
  "Jacuzzi Suite" (5 of these)–spacious, two-person
    whirlpool in view of king bed.

★ **Riverside Inn Resort**   *(541)476-6873*
  just S at 971 SE 6th St. - 97526
  riverside-inn.com
  123 units   *(800)334-4567*   *Moderate-Expensive*
One of the best Rogue River locations in town is the site for the area's largest riverfront lodging. Facilities include an outdoor pool and whirlpool, jet boat boarding dock, gift shop, and river-view restaurant and lounge (see listing). Nearly all of the attractively furnished, recently upgraded rooms have a large private balcony overlooking the river, and two doubles, two queens or a king bed.
  #424,#426–gas fireplace, refrigerator, microwave,
    two-person whirlpool with superb river view
    shared by large private balcony, king bed.
  #367,#267–quiet end, private balcony
    with river rapids view, two queen beds.
  #365,#363,#360,#359–top floor, private
    balcony, fine river view, king bed.

Shilo Inn   *(541)479-8391*
  2 mi. N at 1880 NW 6th St. - 97526
  shiloinns.com
  70 units   *(800)222-2244*   *Moderate*
The local representative of a major Western lodging chain is a
modern two-level motel with an outdoor pool, a sauna and a
steam room. Each comfortably furnished room has a queen or
king bed. Rooms with microwave and refrigerator are available.

Sunset Inn   *(541)479-3305*
  1 mi. N at 1400 NW 6th St. - 97526
  sunset-inn.net
  30 units   *Low-Moderate*
A small outdoor pool is a feature of this attractively refurbished
motel. Each comfortably furnished room has a queen or king bed,
and a microwave and refrigerator upon request.

Super 8   *(541)474-0888*
  2 mi. N at 1949 NE 7th St. - 97526
  super8.com
  79 units   *(800)800-8000*   *Moderate*
This three-story modern motel has an indoor pool and whirlpool.
Each room is comfortably furnished and has one or two queen
beds.

★ **Weasku Inn**   *(541)471-8000*
  6 mi. E at 5560 Rogue River Hwy. - 97527
  weasku.com
  17 units   *(800)493-2758*   *Expensive-Very Expensive*
Weasku Inn is one of the Pacific Northwest's quintessential
romantic retreats. A lodgepole pine fishing lodge (circa 1924) in a
gentle pine forest with lawns and a stream extending to trails by
the Rogue River was painstakingly restored and enhanced in
1997. An expanded Continental breakfast and afternoon wine and
cheese in the lodge or on a pine-shaded river-view deck are
complimentary. Lodge rooms reflect the heritage of the historic
property, while the spacious cabins built near the millennium
showcase a luxurious combination of rustic natural woods and
native rock materials and all contemporary amenities. Cabins in
a forest near the river have a gas-started woodburning fireplace,
big private deck overlooking the river, refrigerator, and queen or
king bed.
  #42,#41–extra-large, sofa and leather armchair
    by a great river-stone raised fireplace, big private
    deck with forest and river view, two-person whirlpool
    with intimate garden view, two-headed rustic-stone
    tile shower, king bed.

Hood River

Hood River is the urbane hub of Oregon's scenic "Garden of Eden." The town extends from the Columbia River waterfront up steep slopes of the gorge into the gentle Hood River Valley at the base of Oregon's most spectacular landmark–glacier-shrouded Mt. Hood. Thanks to a relatively mild four-season climate, lush orchards fill the little basin. The town's largest industry, fruit growing, is also one of its most compelling attractions (scenic fruit loop drives).

In the early 1800s the accounts of Lewis and Clark attracted explorers and fur traders to the Columbia River Gorge. Hood River prospered as a transportation center, and from rich soils and a sheltered climate that led to the first commercial orchard in 1876. Over the years, the area has become the nation's largest source of winter pears, along with a cornucopia of apples, peaches, cherries and other deciduous fruits, plus burgeoning vineyards.

Hood River's downtown is an appealing mix of historic and newer buildings, many offering gorge views from restaurants and lodgings–even from the brewery and well-sited public library. (Unfortunately, there are also parking meters in the only Oregon great town with them.) Restaurants make good use of local fresh food sources, while view lodgings include one of the West's gems, the Columbia Gorge Hotel. Nearby Mt. Hood sustains winter sports year-round. Months of ideal weather support a wealth of summer sports, while windy conditions on the Columbia River make this a favored destination for wind-surfing and kite-boarding at public beaches and parks.

WEATHER PROFILE

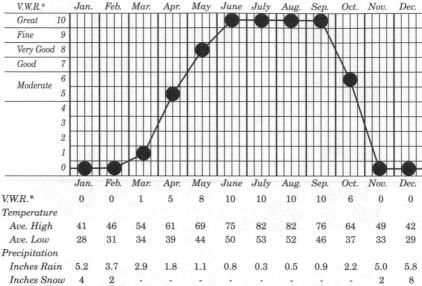

V.W.R.*	Jan.	Feb.	Mar.	Apr.	May	June	July	Aug.	Sep.	Oct.	Nov.	Dec.
V.W.R.*	0	0	1	5	8	10	10	10	10	6	0	0
Temperature												
Ave. High	41	46	54	61	69	75	82	82	76	64	49	42
Ave. Low	28	31	34	39	44	50	53	52	46	37	33	29
Precipitation												
Inches Rain	5.2	3.7	2.9	1.8	1.1	0.8	0.3	0.5	0.9	2.2	5.0	5.8
Inches Snow	4	2	-	-	-	-	-	-	-	-	2	8

* V.W.R. = Vokac Weather Rating: probability of mild (warm & dry) weather on any given day.

BASIC INFORMATION

Population: 5,831
Elevation: 54 feet
Location: 62 miles East of Portland
Airport (regularly scheduled flights): Portland - 48 miles

Hood River, Oregon Chamber of Commerce   (541)386-2000
    just N at 405 Portway Av. - 97031   (800)366-3530
    hoodriver.org

ATTRACTIONS

★ *Bicycling*
Discover Bicycles   *(541)386-4820*
downtown at 116 Oak St.
discoverbicycles.com

Scenic routes featuring Mt. Hood, Columbia River Gorge, and farm trails through the orchards and vineyards south of town beckon with a cornucopia of sights, smells and samples along the way. One of the largest sources for bike rentals and demos in the Northwest has a wide assortment of men's and women's mountain, road and city bikes available hourly, daily and overnight. They also have bikes for sale and all sorts of related clothes and gear and maps. The store is open every day.

★ *Boat Rentals*
Hood River Waterplay   *(541)386-9463*   *(800)963-7873*
just E at the port of Hood River Marina
hoodriverwaterplay.com

Hood River Waterplay is *the* place for rentals and lessons in kayaking, catamaran, sailing, windsurfing and kiteboarding. They have their own private beach plus other sailing sites, and they guarantee that their certified instructors can teach you to windsurf a kiteboard with beginner, intermediate and advanced private lessons. Bring a swimsuit, sunscreen and towel–they'll provide wetsuit, booties and all related equipment.

★ *Boat Rides*
Sternwheeler Columbia Gorge *(541)374-8427 (800)643-1354*
22 mi. W (I-84 exit 44) at Cascade Locks Marine Park-Cascade Locks
sternwheeler.com

For more than twenty years, this triple-deck paddlewheeler has been a popular way to experience the mighty river up close. Two-hour sunset dinner cruises, champagne brunch cruises, holiday and special events cruises, and narrated sightseeing excursions are offered through one of the most spectacular sections of the Columbia River Gorge National Scenic Area. The boat leaves twice daily June through October, and on a modified schedule the rest of the year.

★ **Bonneville Lock & Dam Visitor Center**   *(541)374-8820*
25 mi. W (via I-84 exit 40) - Cascade Locks

Since 1938, Bonneville Dam has supplied electrical power, recreation, navigation, and fish and wildlife protection at one of the most scenic areas in the Columbia River Gorge. The Bradford Island Visitor Center has an underwater viewing room where visitors can watch salmon swim up a fish ladder (usually) from March through November. You can also view the powerhouse and local history exhibits and audiovisual presentations.

★ **Columbia Gorge Sailpark**   *(541)386-1645*
   downtown at Port Marina
A boat basin and swimming beach on the river downtown is the
most readily accessible site for windsurfing. When the breeze is up
(as it often is here in the Gorge), the lawn and beach in the park
by the marina are perfect for watching windsurfers and
kiteboarders show off their skills.

★ **Columbia River Gorge National Scenic Area** *(509)427-8211*
   for 40 mi. in either direction from town   *(800)991-2338*
One of America's most magnificent river valleys is recognized for
the sheer volcanic cliffs that rise hundreds of feet on the Oregon
and Washington sides of the mighty river. Above, grassy plains
give way to luxuriant mixed forests as visitors drive from east to
west for eighty miles between the Deschutes River and Fruitdale
(near Portland). Towering volcanic peaks loom above picturesque
islands, shimmering waterfalls, promontories; and lush vineyards,
orchards, and woodlands contribute to the photogenic and
recreational appeal of this uniquely confined waterway.

Food Specialties

★   **Apple Valley Country Store**   *(541)386-1971*
    5 mi. S at 2363 Tucker Rd.
    applevalleystore.com
In a rustic replica of a Victorian country store, there are more
than 40 varieties of less-sugar, more-fruit jams and jellies (many
of which you can sample). Fresh seasonal fruit pies and cobblers,
and milkshakes featuring huckleberries, marionberries, or
peaches in season are also available in the roadside store. A large
area with shaded and sunny picnic tables adjoins. Open 10-5 daily
except in winter when it's only open on weekends.

★   **The Fruit Company**   *(541)387-3100*   *(800)387-3100*
    5 mi. S (via Hwy. 35) at 2900 Van Horn Dr.
    thefruitcompany.com
Gourmet quality Northwestern and other fruits star in gift
baskets, towers, and premium boxes, and in assorted cheesecakes.
Since 1942, this has become Northern Oregon's largest producer
of Royal Comice Pears (the world's best eating pear). Tractor
tours of the orchards and gift-packing facilities are also offered.
Open daily except Sun. year-round.

★   **Hood River Fruit Loop**   *(541)386-7697*
    35 mi. loop on Hwys. 35 & 281
    hoodriverfruitloop.com
America's largest pear-growing region is represented by a wealth
of fruit stands, berry farms, farm bakeries and more amid
luxuriant orchards in the gentle Hood River Valley between the
grandeur of Mt. Hood and the Columbia River. Highway 35 south

from Hood River has the distinction of being both the fruit orchard mainline and memorably scenic byway beneath towering Mt. Hood to the south and Mt. Adams to the north. Along the way are numerous fruit stands showcasing the remarkable variety and quality of Hood River fruits and related gourmet products.

★ **Kiyokawa Family Orchards**   *(541)352-7115*
   17 mi. S (via Hwy. 35) at 8129 Clear Creek Rd. - Parkdale
   mthoodfruit.com
The Kiyokawa Family Orchards and Fruit Stand combine a breathtaking close-up of Mt. Hood framing the skyline with a one-stop-does-it-all fruit market with seventy kinds of apples and pears. The opportunities are endless for pairing your taste to the right fruit. The big shop has dozens of types of pears and apples and peaches in season on display with tastes. Their preserves also capture the essence of their exquisite fruits. Knowledgeable staff can be very helpful. Their ingeniously designed complete farm experience features u-pick apples, guided group tours, or stroll-through individual tours as additional ways to enjoy this beautiful site. Open daily 9-5 from early September to mid-November, and then self-serve through the end of December.

★ **Packer's Cookie Stop**   *(541)354-1140*
   9 mi. S at 3900 Hwy. 35
   packerorchardsandbakery.com
Packer's country fare is a roadside shop with a wealth of peaches, pears and apples in fall out front, and gourmet fruit syrups, sauces, jams and jellies in the store. Their specialty is a wide assortment of delicious homemade all-natural pear-sweetened cookies and fruit pies. Ice cream, milkshakes and other treats are also available. Tastes are generously offered of almost everything. Open daily spring through fall.

★ **Rasmussen Fruit & Flower Farm** *(541)386-4622 (800)548-2243*
   6 mi. S (via Hwy. 35) at 3020 Thomsen Rd.
   rasmussenfarms.com
This farm is remote but worth it. Surrounded by picturesque orchard-covered slopes of the Hood River Valley, Rasmussen is a cornucopia of all things deciduous. A broad selection of apples, pears and peaches is on display seasonally, and there are all kinds of related gourmet jams, jellies, syrups, sauces, plus delicious ciders and fruit pies made here. The grounds also include a wealth of flowers and vegetables and, in season, there is a popular elephant's-eye-high corn maze. Open daily 9-6 from Oct.-mid-Nov.

★ **International Museum of Carousel Art**   *(541)387-4622*
   downtown at 304 Oak St.
   carouselmuseum.com
The world's largest and most comprehensive collection of antique

carousel art is presented in more than one hundred nostalgic displays filling a large red brick building. You can marvel at antique wooden carousel animals, listen to music from a 1917 Wurlitzer band organ, enjoy a 1900 English carousel, visit their carving and restoration room, or learn the workings of an old steam engine. Open 10-3 Mon.-Thurs., 11-4 Fri.-Sun.

★ **Mt. Hood Railroad**   *(541)386-3556   (800)872-4661*
   downtown at 110 Railroad Av.
   mthoodrr.com
A delightful way to see the luxuriant Hood River Valley is aboard the Mt. Hood Railroad. Narrated excursions run almost daily from mid-April through the end of October. Four-hour trips go 22 miles each way to Parkdale at the base of magnificent Mt. Hood's north face. There is a concession car for snacks and beverages, or bring your own picnic. By reservation, you can also arrange for a multicourse dinner train, brunch train, and special events like murder-mystery or comedy dinner trains; or fruit blossom, autumn, Halloween Express, or Christmas tree seasonal special trains. All trips depart from the historic downtown depot that also has a gift shop.

★ **Multnomah Falls**
   33 mi. W on I-84
Multnomah Falls is the highest in the United States after Yosemite Falls. A network of trails and bridges provides close-up views of the 620-foot sheer drop. Near the base, historic **Multonomah Falls Lodge** offers fine dining and pioneer exhibits.

★ *Windsurfing*
Hood River is the windsurfing capital of America. The gorge funnels breezes down the Columbia River year-round, providing ideal conditions for windsurfing. Several companies in town provide lessons and rent boards, sails and all related equipment. Among the best are:
   Big Winds Hood River   *(541)386-6086   (888)509-4210*
   bigwinds.com
   Hood River Waterplay   *(541)386-9463   (800)963-7873*
   hoodriverwaterplay.com
   Storm Warning   *(541)386-9400   (800)492-6309*
   stormwarning.biz

★ *Wineries*   *(866)413-9463*
   columbiagorgewine.com
Several wineries including the oldest in the Gorge are within a short drive of Hood River. All have individual specialties and produce most Northwestern varietals. Part of the special appeal of this wine district is the scenic drive through bountiful orchards and vineyards overseen by nearby Mt. Hood.

Cathedral Ridge Winery   *(541)386-2882   (800)516-8710*
3 mi. W at 4200 Post Canyon Dr.
cathedralridgewinery.com
Tucked away in luxuriant farmlands above the gorge is a
handsome little winery with a gift shop and well-made
representatives of the Dry Land Oregon classics–pinot noir and
merlot. Their full line of red and white wines is available for
complimentary tastes. Open 11-5 daily and until 6 on Fri.-Sat.

Hood River Vineyards   *(541)386-3772*
3 mi. W at 4693 Westwood Dr.
The oldest certified winery in the Columbia Gorge area is high on
the side of the Hood River Valley above the gorge. The casual
winery tasting room is a good place to try a wide variety of classic
red and white wines, port, and local fruit-derived ports. Tree-
shaded picnic tables overlook vineyards and orchards. Open 11-5
Mar.-Dec., and other times by appointment.

Pheasant Valley Vineyard & Winery *(541)387-3040 (866)357-9463*
5 mi. S at 3890 Acree Dr.
pheasantvalleywinery.com
In the middle of beautiful Hood River Valley is a handsome
tasting room for a winery with a good selection of Northwestern
wines, plus estate-bottled pear wine from organic pears. Generous
tastes next to a large fireplace seating area are offered daily from
11-6. If/when available, rooms in the adjoining bed-and-breakfast
(5 units–Expensive–(541)386-2803, pheasantvalleyorchards.com)
have a terrific garden/vineyards/orchards view of Mt. Hood as the
backdrop to beautifully furnished rooms with a king bed, two-
person whirlpool and private balcony. The "Comice Suite" is
especially notable.

RESTAURANTS

Abruzzo   *(541)386-7779*
1 mi. W at 1810 Cascade St.
D only. Closed Sun.-Mon.   *Expensive*
Abruzzo is a tiny Tuscan trattoria where Northern Italian fare is
served at little tables with benches and chairs and in a heated
adjoining patio.

Bette's   *(541)386-1880*
downtown at 416 Oak St.
B-L.   *Moderate*
Bette's is still a good bet after more than thirty years for
breakfast of traditional American fare and some specials like
homemade cinnamon rolls. The pleasant cafe has windows on
main street and padded booths in the rear.

Big Horse Brew Pub   *(541)386-4411*
downtown at 115 State St.
L-D. Closed Tues.   *Moderate*
Appealing pub grub includes selections like buffalo chili with
jalapeño-honey corn bread, or a half-pound of ale-battered fish
and chips with tequila-citrus slaw. The brews made here are
available as samplers to complement distinctive dishes. The pub
room and dining deck have fine river and mountain views.

Brian's Pourhouse   *(541)387-4344*
downtown at 606 Oak St.
brianspourhouse.com
D only. Sun. brunch in season.   *Expensive*
Creative Northwestern cuisine is featured in unusual dishes like
grilled rack of venison with mushroom truffle risotto or crispy
fried oysters with Maui onion and mango cocktail sauce. A house
was transformed into a casual bistro with a heated shaded deck by
the main street with dining decks by the main street and out back.

★ **Columbia Gorge Hotel**   *(541)386-5566   (800)345-1921*
2 mi. W at 4000 Westcliff Dr.
columbiagorgehotel.com
B-L-D. Plus tea on Sun.   *Very Expensive*
The Columbia Gorge Hotel is the quintessential dining-with-a-
river-view experience in the Northwest. Classic Northwestern
cuisine is featured at all meals. Breakfasts are a five-course
extravaganza that include all sorts of seasonal fruits and berries,
a baked apple and hot apple fritters; old-fashioned oatmeal; eggs
any style with a pork medley of bacon, sausage and chop or fresh
trout; buttermilk pancakes with honey maple syrup; and a
homestyle baking powder biscuit with show-stopping "honey from
the sky." Dinners are similarly intriguing and outstanding,
maximizing top-quality seasonally fresh ingredients like baked
wild salmon stuffed with dill havarti and a sautéed forest
mushroom gateau or porcini-crusted venison medallion finished
in raspberry gorgonzola demi-glaze. For dessert, don't miss apple
tart tatin baked under puff pastry finished tableside with Tillamook
ice cream. Old World formal service and decor cap the romantic
experience in dining rooms lavishly outfitted with linen, candles,
flowers, and a window-wall panorama of the river and gorge.

Egg Harbor Cafe   *(541)386-1127*
just W at 1313 Oak St.
B-L.   *Moderate*
Down-home breakfasts from omelets and scrambles through
pancakes (one with blueberry and banana inside is special) to a
variety of burritos. Padded booths and country-comfortable decor
are enhanced by a picture-window view of the gorge and Mt. Adams.

★ **Full Sail Brewing Company**   *(541)386-2281   (888)244-2337*
  downtown at 506 Columbia St.
  fullsailbrewing.com
  L-D.   *Moderate*
Full Sail Brewing Company has a delightful tasting room and pub
with picture windows and a deck overlooking the Columbia River
and Mt. Baker. This is the place to sample their renowned amber
ale and pale ale and seasonal specialties that are complimentary
for tastes. Their menu ranges from smoked bratwurst through a
house salad with organic greens tossed with toasted hazelnuts,
blue cheese crumbles and raspberry vinaigrette to grilled free-
range bison burger or chipotle salmon sandwich. Worthwhile
tours are also offered, and you can buy t-shirts, hats, and related
gifts as well as six-packs and more of their fine brews.

Hood River Bagel Company   *(541)386-2123*
  downtown at 13 Oak St.
  B-L.   *Moderate*
A wide selection of bagels can be good–when they're fresh.
Outdoor seating is available.

Hood River City Market   *(541)386-9876*
  downtown at 406 Oak Av.
  B-L.   *Moderate*
Assorted breads and pastries are made here including some
distinctive treats like lofty scones or an artichoke roll. Enjoy a
wide selection of coffees and beverages at a few tables surrounded
by tempting displays of quality provisions, and consider their
housemade desserts.

★ **Hood River Hotel**   *(541)386-1900*
  downtown at 102 Oak St.
  hoodriverhotel.com
  B-L-D.   *Expensive*
The hotel's dining room became **The Cornerstone** in mid-2005
with an orientation toward fresh natural ingredients from local
farms, ranches, and water bodies. Carefully prepared dishes from
the wide-ranging menu are served in a smart restaurant and bar,
and at sidewalk-fronting tables on the picturesque main street.

The Mesquitery   *(541)386-2002*
  just S at 1219 12th St.
  L-D. No L Sat.-Tues.   *Moderate*
This roadside restaurant pleases locals with traditional Northwestern fare amid casual wood-trim decor with an expo kitchen or
on a patio. A specialty is homemade desserts like apple crisp, six-
layer chocolate cake and (in season) fresh peach ice cream.

★ **North Oak Brasserie**   *(541)387-2310*
  downtown at 113 Third St.

hoodriverrestaurants.com
L-D. No L Sat.-Mon.   *Moderate*
This underground wine cellar and brasserie offers traditional and creative Italian (like roasted garlic and brie soup) and Northwestern (like pistachio-crusted halibut in three-citrus cream sauce) dishes in intimate candlelit dining areas adjoining a small bar.

★ **6th Street Bistro & Loft**   *(541)490-4908*
   downtown at 509 Cascade Av.
   sixthstreetbistro.com
   L-D.   *Moderate*
Diverse international foods from fresh local ingredients range from chicken satay through organic pear and walnut salad to wild salmon filet. Upstairs, a pool table and snazzy bar adjoin a small dining deck with a Columbia River view. Downstairs is a traditional little bistro by a tree-shaded dining patio.

★ **Stonehedge Gardens**   *(541)386-3940*
   1 mi. W at 3405 Cascade Av.
   hoodriverrestaurants.com
   D only.   *Expensive*
Traditional and innovative Northwestern cuisine using fresh quality seasonal ingredients is showcased in dishes like wild salmon barbecued with a chipotle glaze. Desserts made here are also delicious. Casually elegant dining rooms fill a converted historic mansion surrounded by extensive tree-shaded lawns and gardens that are deservedly popular for outdoor dining in season.

★ **Three Rivers Grill**   *(541)386-8883*
   downtown at 601 Oak St.
   3riversgrill.com
   L-D.   *Expensive*
Three Rivers Grill is one of the best special-occasion dining experiences in the Gorge. Consider wild chinook salmon with sautéed local seasonal vegetables with a lemon cream saffron sauce or hazelnut chicken sautéed with orange, thyme, and hazelnut cream sauce. An assortment of outstanding desserts is also made here. A large corner house has been skillfully transformed into chic dining rooms with a fine view of the gorge and town shared by a delightful adjoining dining deck. (The clean spare elegance is especially evident in the uniquely outfitted ladies room.)

★ **Wild Flower Cafe**   *(541)478-0111*
   6 mi. E at 2nd/Main Sts. - Mosier
   cafewildflower.com
   B-L-D. No B Wed.-Fri. Closed Mon.-Tues.   *Moderate*
Excellent specialties like marionberry-and-hazelnut pancakes, plus traditional American fare and homemade desserts, are served in a warm dining room with gorge views.

LODGINGS

Local lodgings include a full range of options with views of the Columbia River Gorge–from historic hotels through comfortable bed-and-breakfasts to memorable motels. High season is mid-spring through early fall. Rates may be reduced 20% or more at other times.

★ **Columbia Gorge Hotel**   *(541)386-5566*
  2 mi. W at 4000 Westcliff Dr. - 97031
  columbiagorgehotel.com
  40 units   *(800)345-1921*   *Expensive-Very Expensive*
The Columbia Gorge Hotel is one of America's most romantic country lodgings. The restored 1921 hotel is perched on a bluff hundreds of feet above the Columbia River. It is adjacent to the Wah Gwin Gwin Waterfall, the second highest (at 208 feet) year-round fall in the gorge. The building and stream leading to the waterfall are surrounded by extensive arboretum-quality flower gardens and towering pines and oaks. The hotel has been painstakingly restored to its original grandeur from the Roaring '20s when it was a favorite of Rudolph Valentino and other luminaries. A well-played grand piano distinguishes the luxurious firelit lounge. An outdoor patio surrounded by a rock garden has gorge views and breathtaking waterfall views from the lower level. The large dining room (see listing) is richly appointed in full linen and offers an enchanting view of the gorge beyond a window wall. A bountiful gourmet "farm breakfast" is included. All rooms are beautifully furnished including some antiques and regional wall hangings and have either one or two queens or a king bed.
    waterfall rooms (#339,#239)–spacious, above brim of
      waterfall with terrific corner view of gorge and gardens,
      corner (new age fiber-optic) electric fireplace, king bed.
    #229,#329–gas fireplace, corner rooms with grand
      gorge view from queen bed.

Comfort Suites   *(541)308-1000*
  1 mi. W at 2625 Cascade Av. - 97031
  comfortsuites.com
  62 units   *(800)228-5150*   *Expensive*
This three-story Comfort Suites is well outfitted with a large indoor pool, whirlpool, sauna and exercise room. Each spacious room is well furnished and has a microwave, refrigerator and a queen bed, and some view of Mt. Adams.
    #205–two-person whirlpool in room.

Hood River Bed & Breakfast   *(541)387-2997*
  just W at 918 Oak St. - 97031
  hoodriverbnb.com
  3 units   *Moderate-Expensive*

Fine Mt. Adams views are a feature of this comfortable bed-and-breakfast, opened in 2002 within a stroll of downtown. Hearty breakfasts are complimentary. Each nicely furnished room has a private (one detached) bath, a view of the river and distant Mt. Adams, and a queen bed.

"The Sky Room"–spacious, in-bath whirlpool.

★ **Hood River Hotel**   *(541)386-1900*
   downtown at 102 Oak St. - 97031
   hoodriverhotel.com
   41 units   *(800)386-1859*   *Moderate-Expensive*

Hood River's downtown landmark, a 1913 three-story hotel, has been fully restored to casual elegance. Amenities include a handsome new dining room (see listing), whirlpool, sauna, exercise room, and in-house (fee) massage. All of the comfortably furnished rooms have some antiques and quality reproductions and a queen bed. Many of the rooms have a river view.

#310–top floor, corner window views
   of the river, full kitchen.

★ **Hood River Inn - Best Western**   *(541)386-2200*
   just E at 1108 E. Marina Way - 97031
   hoodriverinn.com
   149 units   *(800)828-7873*   *Expensive*

The biggest lodging in town is right by the Columbia River. Amenities include a waterfront restaurant and lounge with a terrific view of the river, gorge and bridge. There is a large outdoor pool and whirlpool, exercise facilities, small private beach and boat dock. Many of the well-furnished rooms have a balcony or patio overlooking the river, a refrigerator, and a choice of two queens or a king bed.

"Bridal Suite"–one bedroom, gas fireplace,
   in-room two-person whirlpool, large private
   patio with river view, king bed.
#515,#415,#315–spacious, gas fireplace,
   fine view from river's edge, queen bed.

Inn at the Gorge Bed & Breakfast   *(541)386-4429*
   just SW at 1113 Eugene St. - 97031
   innatthegorge.com
   5 units   *Moderate-Expensive*

A large century-old home with a wraparound porch now serves as a bed-and-breakfast in a quiet area surrounded by luxuriant gardens. Full gourmet breakfast is complimentary. Each well-furnished unit has some antiques, a private bath, and a queen or king bed. Three rooms have a kitchen or kitchenette.

"Terrace Room"–in-bath whirlpool tub, refrigerator,
   private romantic terrace, antique queen bed.

Lakecliff   *(541)386-7000*
2 mi. W at 3820 Westcliff Dr. - 97031
lakecliffbnb.com
4 units   *Expensive*
A historic mansion (circa 1908) on a large site overlooking the
Columbia River now serves as a comfortable, peaceful bed-and-
breakfast. Hearty breakfast is complimentary. Each well-
furnished room has a private bath (one detached) and a queen
bed. Most also have a river view and a gas fireplace.
  "Daffodil"–gas fireplace, river view.
  "Lilac"–spacious, good river view, gas fireplace,
    private bath across hall.

Meredith Motel   *(541)386-1515*
2 mi. W at 4300 Westcliff Dr. - 97031
22 units   *Low-Moderate*
For nifty deja-vu, Meredith Motel is worth going way out of the
way for. It adjoins a pine-shaded picnic park with a grand gorge
overlook. Built in 1954 and recently remodeled and upgraded, the
single-level motel sports the sleek clean lines of the 1950s with
contemporary amenities. Each well-furnished, compact room with
two doubles or a queen bed also has an awe-inspiring Columbia
Gorge view from the blufftop hundreds of feet above the river.
  #22 (mini-suite)–large room, refrigerator and microwave,
    grand gorge view from two picture windows, queen bed.

Oak Street Hotel   *(541)386-3845*
just W at 610 Oak St. - 97031
oakstreethotel.com
9 units   *(866)386-3845*   *Expensive*
A renovated 1909 house is now a boutique hotel within walking
distance of the heart of town and the marina. Each compact room
is simply furnished, and has a private bath, refrigerator and a
queen bed.
  #5–corner room with good town/river view on two sides.

Panorama Lodge Bed & Breakfast   *(541)387-2687*
4 mi. SE at 2290 Old Dalles Dr. - 97031
panoramalodge.com
5 units   *(888)403-2687*   *Moderate*
Panorama Lodge Bed & Breakfast is aptly named. The
comfortably rustic log home perched on a forested ridge has an
unsurpassed view of Mt. Hood and the Hood River Valley
orchards. Abundant country breakfast with homemade bread and
local fruits is complimentary. Each room is comfortably furnished
and has a queen or king bed.
  "Elliott Gacier Room–large, fine Mt. Hood/valley
    view, king bed.

Sunset Motel   *(541)386-6098*
  1 mi. W at 2300 Cascade St. - 97031
  http://business.gorge.net/sunset/
  14 units   *(800)706-4429*   *Low*
This contemporary little motel with an antique shop has comfortable rooms with a refrigerator and microwave, a queen bed, and a good view of Mt. Adams.

★ **Vagabond Lodge**   *(541)386-2992*
  2 mi. W at 4070 Westcliff Dr. - 97031
  vagabondlodge.com
  42 units   *(877)386-2992*   *Moderate-Expensive*
Tucked into a lush forest-shaded garden near the rim of the Columbia River gorge is a delightful motel where all units have a refrigerator, microwave and one or two queen beds. Some of the well-furnished rooms have an outstanding forest and river view and extra amenities.

  #34,#30–woodburning rock fireplace, corner
     windows, choice river view, two queen beds.
  #23–fine forest/river view, corner, apartment with raised
     stone woodburning fireplace, full kitchen, two queen beds.
  #50,#60–one bedroom, stone (gas) fireplace, private
     balcony with super view of gorge, two queen beds.
  #19-22, #24-27–single-level units, forest/river
     view, one or two queen beds.

Jacksonville

Jacksonville is a treasury of living history. The downtown exudes a genuine Old West feeling, but offers goods and services that are as perfectly attuned to present tastes as the original 19th century businesses were. Preserving the historic edifices is aided by one of the mildest climates in the Northwest and surprisingly light annual rainfall. Temperatures are pleasant from spring through fall, when roadside stands offer a bountiful harvest of regional produce from surrounding truck gardens and orchards including America's best and biggest Comice pears and peaches.

Gold was discovered here in 1851 in one of the state's first strikes. Many substantial brick and stone buildings were constructed before the gold played out in the 1920s. Genteel decay set in until 1963, when volunteers constructed a makeshift stage for the Northwest's first summer outdoor music festival on a pioneer hillside estate with fine natural acoustics and valley views. Today it has grown into one of the West's most acclaimed festivals, with permanent performing arts facilities located on lush, tree-shaded grounds amid colorful gardens a short stroll up a hill from downtown.

The whole town is now a historic district on the National Register of Historic Places–the first in Oregon so designated (in 1966). Nearly 100 well-preserved original buildings house specialty stores, galleries, gourmet restaurants, romantic lodgings and homes. Abundant trails through town, parks, gardens, and one of the most picturesque main streets in the Northwest make it a bonanza for strollers, shoppers, and history buffs.

WEATHER PROFILE

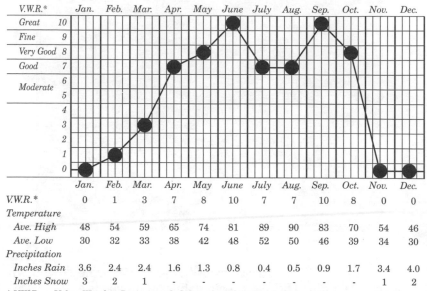

V.W.R.*		Jan.	Feb.	Mar.	Apr.	May	June	July	Aug.	Sep.	Oct.	Nov.	Dec.
Great	10												
Fine	9												
Very Good	8												
Good	7												
Moderate	6												
	5												

	Jan.	Feb.	Mar.	Apr.	May	June	July	Aug.	Sep.	Oct.	Nov.	Dec.
V.W.R.*	0	1	3	7	8	10	7	7	10	8	0	0
Temperature												
Ave. High	48	54	59	65	74	81	89	90	83	70	54	46
Ave. Low	30	32	33	38	42	48	52	50	46	39	34	30
Precipitation												
Inches Rain	3.6	2.4	2.4	1.6	1.3	0.8	0.4	0.5	0.9	1.7	3.4	4.0
Inches Snow	3	2	1	-	-	-	-	-	-	-	1	2

* V.W.R. = Vokac Weather Rating: probability of mild (warm & dry) weather on any given day.

BASIC INFORMATION

Population: 2,235
Elevation: 1,570 feet
Location: 268 miles South of Portland
Airport (regularly scheduled flights): Medford - 9 miles

Jacksonville Chamber of Commerce   (541)899-8118
   downtown at 185 N. Oregon St. (Box 33) - 97530
   jacksonvilleoregon.org
Southern Oregon Reservation Center (541)488-1011 (800)547-8052
   oregonadventure.net

ATTRACTIONS

★ **Applegate Lake**   *(541)899-1812*
   24 mi. SW via Hwy. 238
Deep in the Rogue River-Siskiyou National Forest is this scenic recreational reservoir on the Applegate River. Dense forests blanket the slopes of the gentle Siskiyou Mountains around the lake. Fishing is popular, with catches ranging from native cutthroat and Rainbow trout in the deeper portions to perch and crappie in warmer, shallow areas. Numerous campgrounds and a trail system around the 18-mile shoreline, swimming, picnicking, boating, and windsurfing are also enjoyed.

★ **Beekman Woods**
   just E (via California St.) on Laurelwood St.
Beekman Woods is the crown jewel in the "necklace of woodlands" surrounding Jacksonville. The evolving Woodlands Park and Trail System now includes more than 300 acres and nine miles of recreational trails.

★ *Bicycling*
   Cycle Analysis   *(541)899-9190*
   downtown at 535 N. 5th St.
   cycleanalysis.net
Jacksonville's idyllic location at the junction between the orchards and farmlands of Bear Creek Valley and gentle mountains rising above town is perfect for bicycling adventures. Mountain bikes can be rented here for two hours or all day (except Mon.) to explore miles of separated bikeways and scenic byways in the lush valley or gentle mountains.

★ **Britt Festivals**   *(541)779-0847*   *(800)882-7488*
   downtown at 216 W. Main St.
   brittfest.org
Britt Festivals are the Northwest's premier outdoor showcase for music and performing arts. Dozens of concerts from June through mid-September feature world class artists in music ranging from classical, jazz and blues to pop, folk, blue grass and country. Music lovers appreciate the relaxing atmosphere of stadium seating in a natural amphitheater surrounded by pines, madrones, and a 200-foot redwood planted in 1862.

Food Specialties
★   **Gary West Gourmet Food**   *(541)772-4172*   *(800)833-1820*
   just N at 690 N. 5th St.
   garywest.com
Gary West has developed, since 1966, into the premier source of meat products in the Northwest. Several different kinds of outstanding beef jerky (including certified Angus beef hickory-smoked steak strips), wild game jerky, smoked ham, and sausages

are complemented by related condiments and gourmet gifts. Samples are generously available, and there is tasting of premium Oregon vintages. Open 9-6 Mon.-Sat. Closed Sun.

★ **Good Bean Coffee** *(541)899-8740 (800)480-4036*
  downtown at 165 S. Oregon St.
  goodbean.net
A handsome brick building off main street has been effectively transformed into a popular coffeehouse/roastery where you can enjoy premium blends and related light fare. Consistent fine premium coffee varieties are achieved in part thanks to air roasting, rather than drum roasting, of the beans.

★ **The Rogue Creamery** *(541)665-1155 (866)665-1155*
  6 mi. NE at 311 N. Front St. - Central Point
  roguecreamery.com
The Rogue Creamery has been producing fine artisan cheeses since 1935. They have earned acclaim, including "World's Best Blue Cheese" at the 2003 World Cheese Awards in London–for Rogue River Blue. In addition to three kinds of outstanding blue cheese, they also make more than a dozen cheddars, plus Monterey jack. Samples are generously offered. Open Mon.-Sat. 9-5 and Sun. noon-5.

Jacksonville Cemetery
  downtown at the end of E St.
In this unusual place you can feel the scenic tranquility of the tucked-away historic village while walking among gravesites of early pioneers and townspeople buried here since 1859.

★ **Jacksonville Museum of Southern Oregon History** 773-6536
  downtown at 206 N. 5th St.
  sohs.org
The Southern Oregon Historical Society was organized in 1946 to save the Jackson County Courthouse (circa 1883). They now operate the Jacksonville (and children's) museum in the imposing landmark, plus the history store, a research library, the C.C. Beekman House, and Hanley Farm. Exhibits focus on the history of Peter Britt, Jacksonville, and the Rogue Valley.

★ *Wineries*
  Rogue Valley Wine Center *(541)512-2955 (866)512-2955*
  6 mi. E at 2310 Voorhies Rd. - Medford
  edenvalleyorchards.com
Their tasting room is host to Eden Valley Estate Wines (and selected boutique wineries). Guests enjoy samples of chardonnay, pinot noir, viognier, and cabernet franc in a stylish setting, stroll through colorful gardens and demonstration vineyards, and (in fall) sample grapes straight from the vine. Open Mon.-Sat. 10-6 and Sun. 12-4; in winter, Tues.-Sat. 10-5 and Sun. 12-4.

Valley View Winery   *(541)899-8468   (800)781-9463*
valleyviewwinery.com
9 mi. SW at 1000 Upper Applegate
Valley View is one of the best area producers of Northwestern wine. It has a stylish tasting area, expansive wine and gift shop, tours, and picnic tables with fine vineyard, gardens and mountain views. The **Valley View Winery Jacksonville Tasting Room** (125 W. California St.) is a tasting room and gift shop in the heart of town offering generous tastes. Both are open 11-5 daily.

RESTAURANTS

Applegate River Ranch House   *(541)846-6690*
16 mi. SW (on Hwy. 238) at 15100 Hwy. 238 - Applegate
applegateriverlodge.com
D only. Closed Mon.-Tues.   *Moderate*
The Applegate restaurant is next to the lodge by the river. Contemporary Northwestern fare ranges from steamer clams (when available) in a chardonnay broth to baby back ribs, rack of lamb or boneless duck breast broiled over red oakwood. For dessert, try the homemade hula pie. Pine log construction with a wood-trimmed dining room and deck overlooking the Applegate River contribute to the rustic charm of this getaway restaurant.

Back Porch BBQ   *(541)899-8821*
just N at 605 N. 5th St.
L-D.   *Moderate*
For authentic Texas Hill Country barbeque, try Back Porch BBQ, where meats are smoked on the premises and served with all the trimmings. The down-home outpost in an Old West themed setting also offers assorted half-pound burgers, Tex-Mex dishes, homemade pies and other desserts, and microbrewed beers.

Bella Union Restaurant & Saloon   *(541)899-1770*
downtown at 170 W. California St.
bellau.com
L-D.   *Moderate*
Italian comfort foods including all sorts of pizzas and unusual treats like a salmon burger are served in colorful relaxed dining rooms, and on a heated patio covered by a century-old wisteria vine. You can also dine with drinks in a saloon with much-trod wooden floorboards that evoke the building's Victorian heritage.

★ **Caterina's Trattoria**   *(541)899-6975*
just N at 505 N. 5th St.
D only. Closed Mon.-Tues.   *Expensive*
Appealing selections of traditional and creative Italian dishes range from fresh hand-cut lasagne or lemon-rosemary chicken to roasted lamb rack dijon-encrusted in a port wine demi-glaze.

Delicious breads and desserts are also made here fresh daily and served in the modish wood-trimmed trattoria.

★ **Country Cottage Cafe & Bakery**   *(541)899-2900*
   downtown at 230 E. C St.
   B-L.   *Moderate*
This is *the* place for breakfast in Jacksonville. Enjoy crepes, waffles, or a delicious omelet. Or, how about a super-sized blackberry streusel muffin, buttery croissant, or cinnamon roll made here? Creative soups, salads and sandwiches are featured later, along with mile-high chocolate banana cream pie and other luscious desserts made in this appealing side-street cafe/bakery.

★ **Gogi's Restaurant**   *(541)899-8699*
   downtown at 235 W. Main St.
   gogis.net
   D only. Closed Mon.-Tues.   *Expensive*
Gogi's is an unsurpassed destination for "New Northwestern" cuisine. The chef/owner has a genuine passion for coaxing award-winning flavors from the freshest and finest seasonal products from local and regional sources. House-smoked salmon with apple slaw basil vinaigrette and Crater Lake blue cheese is a classic example. So is mahogany-grilled breast of duck with wild rice and dried cranberry reduction sauce. Housemade desserts are similarly stellar. The dining room has an easygoing elegance that complements the sophisticated gourmet fare.

★ **The Jacksonville Inn**   *(541)899-1900*
   downtown at 175 E. California St.
   jacksonvilleinn.com
   B-L-D. No B-L Mon. Sun. brunch.   *Moderate-Expensive*
Acclaimed Continental cuisine with a Northwestern topspin has been featured for many years in dishes like stuffed hazelnut chicken or wild salmon with shitake mushrooms and cilantro sauce. Save room for elegant desserts made here like three-layer hazelnut meringue filled with whipped cream and fresh raspberries. Diners have a choice of Victorian elegance in a romantic candlelit cellar or upstairs in a plush nostalgic dining room. The nostalgic Civil War-era building (on the National Historic Register) also houses a gourmet food and wine shop.

Las Palmas   *(541)899-9965*
   downtown at 210 E. California St.
   L-D.   *Moderate*
Mazatlan seafood is the highlight of Las Palmas in dishes like shrimp sautéed with mushrooms in a creamy white sauce or crab enchiladas. A wealth of traditional Mexican dishes is also served including sopaipillas for dessert. There is a choice of casual colorful dining rooms or a landscaped patio out back.

★ **McCully House Inn**   *(541)899-1942*
   downtown at 240 E. California St.
   mccullyhouseinn.com
   D only.   *Moderate*
At McCully House, classic Northwestern cuisine is showcased in dishes like hazelnut-crusted chicken with lemon-tarragon cream sauce or grilled duck breast with lingonberry sauce, or grilled lamb chops with mint basil and pine nut sauce. For dessert, housemade chocolate souffle is always popular. Intimate casually elegant dining rooms include a glassed-in garden-view solarium and outdoor dining in summer.

LODGINGS

Lodgings are relatively scarce, but invariably distinctive and appropriate for the historic setting. Most are within a stroll of the heart of town. Many highway-front lodgings are in nearby Medford, including several bargain motels. High season is late spring to early fall. Rates may be reduced 20% or more at other times.

★ **Applegate River Lodge**   *(541)846-6690*
   16 mi. SW at 15100 Hwy. 238 (Box 3282) - Applegate 97530
   applegateriverlodge.com
   7 units   *Expensive*
The Applegate River Lodge opened in 1997 on a choice location by the Applegate River next to their notable restaurant (see listing). The little river is swimmable here, and there is a small park/beach across from the lodge. Each of the large, well-furnished rooms has a Northwestern theme, a private bath with a two-person whirlpool, a private deck overlooking the river and historic Pioneer Bridge, and a queen or king bed.

★ **Bybee's Historic Inn**   *(541)899-0106*
   1 mi. N at 883 Old Stage Rd. (Box 597) - 97530
   bybeeshistoricinn.com
   6 units   *(877)292-3374*   *Expensive*
A classic Revival Victorian home on the National Historic Register, centered on expansive landscaped grounds that include a gazebo and koi pond, now serves as a charming getaway bed-and-breakfast. Full breakfast and guest refrigerator with sodas, ice cream, etc., and fresh baked cookies, are complimentary. Each room is attractively furnished, including some antiques, all contemporary amenities, and a queen or king bed.
   "Elizabethan Room"–candlelit fireplace, two-
      person whirlpool in view of queen bed.
   "Renaissance Room"–two-person whirlpool,
      double-head shower, canopy queen bed.

★ **The Jacksonville Inn**   *(541)899-1900*
   downtown at 175 E. California St. (Box 359) - 97530
   jacksonvilleinn.com
   12 units   (800)321-9344   Expensive-Very Expensive
The Jacksonville Inn is one of the Northwest's most venerable landmarks. The small hotel, in an 1861 two-story brick landmark on the National Historic Register, shares the building with a restaurant (see listing) and a gift shop that is a fine source for premium wines and gourmet products of the region. Breakfast at the inn and bicycles are complimentary. Each of the eight hotel rooms is beautifully furnished with authentic Western antiques, and has a private bath, all contemporary conveniences, plus extra amenities and a queen bed. Nearby beautifully furnished private cottages also cater to romance with a luxurious Victorian theme.
   "Honeymoon Cottages" (4 of these)–two-person in-room
      whirlpool, steam shower, gas fireplace, sitting room,
      private patio, entertainment center, canopy king bed.
   "Peter Britt Room" (in hotel)–two-person in-room
      whirlpool, canopy queen bed.

Jacksonville's Magnolia Inn   *(541)899-0255*
   downtown at 245 N. 5th St. (Box 1319) - 97530
   www.magnolia-inn.com
   9 units   (866)899-0255   Expensive
A 1920s apartment has been transformed into a simply stylish inn with a gift shop. Expanded Continental breakfast is complimentary. Each comfortably furnished room has all contemporary amenities including a private bathroom and queen bed.

McCully House Inn   *(541)899-1942*
   downtown at 240 E. California St. (Box 13) - 97530
   mccullyhouseinn.com
   3 units   (800)367-1942   Expensive
Behind a white picket fence on a large corner lot is McCully House (on the National Historic Register), painstakingly restored to its 1861 origins. Beautiful surrounding gardens include more than 80 varieties of Jackson & Perkins' test roses. Downstairs is a fine restaurant (see listing) with numerous wall hangings by local artists for sale. Full breakfast in the dining room or garden is complimentary. Upstairs, each guest room is well furnished including antiques, a private bath and queen or king bed.
   "McCully Room"–antique clawfoot tub with
      shower, gas fireplace, queen bed.

Orth House Bed & Breakfast   *(541)899-8665*
   downtown at 105 W. Main St. (Box 1437) - 97530
   orthbnb.com
   3 units   (800)700-7301   Expensive

A classic brick Victorian home by the heart of town has been skillfully transformed into a bed-and-breakfast that captures the Gold Camp spirit of its 1880 origins with a wealth of quality original and reproduction antiques. A full breakfast is complimentary. Each well-furnished room includes nostalgic furnishings, a private bath and one or two queens or a king bed.

"Josie's Room"–spacious, town-view windows, in-room
   clawfoot tub, shower in view of brass king bed.

The Stage Lodge   *(541)899-3953*
   just N at 830 N. 5th St. (Box 1316) - 97530
   stagelodge.com
   27 units   *(800)253-8254*   *Moderate-Expensive*
The Stage Lodge, Jacksonville's only traditional motel, hints at the nostalgic Old West theme. Each well-furnished unit includes contemporary comforts, small refrigerator, and queen or king bed.

"suites" (2 of these) gas fireplace in living room,
   two-person in-bath whirlpool, wet bar,
   microwave and refrigerator, queen bed.

★ **TouVelle House Bed & Breakfast**   *(541)899-8938*
   just N at 455 N. Oregon St. (Box 1891) - 97530
   touvellehouse.com
   6 units   *(800)846-8422*   *Expensive*
Crowning a knoll a short stroll from the heart of the village is one of the area's most stately mansions (circa 1916). Expansive grounds include beautiful gardens, a fountain, and a heated pool (in season). Full gourmet breakfast, and fresh lemonade or warm beverages in the afternoon, are complimentary. Each room in the three-story home is well furnished with antiques and period artworks, intimate views, a private bath, and a queen or king bed.

"The Garden Suite"–spacious, sitting room, many garden-
   view windows, Roman tub for two, queen bed.
"Frank TouVelle's Room"–large corner room, gardens/
   mountain view, balcony, king bed.

Under the Greenwood Tree   *(541)776-0000*
   2 mi. E at 3045 Bellinger Ln. - Medford 97501
   greenwoodtree.com
   4 rooms   *Expensive*
A substantial historic country home now serves as a romantic bed-and-breakfast hideaway on ten landscaped acres that include luxuriant gardens, a honeysuckle and rose gazebo, Civil War era farm buildings, and a family of friendly llamas. A gourmet country breakfast, tea and treats in the afternoon, and use of bicycles are complimentary. Each cozy room is well furnished with antiques and contemporary amenities, a private bath, intimate garden views, extras, and a double or queen bed.

Joseph

Joseph is the hidden jewel among Oregon's treasury of great towns. Resplendent snow-capped peaks provide a picture-perfect backdrop to a lineup of Old West-style buildings further distinguished by abundant colorful landscaping and majestic life-size bronzes. The arrow-straight main street aims directly toward nearby Wallowa Lake and the alpine grandeur of the Eagle Cap Wilderness. These attractions and the surrounding national forest provide endless ways for outdoor enthusiasts to enjoy the full-four-season climate.

The town's remote location miles from major cities has kept the population small in this isolated outback. Early settlers in the late 1800s named the town after Chief Joseph, the renowned American Indian who especially loved this region. Agriculture, timber, art, and tourism have always been the key industries. The town's first bronze foundry opened in 1982, providing jobs for artists drawn here by the inspiring setting (which has resulted in the nation's most elaborate collection of fine public bronze art on permanent display along the main street).

The growing selection of specialty shops, studios and art galleries, restaurants and inns is delightfully individualized. Nearby, unlimited recreation opportunities include all kinds of day-use sports like boating, hiking, fishing, swimming, horseback riding, river running and rock climbing in summer. More exotic options include parasailing, llama treks, multiday (hunting or fishing) pack trips, or wildlife photography in the still-pristine high Wallowas.

Joseph

WEATHER PROFILE

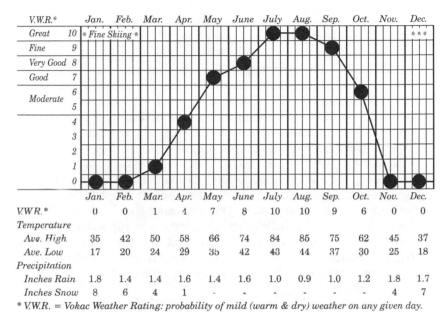

V.W.R.*	Jan.	Feb.	Mar.	Apr.	May	June	July	Aug.	Sep.	Oct.	Nov.	Dec.
V.W.R.*	0	0	1	4	7	8	10	10	9	6	0	0
Temperature												
Ave. High	35	42	50	58	66	74	84	85	75	62	45	37
Ave. Low	17	20	24	29	35	42	43	44	37	30	25	18
Precipitation												
Inches Rain	1.8	1.4	1.4	1.6	1.4	1.6	1.0	0.9	1.0	1.2	1.8	1.7
Inches Snow	8	6	4	1	-	-	-	-	-	-	4	7

* V.W.R. = Vokac Weather Rating: probability of mild (warm & dry) weather on any given day.

BASIC INFORMATION

Population: 1,054
Elevation: 4191 feet
Location: 317 miles East of Portland
Airport (regularly scheduled flights): Lewiston, WA - 72 miles

Wallowa County Chamber of Commerce (541)426-4622
  5 mi. N at 115 Tejaka Lane (Box 427) - Enterprise 97828
  wallowacountychamber.com (800)585-4121
  josephoregon.com

ATTRACTIONS

Aerial Tramway
★ **Wallowa Lake Tramway**   *(541)432-5331*
6 mi. S at 59919 Wallowa Lake Hwy.
wallowalaketramway.com
The Wallowa Lake Tramway is the steepest, and one of the most thrilling, aerial rides in America. Four-person cable cars go from a base elevation of 4,450 feet to the top of Mt. Howard at 8,150 feet above sea level in fifteen minutes–a distance of nearly four miles. The patio deck adjacent to the top of the tram is a great place to enjoy beer or wine with a light meal or snacks from the **Summit Grill** ("the Northwest's highest restaurant") or your own picnic with a breathtaking backdrop. The top of the tram serves as a trailhead for a wealth of trails and loops to spectacular viewpoints and picnic sites. Do not miss the Wallowa Valley Overlook Trail (¾ mile) for a glorious perspective on the mountains, Wallowa Lake, Joseph, and the lush valley below. Bring your mountain bike for an easy but memorable five- to fifteen-mile bike ride down from the summit.
Boat Rentals
★ **Wallowa Lake Marina**   *(541)432-9115*
6 mi. S at Wallowa Lake Marina
wallowalake.net/wallowa/lakemarina.html
From May to mid-September, you can rent canoes, rowboats, pontoon boats or motorboats by the hour (or day). This is also the place to secure fishing guides, hiking information and gifts.
★ **Bronze Foundry Tours**
Joseph's main street is a unique showcase for eight monumental bronze sculptures (owned by the city) cast locally. Stirring renditions of a soaring eagle, cougar, prowling wolves, and many other bronzes are exhibited in lovely gardens by prime intersections along Main Street. The number of local foundries and the public art have earned Joseph distinction as the "Bronze Capital of the Northwest." Tours of local foundries and galleries complete the experience.
Kelly's Gallery on Main   *(541)432-3116*
downtown at 103 N. Main St.
josephbronze.net
Tours leave from Kelly's (where bronzes and other fine art are displayed and sold) on Friday and Saturday to **Joseph Bronze**, the foundry just north of town. Museum-quality bronzes of all sizes from monumental to intimate are on display.
Valley Bronze Gallery   *(541)432-7445*
downtown at 18 S. Main St.
valleybronze.com

The largest bronze foundry in Joseph (started in 1982) is a delightful showcase for bronze sculptures of all sizes. The dramatic bronze horse sculpture on main street is a stirring example of their work. One tour daily (by reservation) goes from here to the **Valley Bronze of Oregon** (the nearby foundry)–one of America's largest.

★ **Downtown**
  downtown on Main St.
The recently renovated heart of Joseph is a perfect cultural complement to the natural grandeur of the setting. Sensitive architecture, impressive public art and extensive landscaping combine to make the right foreground for this alpine haven. Views to the south are punctuated by the enormous front range of the Wallowas towering over downtown. Strollers are also rewarded with a wealth of fine art galleries, restaurants and recreation-oriented specialty shops on Main Street.

★ **Eagle Cap Excursion Train**   *(541)963-9000   (800)323-7330*
  24 mi. NW on Hwy. 82 - Wallowa
  eaglecaptrain.com
For memorably scenic rail adventures, don't miss this train that showcases otherwise inaccessible canyons on Saturday trips from June through October. The longest and most popular route is the "Two Rivers Run" that goes from the village of Wallowa through the spectacular Grand Ronde River Canyon (inaccessible to autos) and ends near the delightfully unassuming Western village of Elgin. The seven-hour round-trip covers sixty-three miles. Lunch, beverages and a snack are included. The "Valley Voyage" goes round-trip from Wallowa to Joseph, covering nearly fifty miles in seven hours.

★ *Fishing*
Steelhead and rainbow trout fishing on Wallowa Lake (and River) and nearby streams is some of Oregon's finest. Local guides to outfit you with the right equipment, take you to the best holes, and arrange whitewater floats include:
  Backcountry Outfitters   *(541)426-5908   (800)966-8080*
  backcountryoutfittersinc.com
  Eagle Cap Fishing Guides   *(541)432-9055   (800)940-3688*
  wallowa.com/eaglecap
  Joseph Fly Shoppe   *(541)432-4343*
  josephflyshop.com
  Ninebark Outfitters   *(541)426-4855   (877)646-3275*
  ninebarkoutfitters.com
  Food Specialties
★   **Betty's Kitchen**   *(541)432-8181   (877)399-0442*
  downtown at 304 S. Lake St.

bettys-kitchen.com

A full line of homemade (no preservatives or additives) specialty foods like huckleberry jam, homemade salsa, candies, breads and many more "yummies for the tummy" can be purchased individually or assembled into gift baskets. When Betty's door is open, visitors are invited into Betty's kitchen to sample what's cooking and to purchase items from her extensive catalog.

★ **Hells Canyon National Recreation Area**   *(541)426-5546*
   24 mi. SE via Hwy. 82 & F.S. Road 39 N

Hells Canyon is North America's deepest gorge–almost 8,000 feet from Devil Mountain to Granite Creek below. The Snake River surges for 71 free-flowing miles along the Oregon-Idaho border. In this near-wilderness, wildlife ranges from mountain goats and elk to cougars and bears. Salmon, steelhead and rainbow trout are the popular game fish, but it is said that sturgeon more than ten feet long also inhabit the Snake River. Powerboats, float trips, and backpacking provide scenic access. Highway 82 and FS 39N extend to an awesome panorama from Hells Canyon Overlook across the designated wilderness portion of the canyon to the river. Hells Canyon National Recreation Area Headquarters, at the Wallowa Mountains Visitor Center (see listing), has permits, maps, road conditions and details about whitewater rafting, jet-boat trips, fishing and hunting excursions.

★ **Hells Canyon Scenic Byway**   *(541)426-4978*
   via Hwys. 82, 86, & FS 39
   hellscanyonbyway.com

This 218-mile paved road loops through both Joseph and Baker City as it encircles the snow-tipped Wallowa Mountains. It is one of only 21 designated "All-American Roads" in the United States–the highest scenic designation in the federal highways system. Recreational opportunities along the byway, especially between the Snake River and Wallowa Lake and Mountains, are unlimited in summer. The road is usually open only from Memorial Day until the first big snowstorm.

Horseback Riding

★   **Eagle Cap Pack Station**   *(541)432-4145 (800)681-6222*
    6 mi. S at 59761 Wallowa Lake Hwy.
    eaglecapwildernesspackstation.com

At the south end of Lake Wallowa, this outfitter conducts guided rides lasting one, two, four, or eight hours, and arranges multi-day pack trips into the adjacent Eagle Cap Wilderness.

★   **Ninebark Outfitters**   *(541)426-4855   (877)646-3275*
    39 mi. N
    ninebarkoutfitters.com

Horseback pack trips begin at a near-wilderness lodge and go to wilderness drop camps, tent camps, or their wilderness cabin. Adventures from any base camp can be customized to feature fishing, hunting, hiking and/or photography.

★ *Parasailing*
  Eagle Cap Pack Station   *(541)432-4145*   *(800)681-6222*
  6 mi. S at 59761 Wallowa Lake Hwy.
From the marina you can charter a fast boat trip out onto the lake where you can enjoy a thrilling over-the-lake cruise while parasailing behind the boat. Available daily May through Sept.

★ *River Running*
Guided whitewater rafting trips are popular on nearby clear streams in picturesque canyons in late spring and summer. Day trips and longer can be arranged at:
  North Star River Odysseys, LLC   *(541)432-4343*
  josephflyshop.com
  Winding Water River Expeditions   *(541)432-0747*
  windingwatersrafting.com
  Wallowa County Museum   *(541)423-6095*
  downtown at 110 S. Main St.
  co.wallowa.or.us/museum
The area's first bank (circa 1888), on the National Historic Register, now houses a wealth of historical memorabilia from pioneer days. The Nez Perce Room is dedicated to Chief Joseph's tribe, and includes a teepee. The museum shop sells books and souvenirs. Open 10-5 daily from late May to mid-Sept.

★ **Wallowa County Park**
  1 mi. S on Hwy. 82
The north shore of Wallowa Lake has been made into a local park with extensive lawns extending to a sandy and gravely beach with an outstanding view down to the fjord-like lake to towering peaks. A boat ramp and restrooms are available.

★ **Wallowa Lake**   *(800)585-4121*
  6 mi. S on Wallowa Lake Hwy.
  wallowalake.net
Wallowa Lake is the top destination in Eastern Oregon for fresh water recreation. It fills a long-gone glacial trough for five miles between a lush pine forest surrounded by craggy peaks and a sage-covered terminal moraine where the ancient glacier stopped in the broad Wallowa Valley beyond the mountains. Boating, waterskiing, parasailing, fishing and swimming are all popular during summer. Hiking, backpacking, mountain biking, and horseback riding are enjoyed around the lake and and beyond in the vast Eaglecap Wilderness. A visitor-friendly village in the pines by the south end of the lake offers all kinds of food, lodgings, and recreation opportunities.

★ **Wallowa Lake State Park**   *(541)432-4185   (800)452-5687*
  6 mi. S (on Hwy. 82) at 72214 Marina Lane
  oregonstateparks.org
The entire scenic south shore of Wallowa Lake has been developed into one of the Northwest's most deservedly popular state parks. Extensive lawns sprinkled with towering pines extend to a sandy beach between the outlet of the picturesque little Wallowa River and the lake's only marina. The enormously popular day-use-only shore area is backed by a big full-service campground in the forest on the flat lands by the river surrounded by majestic peaks. Boating, sailing, parasailing, fishing and canoeing are popular. On warm days, swimming (in spite of the cold water) is popular on the clear, deep lake.

★ **Wallowa Mountains Visitor Center**   *(541)426-5546*
  6 mi. NW at 88401 Hwy. 82 - Enterprise
Perched high on a rim overlooking the Wallowa Valley and the magnificent mountain range beyond is an impressive wood-trim building with a not-to-be-missed picture-window alpine view and interactive diaramas related to forest features like camping, hunting, fishing and river running. The is also a good source of maps and trail guides and related material about the region's recreation opportunities.

★ **Wallowa-Whitman National Forest**   *(541)426-5546*
  begins 3 mi. S
  fs.fed.us/r6/w-w
Joseph is surrounded by one of the West's biggest national forests, which also includes a large area west of Baker City. The forest's crown jewel, however, begins just three miles south of Joseph. The majestic **Eagle Cap Wilderness** is the largest wilderness in Oregon. Bare granite peaks and ridges tower over high alpine lakes, flower-filled meadows and U-shaped glacial valleys. Cold, clear streams and waterfalls with deep pools hidden by dense pine forests lure fishermen with golden trout. Backpackers, hikers and climbers may catch glimpses of bald eagles, bighorn sheep and mountain goats among the diverse wildlife here. More than 500 miles of trails lead to campsites amid grandeur far from civilization. For maps and detailed information about recreation passes and wilderness permits, go to the Wallowa Mountains Visitor Center (see listing).

★ *Winter Sports*
  Ferguson Ridge   *(541)432-4170*
  8 mi. SE on Tucker Donn Rd.
For a deja-vu downhill ski experience that is a throwback to an earlier time (with only a rope and T-bar), try the scenic little ski area at Ferguson Ridge. The vertical drop is 640 feet and the

longest run is close to a mile. There are rentals, a day lodge, a terrain park and half pipe for snowboarders, and cross-country ski trails. Open December to mid-March on weekends.

Wing Ridge Ski Tours   *(541)426-4322   (800)646-9050*
wingski.com
Cross-country skiing and guided hut-to-hut multi-day tours can be arranged here for scenic trips to shelters in the Wallowas.

RESTAURANTS

Boeve's General Store & Pub   *(541)432-9292 (888)432-9292*
6 mi. S at 72784 Marina Lane
boeves.com
L-D.   *Moderate*
This is a fine place to stock up on provisions while enjoying the pine-forested campgrounds, picnic tables and lodgings just south of Wallowa Lake. There is a rustic little pub with a good selection of Northwestern comfort foods and beers.

Cloud 9 Bakery   *(541)426-3790*
5 mi. N at 105 SE 1st St. - Enterprise
B-L. Closed Sat. & Sun.   *Low*
Assorted soups, salads and sandwiches are served along with a variety of donuts, pastries and cookies on display in this warm wood-trim cafe. The multigrain roll is a specialty.

★ **Embers Brewhouse**   *(541)432-2739*
downtown at 206 N. Main St.
L-D.   *Moderate*
More than a dozen tap beers (made elsewhere) can be enjoyed with traditional or creative pizzas and big calzones (the combo with pepperoni, sausage, mushrooms, and olives is outstanding). There are some tables inside, but the split-level tree-shaded deck and porch are *the* place to be when weather is good. The view of Main Street and towering nearby mountains is memorable.

★ **Mountain Air Cafe**   *(541)432-0233*
downtown at 4 S. Main St.
eoni.com/~mtnair
B-L.   *Moderate*
Some of the finest breakfasts in Northeastern Oregon are served at the Mountain Air Cafe. Careful attention to fresh ingredients assures fine quality for all sorts of omelets, plate-filling pancakes and other tasty breakfast selections. Big housemade raisin-filled cinnamon rolls are another treat, as are seasonal and cream pies, fresh-baked bread and fudge served in the warm comfortable coffee shop. Gallery art is displayed for sale on one wall and a picture-window view of the mountains is on the other. Don't miss the **Natural Wildlife Museum** accessed through the cafe, a

remarkable 100-foot-long showcase of every kind of major animal living in the region. Each is doing what comes naturally–some spectacularly like a mountain lion attacking a buck deer. Well-done murals enhance the dramatic impact of the panoramic exhibit.

Old Town Cafe   *(541)432-9898*
downtown at 8 S. Main St.
B-L.   *Moderate*
In addition to a good selection of down-home country fare, there are innovative specialties like "hole-in-one" (two eggs cooked inside toast topped with bacon, cheddar and green chili). The cafe is deservedly popular. A colorful flower-strewn little patio adjoins.

Outlaw Restaurant and Saloon   *(541)432-4321*
downtown at 108 N. Main St.
L-D.   *Moderate*
Half-pound burgers, specialty burgers, potato skins and other comfort foods can be enjoyed with assorted beers on tap in a casual Western-themed dining room with a wood-toned adjoining saloon.

★ **Rimrock Inn**   *(541)828-7769*
39 mi. N at 83471 Lewiston Hwy. - Enterprise
rimrockrestaurant.com
L-D. Closed Sun.-Mon.   *Moderate*
Rimrock Inn is the most remarkable dining destination in Northeastern Oregon. Updates of American classic entrees and a specialty dish each evening are skillfully prepared from scratch with quality ingredients. The homemade pies from fresh seasonal fruits are a perfect finish to "fine dining on the edge." A handsome old roadhouse has been transformed into an upscale dinner house where tables set with full linen and candles overlook a panoramic view of immense Joseph Canyon.

Russells at the Lake   *(541)432-0591*
6 mi. S at 59984 Wallowa Lake Hwy.
L-D. Closed Oct.-Apr.   *Moderate*
Fresh trout and salmon prepared several ways highlight a menu with a wealth of traditional and designer fare. A simply comfortable wood-trimmed dining room overlooks the surrounding pine forest.

Stubborn Mule Saloon & Steakhouse   *(541)432-6853*
downtown at 104 S. Main St.
L-D. Closed Mon.   *Moderate*
This cafe and bar combines casual food and drinks amid Western wood-trim decor that includes pool tables and shuffleboard.

Terminal Gravity Brew Pub   *(541)426-0158*
6 mi. N at 803 SE School St. - Enterprise
L-D. No L Sun. Closed Mon.-Tues.   *Moderate*
India Pale Ale is the hallmark of this microbrewery with a little upstairs dining room featuring creative pub grub.

Vali's Alpine Restaurant & Delicatessen   *(541)432-5691*
6 mi. S at 59811 Wallowa Lake Hwy.
D only. Closed Mon.-Tues.   *Moderate*
Hearty Eastern European fare like schnitzel or chicken paprikas
is served as the entree of the day in this warm wood-toned
mountain cabin in the pines. Dinner reservations are required.

Wallowa Lake Lodge   *(541)432-9821*
6 mi. S at 60060 Wallowa Lake Hwy.
wallowalakelodge.com
B-D.   *Moderate*
For breakfast, the Lodge's specialty is an Oregon classic–honey-
wheat hazelnut pancakes with marionberry butter. Contemporary
American standards each evening like rib steak and trout
almondine are featured on a limited menu in a large wood-trim
dining room with a view of the lake from the historic lodge.

★ **Wildflour Bakery**   *(541)432-7225*
downtown at 600 N. Main St.
B-L. Closed Tues.   *Moderate*
A limited selection of housemade pastries, breads and cookies is
on display. Breakfast specialties like omelets, sourdough or
cornmeal pancakes are served in the morning, and light dishes at
lunch, in the adjoining coffee shop overlooking the mountains and
a large deck that is deservedly popular in warm weather.

LODGINGS

Lodgings in the area are relatively scarce and uniformly small.
Almost all reflect the area's mountain mystique. High season is
May to September. Rates may be 30% or more less at other times.
Some properties close from fall through spring.

★ **Bronze Antler Bed & Breakfast**   *(541)432-0230*
downtown at 309 S. Main St. (Box 74) - 97846
bronzeantler.com
3 units   *(866)520-9769*   *Expensive*
The Bronze Antler is northeastern Oregon's premier bed-and-
breakfast. A well-landscaped arts-and-crafts-style home (circa
1925) a stroll from downtown was skillfully transformed into the
inn. A full gourmet breakfast is complimentary. So are port or
sherry and fresh baked goods (like tasty brownies) in the evening,
and soft drinks in the guest refrigerator. Each cozy room is
attractively furnished, including some European antiques and
extra touches, a private bath, a view of the mountains, and a
queen bed.
    "Chief Joseph Mountain Room"–splendid mountain view.

Chandlers' Inn   *(541)432-9765*
just S at 700 S. Main St. (Box 243) - 97846

josephbedandbreakfast.com
5 units   *Moderate-Expensive*
A streamside gazebo enhances this rustic wood-trim bed-and-breakfast. Full breakfast and coffee, tea and cookies are complimentary. Each simply furnished room has a queen or king bed. Two rooms share a bath.
   #2–private bath, choice mountain view from king bed.
★ **Eagle Cap Chalets**   *(541)432-4704*
   6 mi. S at 59879 Wallowa Lake Hwy. - 97846
   eaglecapchalets.com
   37 units   *Moderate-Expensive*
An indoor pool, whirlpool, miniature golf and an espresso bar are features of this wood-trim complex in the pines a stroll from Wallowa Lake. There is a wide range of comfortably furnished condos, cabins and simply furnished chalet rooms offering a gas fireplace, private decks, kitchens, and queens or a king bed.
   Cabin #8–studio, in-bath whirlpool, gas (metal) fireplace,
      small kitchen, private deck, queen bed.
Flying Arrow Resort   *(541)432-2951*
   6 mi. S at 59782 Wallowa Lake Hwy. - 97846
   flyingarrowresort.com
   18 units   *Moderate-Expensive*
The picturesque little Wallowa River follows a rocky course past this cabin complex to nearby Wallowa Lake. Pine-shaded grounds include a pool and whirlpool. Each simply furnished cabin has a kitchen and twin, double, queen or king beds in one- to four-bedroom units. Several have a riverside deck and/or a gas or woodburning fireplace.
Indian Lodge Motel   *(541)432-2651*
   downtown at 201 S. Main St. (Box 420) - 97846
   eoni.com/~gingerdaggett/
   16 units   *(888)286-5484*   Low
This single-level small motel is convenient to the heart of town. Each comfortably furnished room has all contemporary amenities, including a refrigerator and doubles, queen or king bed.
Matterhorn Swiss Village   *(541)432-4071*
   6 mi. S at 59950 Wallowa Lake Hwy. - 97846
   matterhornswissvillage.com
   7 units   *(800)891-2551*   *Moderate-Expensive*
In tall pines beyond the south end of Lake Wallowa is a little cottage complex with a cafe and gift shop. Each simply furnished cottage (from studio to two bedroom) has a kitchen, a private bath, and a choice of bed sizes.
   #6–one bedroom, gas fireplace, full kitchen,
      private deck, queen bed.

Ponderosa Motel   *(541)426-3186*
5 mi. N at 102 E. Greenwood - Enterprise 97828
33 units   *Moderate*
Ponderosa Motel is in the heart of Enterprise. Each well-furnished unit is attractively decorated with rough-hewn Ponderosa pine accents and has one or two queens or a king bed.

★ **Rama Inn - Best Western**   *(541)426-2000*
6 mi. N at 1200 Highland Av. - Enterprise 97828
enterpriseramainn.com
53 units   *(888)726-2466*   *Moderate-Expensive*
High on a rim overlooking a broad fertile valley backed by an immense mountain range is a relatively new lodging that is the area's biggest and most complete. Facilities include an indoor pool, whirlpool, sauna, and exercise room, and guests receive a complimentary expanded Continental breakfast. Each well-furnished room has a refrigerator, microwave, and one or two queens or a king bed. Many have a fine view of the mountains.
    #235,#231,#121–captivating mountain views,
       in-room two-person whirlpool, king bed.

Strawberry Wilderness Bed & Breakfast   *(541)432-3125*
just W at 406 W. Wallowa Av. - 97846
lbsites.com/strawberrywbb
3 units   *Moderate*
A large, recently built log home serves as a bed-and-breakfast and art gallery near downtown. A hearty country-style breakfast is complimentary. Rooms are comfortably furnished, with private or shared bathroom, and a choice of twins, queen or king bed.

★ **Wallowa Lake Lodge**   *(541)432-9821*
6 mi. S at 60060 Wallowa Lake Hwy. - 97846
wallowalakelodge.com
30 units   *Moderate-Expensive*
The area's most historic lodging (circa 1923) is Wallowa Lake Lodge situated in a tranquil forest adjacent to where the rocky little Wallowa River enters Wallowa Lake. A picturesque firelit lobby with several windows overlooking the lake adjoins the big wood-trimmed dining room (see listing). Each lodge room is individually nicely furnished with period antiques, a view of the forest or lake, and twins or one or two queen beds. There are also eight comfortably outfitted knotty-pine cabins with woodburning fireplaces on the expansive pine-shaded site.
    "Spruce"–one bedroom, full kitchen, stone woodburning
       fireplace, private lake and forest view deck, queen bed.
    "Two Bedroom Cabin" (3 of these)–full kitchen, stone
       woodburning fireplace, private forest/river view deck,
       double and queen bed.

Lincoln City

Lincoln City is the oceanfront-view capital of the Pacific Northwest. More local dining rooms and lodgings feature window-wall panoramas of seascapes than anywhere else along the Oregon and Washington coast. This is partially because Lincoln City sprawls for more than seven miles along a shoreline distinguished by gentle bluffs and broad sandy beaches. The location of the heart of town is debatable. But, an important small nucleus of restaurants, shops, and lodgings has been built on both sides of the world's shortest river (a few hundred feet in length). The temperate climate is notably windy, so kite flying is popular much of the year. In winter, storm-watching has become the town's main attraction when gigantic windwhipped surf pounds against beaches and bluffs.

Unlike most Oregon towns, the local economy was never based on fishing, lumber or minerals. Instead, residents have always been oriented toward fulfulling the needs of travelers and vacationers. Tourism was given a major boost by the completion of the Oregon Coast Highway (US 101) during the 1930s. In 1965, five villages incorporated as one town to better coordinate their appeal to visitors.

Today, Lincoln City is one of the largest and most popular coastal vacation destinations—with something for all age groups. Galleries, shops, restaurants and lodgings are spread along the coast and main highway throughout the length of town. Collectively, they represent all ranges of price and quality, including some of the Oregon coast's finest tourist facilities.

WEATHER PROFILE

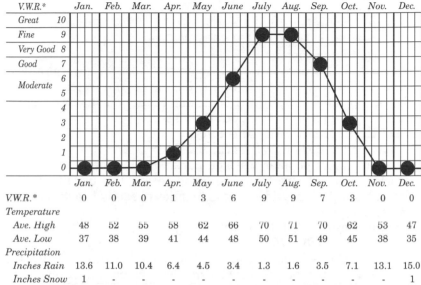

V.W.R.*		Jan.	Feb.	Mar.	Apr.	May	June	July	Aug.	Sep.	Oct.	Nov.	Dec.
Great	10												
Fine	9												
Very Good	8												
Good	7												
Moderate	6 / 5												

V.W.R.*	Jan.	Feb.	Mar.	Apr.	May	June	July	Aug.	Sep.	Oct.	Nov.	Dec.
	0	0	0	1	3	6	9	9	7	3	0	0
Temperature												
Ave. High	48	52	55	58	62	66	70	71	70	62	53	47
Ave. Low	37	38	39	41	44	48	50	51	49	45	38	35
Precipitation												
Inches Rain	13.6	11.0	10.4	6.4	4.5	3.4	1.3	1.6	3.5	7.1	13.1	15.0
Inches Snow	1	-	-	-	-	-	-	-	-	-	-	1

* V.W.R. = Vokac Weather Rating: probability of mild (warm & dry) weather on any given day.

BASIC INFORMATION

Population: 7,437
Elevation: 80 feet
Location: 84 miles Southwest of Portland
Airport (regularly scheduled flights): Portland - 91 miles

Lincoln City Visitor & Convention Bureau   (541)996-1274
  downtown at 801 SW Hwy. 101, Suite 1 - 97367   (800)452-2151
  oregoncoast.org
Lincoln City Chamber of Commerce   (541)994-3070
  2 mi. N at 4039 NW Logan Rd. (at Hwy. 101) (Box 787) - 97367
  lcchamber.com

ATTRACTIONS

★ *Boat Rental*
Blue Heron Landing Boat Rental   *(541)994-4708*
2 mi. N (near Hwy. 101) at 4006 W. Devils Lake Rd.
blueheronlanding.net
Devils Lake borders Lincoln City on the west for several miles.
The best way to enjoy the scenic lake is on the water. Canoes,
kayaks, paddleboats, fishing boats and other personal watercraft
can be rented here by the hour or longer.

★ **"D" River Beach Wayside Park**
downtown at Hwy. 101/1st St. SE
Oregon's most popular wayside park was developed where the
world's shortest river flows into the ocean. The usually sunny
beachfront park provides access to miles of sandy beaches to the
north and south.

★ **Depoe Bay**   *(541)765-2889*
13 mi. S on Hwy. 101 - Depoe Bay
An appealing village has grown up around a tiny rock-bound
harbor that may be the world's smallest. A sea wall promenade
and bridge are the best places for watching sportfishing and
pleasure boats negotiate the harrowingly narrow, rock-lined
channel between the harbor and the sea. Just west of the
promenade are "spouting horns"–natural rock formations
throwing geyserlike sprays of surf high in the air. Various
sightseeing and deep-sea fishing trips (see listing) depart from the
harbor daily. Several restaurants and lodgings (see listings) offer
picture-window views of the exciting coastline.

★ **Devils Lake State Park**   *(541)994-2002*   *(800)551-6949*
just NE on 6th Dr.
oregonstateparks.org
This in-town campground offers full-service tent, RV and yurt
sites next to a popular three-mile-long freshwater lake separated
from the ocean by the 440-foot-long "D" River, the shortest river
in the world. Swimming is popular at Sand Point Park (on the
eastern shore) because the lake is relatively warm in summer.
Sunbathing, boating, and fishing are also popular. Boats of
various kinds can be rented at Blue Heron Landing (see listing).

★ **Fogarty Creek State Park**   *(800)551-6949*
10 mi. S on Hwy. 101 - Depoe Bay
oregonstateparks.org
A small, crystal-clear stream tumbles out of a forest and across a
broad sandy beach before emptying into a sheltered cove. The
state has provided dressing rooms and picnic facilities. It is an
idyllic site for picnicking, sunbathing, swimming (for the hearty),
beachcombing, and surf fishing.

Food Specialties

Barnacle Bill's Seafood Market *(541)994-3022*
  1 mi. N at 2174 NE Hwy. 101
This open-air fish stand features smoked, fresh, and canned salmon and other fish, plus walkaway shrimp and crab cocktails.

★ **Mr. Bill's Village Smokehouse** *(541)994-4566* *(888)672-4557*
  2 mi. S at 2981 SW Hwy. 101
  mrbillsvillagesmokehouse.com
Mr. Bill's is open every day, with a fine selection of alder-smoked fish including various kinds of salmon jerky in season, plus smoked meats and fish on a stick for tempting treats, or to go.

★ **Freed Gallery** *(541)994-5600*
  4 mi. S at 6119 SW Hwy. 101
  freedgallery.com
The Oregon coast's most sophisticated art gallery is in an architecturally distinctive large building adjoining a unique sculpture garden of wind-driven objects of art. The two-level interior showcases a wealth of post-modern wall hangings, sculpture, furniture, and unique objects of art like an arresting chess set and high-tech prismatic glass pyramids. Closed Tues.

Golf

★ **Salishan Golf Course** *(541)764-2471*
  7 mi. S on Hwy. 101 - Gleneden Beach
The famed resort's magnificent 18-hole championship golf course provides panoramic ocean views and lush green fairways in a sylvan setting. It is open to the public and includes a pro shop, club and cart rentals, a driving range, and a fine view restaurant and lounge (see listing).

★ *Horseback Riding*

Ocean Trails Riding Stable *(541)994-4849*
  8 mi. N on Hwy. 101 - Neskowin
Hour-long guided horseback rides on a sandy ocean beach can be reserved from mid-May through September.

★ *Sportfishing*
  13 mi. S (on Hwy. 101) at mouth of harbor - Depoe Bay
Salmon fishing is one of the major attractions of the Oregon coast. Nearby Depoe Bay is home port to several fishing charters in the world's smallest natural harbor. Salmon trolling and other deep-sea fishing, and whale watching excursions, are featured.

Charterboat Reel Nauti *(541)921-1628*
  fishoregoncoast.com
Dockside Charters *(541)765-2545* *(800)733-8915*
  docksidedepoebay.com
Tradewinds Charters *(541)765-2345* *(800)445-8730*
  tradewindscharters.com

Warm Water Feature
  Lincoln City Swimming Pool   *(541)994-5208*
  1 mi. N at 2150 NE Oar Av.
Visitors are welcome to swim in the city's Olympic-sized pool in the recently expanded community center that now also includes a fitness center and gym. Swimming hours are designated.

RESTAURANTS

★ **Bay House**   *(541)996-3222*
  4 mi. S at 5911 SW Hwy. 101
  bayhouserestaurant.com
  D only. Sun. brunch. Closed Mon.   *Very Expensive*
The Bay House is the Northwest's finest coastal dinner house. For many years, this has been a landmark destination for Northwestern cuisine, consistently prepared with skill and creativity using top-quality seasonal ingredients from the sea and land. Regional delights like kumamoto oysters on the half shell, troll-caught wild Columbia River salmon, or roasted hazelnut-crusted free-range chicken breast contribute to the Bay House's continuing acclaim. Seasonally fresh and innovative desserts provide a perfect ending for special-occasion dining. Two split-level dining rooms are outfitted with full crisp linen, crystal, unusual china and candle, and provide each diner with a romantic view of Siletz Bay.

★ **Blackfish Cafe**   *(541)996-1007*
  1 mi. N at 2733 NW Hwy. 101
  blackfishcafe.com
  L-D. Closed Tues.   *Moderate*
The Blackfish Cafe is one of the Oregon coast's best destinations for fine dining. A short list of entrees describes skillfully prepared seasonal specialties like skillet-roasted troll-caught wild Oregon salmon basted with fennel lime butter, or citrus-marinated grilled breast of duck with local marionberries, or grilled brochette of Northwestern spring lamb with lemon mint. Desserts made here like apple tart with cinnamon-ginger ice cream are similarly delicious. The simply stylish dining room reflects the easygoing sophistication of the cuisine.

Dory Cove Restaurant   *(541)994-5180*
  3 mi. N at 5819 Logan Rd.
  www.dorycove.com
  L-D.   *Moderate*
This first-rate family-oriented fishhouse features an impressive variety of seafoods in all-American renditions like beer-battered crab legs and broiled salmon filets, plus assorted burgers and other landlubber favorites. The large, casual-and-usually-crowded

dining room has an old-time seaside fishhouse feeling, and a distant view of the ocean.

Gracie's Sea Hag Restaurant   *(541)765-2734*
13 mi. S at 58 E Hwy. 101 - Depoe Bay
B-L-D.   *Moderate*
Northwestern-style food offered here, including fresh-daily cinnamon rolls, is plain and plentiful. The simply furnished dining room has sported nautical decor since 1963.

★ **The Inn at Spanish Head**   *(541)996-2161*
2 mi. S at 4009 SW Hwy. 101
spanishhead.com
B-L-D. Sun. brunch.   *Moderate*
Fathoms Restaurant and Bar, on the top (10th) floor of the Inn at Spanish Head, offers fine dining with an emphasis on seafood and steak. Consider dishes like smoked halibut chowder, or Dungeness crabcakes, or salmon in parchment paper. Delicious desserts like peanut butter pie are also served in dining areas that offer a breathtaking window-wall-on-two-sides view to the sand and surf far below. A firelit lounge with armchair comfort shares the awesome view.

★ **Kernville Steak & Seafood House**   *(541)994-6200*
6 mi. S at 186 Siletz Hwy.
kernvillesteakhouse.com
L-D.   *Expensive*
Charbroiled steaks are the specialty with all the right support dishes. Choices include filet mignon or a 22-ounce Porterhouse. The menu also features ocean-fresh seafoods and some pork, chicken and vegetarian dishes, plus desserts like hazelnut apple cake. Stylish wood-trimmed dining rooms have a spectacular view of the Siletz riverfront, shared with a romantic lounge enhanced by unique wall hangings and occasional live entertainment.

★ **Kyllo's**   *(541)994-3179*
downtown (on Hwy. 101) at 1110 NW First Court
L-D.   *Moderate*
All-American dishes with an emphasis on fresh regional seafoods are given careful attention. A large avant-garde dining room thrusts over the tiny "D" River where it meets the ocean on a broad sandy beach. Floor-to-ceiling window walls give each diner in the large multi-room restaurant a close-up view of surf and sand. The big firelit lounge shares the view and has outdoor seating.

Lil Sambo's Restaurant   *(541)994-3626*
2 mi. N at 3262 NE Hwy. 101
B-L-D.   *Moderate*
Here's a good place for hungry families, nostalgia buffs, and early

risers. There's no finesse—just big portions of omelets and biscuits, pancakes, and other American standards for breakfast (served all day) and other meals. Plastic booths and tables support the "1950s retro feel," and there is a large gift shop.

McMenamins Lighthouse Pub & Brewery   *(541)994-7238*
  2 mi. N at 4157 N. Hwy. 101 in Lighthouse Square
  mcmenamins.com
  L-D.   *Moderate*
The Oregon coast's premier "boutique brewery" offers complimentary tastes of their brews. Creative pub grub like creamy sharp cheddar and ale with crabmeat fondue or halibut fish and chips hand-dipped in their own ale batter is featured with their fine selection of ales on draft. The warm wood-toned dining areas overlook brew kettles from two levels.

Mo's   *(541)996-2535*
  3 mi. S at 860 SW 51st St.
  moschowder.com
  L-D.   *Low*
Seafood is offered in the family-oriented local representative of a Newport-based chowder house chain. The real feature is a waterfront view of Siletz Bay from two sides of the large, very casual dining room where picnic table seating overlooks the scene.

★ **Otis Cafe**   *(541)994-2813*
  6 mi. NE (on Hwy. 18) at 1259 Salmon River Hwy. - Otis
  B-L-D. No D Mon.-Thurs.   *Moderate*
The Oregon coast's most famous roadside foodie landmark is the Otis Cafe. The homemade meals are tributes to American-style cuisine—highlighted by all sorts of delicious homemade pies (don't miss the apple crunch when they have it), breads, cinnamon rolls, and even their own mustard. Wood booths, windows on three sides, and a counter lend homespun charm to the tiny roadside cafe that has pleased crowds for many years.

Pier 101   *(541)994-8840*
  downtown at 415 SW Hwy. 101
  L-D.   *Moderate*
Seafood dishes have been served in this family-oriented, wood-trimmed dining room with nautical decor for more than thirty years. A lounge adjoins.

★ **Rockfish Bakery**   *(541)996-1006*
  1 mi. N at 3026 NE Hwy. 101
  B-L. Closed Tues.   *Moderate*
The Rockfish Bakery is the best source of pastries, traditional and designer breads, and desserts in Lincoln City. Displays showcase skillfully prepared choices that are served to go or at simply comfortable tables in the little bakery cafe.

★ **Salishan Lodge**   *(541)764-3632*
   7 mi. S at 7760 Hwy. 101 - Gleneden Beach
   salishan.com
   B-L-D.   *Moderate-Very Expensive*
Northwestern specialties are the emphasis in Salishan's main
dining room, **The Dining Room** (D only–Very Expensive).
Consider line-caught wild Oregon salmon, Oregon blue cheese
souffle, or Oregon elk steak. Desserts made here feature local
fruits like marionberry cobbler or poached pear. Diners at
casually elegant candlelit table settings enjoy a window-wall view
of the resort's artful landscaping and a distant view of the ocean.
The Sun Room (B-L-D–Moderate) features light Northwestern
dishes at all meals in a large comfortable dining room overlooking
the lush forest and golf course. At **Attic Lounge**, relax with a
beverage in a room enhanced by local art, a huge stone fireplace,
and billiards.

★ **Side Door Cafe**   *(541)764-3825*
   7 mi. S at 6675 Gleneden Loop Rd. - Gleneden Beach
   sidedoorcafe.com
   L-D.   *Expensive*
Their seafood chowder is outstanding–chunks of salmon, halibut,
shrimp, mussels and clams with a light-bodied sherry-cream base
and a hint of fresh dill. Fresh local seafood and local organic
produce are featured in all of the flavorful creative dishes served
here like shrimp quesadillas, salmon burgers, or sesame-seared
Columbia River sturgeon. Save room for one of the award-winning
desserts like white chocolate banana cream pie. The comfortably
stylish dining room has an open, airy feeling in a transformed old
brick-and-tile factory building that also houses **Eden Hall**, a 200-
seat concert/banquet room popular for public/private music and
theatrical entertainment.

Spouting Horn   *(541)765-2261*
   13 mi. S at 110 SE Hwy. 101 - Depoe Bay
   B-L-D. Closed Tues.   *Moderate*
Old-fashioned seafood dishes are offered in a comfortably
furnished restaurant that has been in operation for more than
seventy years. The crowd-pleaser is the upstairs room with a
spectacular window-wall view of tiny Depoe Bay and the inlet
bridge. A cozy bar shares the scene.

★ **Surfrider Resort & Restaurant**   *(541)764-2311*
   10 mi. S at 3115 NW Hwy. 101 - Depoe Bay
   surfriderresort.com
   B-L-D.   *Moderate*
Contemporary Northwestern dishes featuring seasonal seafoods
and fresh produce are served in a comfortable dining room with a

two-sided window-wall view of a magnificent seascape where Fogarty Creek empties into the Pacific Ocean. Delicious desserts are showcased at the entrance.

★ **Tidal Raves Seafood Grill**   *(541)765-2995*
  13 mi. S at 279 Hwy. 101 - Depoe Bay
  L-D.   *Moderate*
Contemporary Northwestern dishes with an emphasis on regional seafood like Dungeness crab casserole or rockfish linguini or grilled salmon with rock shrimp risotto enliven a creative American menu. Apart from the food, the awesome window-wall view of surf breaking in a picturesque cove far below the comfortable split-level dining room is a spell-binding crowd-pleaser.

★ **The Wildflower Grill**   *(541)994-9663*
  2 mi. N at 4250 NE Hwy. 101
  B-L-D. No D Sun. & Mon.   *Moderate*
The Wildflower Grill serves some of the Oregon coast's most creative breakfasts. Consider seafood omelet with local crab and shrimp and three cheeses topped with hollandaise, or french toast dipped in eggs, cinnamon, and orange juice. Muffins and all breads are baked here, too. All kinds of po' boys are a good bet for lunch. Dinners emphasize Northwestern classics. A historic roadside home has been skillfully transformed into several cozy dining areas and an attractive deck with a forest view.

LODGINGS

More noteworthy lodgings overlook the ocean in the Lincoln City area than in any other town in the Northwest. Numerous fine accommodations have choice beachfront locations, and an even larger number of surprisingly inexpensive motels are inland along Highway 101 through town. High season is July through September. Many lodgings offer 30% and greater reductions apart from summer.

Beachwood Oceanfront Motel   *(541)994-8901*
  2 mi. N at 2855 NW Inlet Av. - 97367
  beachwoodmotel.net
  28 units   *(800)725-5765*   *Moderate-Expensive*
This older motel is on a bluff by the beach. Each unit is comfortably furnished and has a queen or king bed.
  "oceanfront jacuzzi room"–gas fireplace, refrigerator,
    microwave, wet bar, private balcony and big two-
    person whirlpool share ocean view with king bed.
  "oceanfront beach building" (6 of these)–
    ocean-view private balcony, gas fireplace,
    refrigerator, microwave, queen or king bed.

★ **Channel House**   *(541)765-2140*
  13 mi. S on Hwy. 101 (Box 56) - Depoe Bay   97341
  channelhouse.com
  14 units   *(800)447-2140*   *Very Expensive*
Channel House is the most romantic oceanfront getaway for adults in the Northwest. Perched in the rocks where the ocean enters the harrowing channel into tiny Depoe Bay is a superb little contemporary inn with a classic "Oregon coast" look and feel. Expanded Continental breakfast is served in a room with an unparalleled view of intimate nautical grandeur. There is a gift shop of fine Northwest-related items. Each beautifully furnished unit has an unsurpassed ocean or channel view and all contemporary amenities. Most rooms have a gas fireplace, a two-person whirlpool on a private outdoor deck, and a queen bed.
  "The Admiral's Suite"–(top floor), gas fireplace, corner
    view of ocean and channel from private deck,
    two-person whirlpool, queen bed.
  "The Whale Watch Suite"–(second floor), as above.
  "Fore Deck"–corner by channel inlet and ocean with
    gas fireplace, two-person whirlpool on private deck
    with view shared by queen bed.
  "The Captain's Quarters"–(top floor), gas fireplace, very
    private ocean/channel view from deck, two-person
    whirlpool, queen bed.
  "The Cuckoo's Nest"–(top floor), two gas fireplaces, full
    kitchen, large private deck with two-person whirlpool
    shares ocean view with queen bed.
  "Suite Salt Air"–gas fireplace, ground floor with
    ocean/channel views shared by large deck with
    two-person whirlpool and king bed.

Chinook Winds Casino Resort   *(541)994-3655*
  2 mi. N at 1501 NW 44th St. - 97367
  chinookwindscasino.com
  247 units   *(877)423-2241*   *Moderate-Very Expensive*
A longtime peaceful oceanfront hotel was recently transformed. It is now owned and operated by the Siletz Indians as an action-oriented casino open 24 hours every day with Vegas-style gambling. It also has an indoor pool, whirlpool, sauna, gift shop, arcade, restaurant, deli, entertainment lounge, and showroom. Each standard hotel room has a queen bed. Ocean-view rooms and suites have one or two queens or a king bed.

★ **Coho Inn**   *(541)994-3684*
  1 mi. N at 1635 NW Harbor Av. - 97367
  thecohoinn.com
  50 units   *(800)848-7006*   *Moderate-Expensive*

All rooms are oceanfronting in this modern blufftop motel with an indoor pool, whirlpool, sauna and exercise room. Each well-furnished unit has a surf view and a queen or king bed.

"fireplace suite" (12 of these)–one bedroom, kitchen, gas
   fireplace, private ocean-view balcony or patio, two queen beds.

Comfort Inn   *(541)994-8155*
downtown at 136 NE Hwy. 101 - 97367

30 units   *(800)423-6240*   *Expensive*

One of the best representatives of the contemporary lodging chain is in the heart of town, a short stroll from the ocean and "D" River Wayside. Expanded Continental breakfast and fresh cookies are complimentary. Each spacious, well-furnished room has a refrigerator, microwave, a private balcony (some with partial ocean view) and a queen or king bed.

"NK1" (2 of these)–one bedroom, in-room two-person
   whirlpool, gas fireplace, private ocean-view balcony,
   king bed.

★ **Cozy Cove**   *(541)994-2950*
downtown at 515 NW Inlet Av. - 97367
coastalguidebooks.com

70 units   *(800)553-2683*   *Moderate-Expensive*

One of Oregon's most sybaritic lodgings is a contemporary ocean-front complex adjoining the sandy beach in the heart of town. Amenities include private beach access, large outdoor pool, whirlpool and sauna. Each of the attractively furnished units has a queen bed. Most have a close-up surf view.

#308,#309,#315,#316,#203,#208,#309,#215,#216–raised
   gas fireplace, refrigerator, microwave, private floor/ceiling
   glass-doored balcony, raised two-person in-room whirlpool
   in alcove by fine ocean view.

"D" Sands Condominium Motel   *(541)994-5244*
downtown at 171 SW Hwy. 101 - 97367
dsandsmotel.com

63 units   *(800)527-3925*   *Expensive*

An oceanfront indoor pool and whirlpool, plus a surfside location, are features of this modern motel. Each individually comfortably furnished unit has a private balcony or patio with an ocean view, kitchen, and a queen or king bed.

"deluxe fireplace suite" (16 of these)–one bedroom, private
   ocean-view balcony, gas fireplace, kitchen, king bed.
"queen mini-suite" (8 of these)–studio, private ocean-view
   balcony, gas fireplace, kitchen, Murphy queen bed.

Dock of the Bay   *(541)996-3549*
3 mi. S at 1116 SW 51st St. - 97367
allseasonsvacation.com

22 units   *(800)362-5229*   *Expensive*

This recently built condominium-style motel fronts on Siletz Bay. Amenities include a whirlpool and access to a sandy beach. In addition to contemporary decor and furnishings, each unit (one- and two-bedroom) has a kitchen, woodburning fireplace, private balcony with a waterfront view, and one or two queen beds.

Edgecliff Motel   *(541)996-2055*
2 mi. S at 3733 SW Hwy. 101 - 97367
lincolncity.com/edgecliff
44 units   *(888)750-3636*   *Moderate-Expensive*

This long-established motel perched on the rim of a hill was recently expanded and upgraded. The units have an unobstructed ocean view. There is a private beach access. Each comfortably furnished room has a refrigerator, microwave, gas fireplace and one or two queens or a king bed. Some have a private balcony.

"Honeymoon Suite"–two-person whirlpool
    shares ocean view with king bed.
"New Studio with whirlpool" (several)–private ocean-view
    two-person in-room whirlpool, king bed.
"New Studio with balcony" (several)–private ocean-view
    balcony, in-bath whirlpool, king bed.

★ **Inn at Arch Rock**   *(541)765-2560*
13 mi. S at 70 NW Sunset St. (Box 1516) - Depoe Bay 97341
innatarchrock.com
13 units   *(800)767-1835*   *Moderate-Very Expensive*

Inn at Arch Rock is a historic complex with a splendid blufftop setting overlooking Depoe Bay. In is *the* place to watch great grey whales up-close in one of the few areas on the Pacific Coast where they spend extended periods of time close to shore. An expanded Continental breakfast is complimentary. Each comfortably furnished unit (up to two bedrooms) has all contemporary conveniences plus a microwave and small refrigerator, and one or two queen beds.

"Seagull's Nest Room" (#11)–awesome view of the
    entire bay, gas fireplace, vaulted ceiling, queen bed.
"Perch Room" (#10)–big corner windows with spectacular
    ocean panorama, kitchenette, gas fireplace, two queen beds.
"Eagle's Nest Room" (#12)–gas fireplace, romantic
    ocean view, vaulted ceiling, queen bed.

★ **The Inn at Spanish Head**   *(541)996-2161*
2 mi. S at 4009 SW Hwy. 101 - 97367
spanishhead.com
120 units   *(800)452-8127*   *Expensive-Very Expensive*

One of Lincoln City's largest lodgings is an oceanfronting ten-level condominium motel that extends from a high blufftop to a large outdoor pool by the beach. Other amenities include an ocean-view whirlpool, saunas, exercise and recreation room, plus an ocean-view restaurant (see listing) and lounge. Each individually nicely furnished unit has a refrigerator and micro-wave or full kitchen, full ocean view, and one or two queen beds.

Lincoln City Inn   *(541)996-4400*
  downtown at 1091 SE 1st St. - 97367
  www.lincolncityinn.com
  59 units   *(800)870-7067*   *Moderate-Expensive*
The ocean is across a highway and parking lot from this four-story contemporary motel, and there is a whirlpool. Each comfortably furnished room has a microwave and refrigerator, and a tiny standing deck past a floor-to-ceiling window and queen or king bed.
  #401,#301–spacious, raised two-person whirlpool,
    ocean view across highway from king bed.

★ **Lincoln Sands Suites - Best Western**   *(541)994-4227*
  downtown at 535 NW Inlet Av. - 97367
  bestwestern.com/lincolnsandsinn
  33 units   *(800)445-3234*   *Expensive-Very Expensive*
One of the Oregon coast's best oceanfront lodgings is the Lincoln Sands Suites (Best Western). Amenities, in addition to direct access to beach and ocean, include an outdoor pool and whirlpool, sauna, and exercise room. Each beautifully decorated one- or two-bedroom unit is equipped with a fine ocean view, a private patio or balcony, full deluxe kitchen, and a queen or king bed.
  "spa suite" (4 of these)–extra-large, raised gas
    fireplace, two-person whirlpool with ocean view
    shared by large private balcony and king bed.

★ **Looking Glass Inn**   *(541)996-3996*
  3 mi. S at 861 SW 51st St. - 97367
  lookingglass-inn.com
  36 units   *(800)843-4940*   *Moderate-Expensive*
The Looking Glass Inn is a contemporary motel with a special location overlooking both the adjoining bay and nearby ocean only a short stroll away. All features are in the beautifully furnished rooms which were recently completely remodeled and upgraded. Most include a kitchen and bay view, and a choice of one or two queen or king bed. Some also have a gas fireplace, a two-person whirlpool and ocean view.
  #304,#303,#302,#301,#217,#215–superb bay and ocean
    views and a large private balcony, two-person whirlpool
    in room, full kitchen, gas fireplace, bay view from king bed.

★ **The Nantucket Inn**   *(541)996-9300*
  2 mi. N at 3135 NW Inlet Av. - 97367

www.thenantucketinn.com
5 units   *Expensive*
The Nantucket Inn (circa 2001) combines the quaint appeal of a
New England beach house with a wealth of 21st-century
amenities. Just steps from the beach, each beautifully furnished
one- or two-bedroom suite has a gas fireplace, kitchenette, two-
person whirlpool tub, and a queen or king bed in each bedroom.
Most have a private oceanfront deck.
   "The Penthouse Suite"–studio, on top floor, fine surf
      views from private balcony and four-poster queen bed.
   "Yester Year Suite," "A Day at the Beach"–
      one bedroom, living room with gas fireplace,
      great surf views from deck and king bed.
   "The Shoreline Suite"–two bedrooms, spacious,
      full kitchen, living room with river-rock gas fire-
      place, great surf-view deck, queen and king bed.
★ **Nelscott Manor**   *(541)996-9300*
   2 mi. S at 3037 SW Anchor Av. - 97367
   www.nelscottmanor.com
   5 units   *Very Expensive*
This three-story wood-trim building completed in 2003 is a
romantic getaway-by-the-sea with direct access to miles of sandy
beach. Each beautifully furnished suite has an oceanfront view
from a private covered deck, kitchenette, in-room two-person
whirlpool, gas fireplace, and a queen or king bed in each bedroom.
   "Executive Bella Suite"–spacious, top floor, kitchen,
      living room with gas fireplace, dual-head shower,
      private balcony with two-person whirlpool shares
      fine ocean view with in-room two-person whirlpool
      and king bed.
   "Nautica Suite"–one bedroom, kitchenette, gas fireplace,
      private ocean-view deck, two-head shower, in-room
      large whirlpool, fine ocean view from queen bed.
Nordic Oceanfront Inn   *(541)994-8145*
   1 mi. N at 2133 NW Inlet Av. - 97367
   nordicoceanfrontinn.com
   53 units   *(800)452-3558*   *Expensive*
This contemporary blufftop motel with easy access to the broad
sandy beach also has an indoor pool, whirlpool, and saunas.
Expanded Continental breakfast is complimentary. Each well-
furnished unit has a refrigerator, microwave, full ocean view, and
one or two queen beds or a king bed.
   #318,#218–studio, raised gas fireplace, dual-head
      shower, raised two-person whirlpool by picture-window
      view of adjacent beach/ocean shared by queen bed.

★ **The O'dysius Hotel** *(541)994-4121*
downtown at 120 NW Inlet Court - 97367
odysius.com
30 units *(800)869-8069* *Expensive-Very Expensive*
The O'dysius Hotel is one of the central coast of Oregon's most sophisticated lodgings. The small luxury hotel is in a five-story building that opened in 1999 on a rise in the heart of Lincoln City overlooking the "D" River and nearby ocean. Amenities include a complimentary evening appetizers-and-wine social, and an expanded Continental breakfast brought to the room. There is a gift gallery that also includes Northwest wines for sale. Each spacious room is beautifully individually furnished and has an in-bath whirlpool tub, stocked (honor) refrigerator, raised gas fireplace, small private balcony, extra amenities, plus a queen or king bed. Many of the rooms have an ocean view.
   "Grand Suites" (#5001,#5007)–two bedrooms,
      in-room two-person whirlpool, queen and king beds.
   #5002 thru #5006–top floor, fine ocean view, queen bed.

Ocean Terrace *(541)996-3623*
3 mi. S at 4229 SW Beach Av. - 97367
oceanterrace.com
41 units *(800)648-2119* *Moderate-Expensive*
A three-level condo occupies a site on a bluff above a broad sandy beach. Amenities include a large indoor pool with whirlpool jets, saunas, and a game room with ping pong and pool. Each spacious, comfortably furnished one-bedroom unit in the newer beachfront includes a kitchen, living room with a floor/ceiling sliding glass door view of the surf, and a queen or king bed.

Pelican Shores Inn *(541)994-2134*
2 mi. N at 2645 NW Inlet Av. - 97367
pelicanshores.com
35 units *(800)705-5505* *Moderate-Expensive*
This studio- to two-bedroom apartment motel has a choice oceanfront site, and there is an indoor pool. Each comfortably furnished unit has a refrigerator and a queen or king bed.
   "fireplace suite" (10 of these)–kitchenette,
      gas fireplace, surf view from queen bed.

Sailor Jack Motel *(541)994-3696*
just N at 1035 NW Harbor Av. - 97367
41 units *(888)432-8346* *Moderate-Expensive*
The surf is flood-lit at night, and there is easy beach access. Apart from a sauna, amenities are in comfortable units, each with an ocean view, refrigerator, microwave, and queen or king bed.
   "jacuzzi room"(3 of these)–in-room
      two-person whirlpool, king bed.

★ **Salishan Lodge**   *(541)764-2371*
　　7 mi. S at 7760 Hwy. 101 (Box 118) - Gleneden Beach 97388
　　salishan.com
　　205 units　　　　*(888)725-4742*　　　　*Moderate-Expensive*
Exquisite sensitivity was applied in synthesizing luxurious leisure
facilities with a natural Oregon landscape. The result is Salishan,
a large (350 acres) renowned resort where contemporary low-rise
buildings are sequestered into manicured grounds a half-mile from
the ocean. Amenities include extensive nature trails, a big indoor
pool, whirlpool, saunas, state-of-the-art fitness center, 18-hole
putting course, nature trails, and (for a fee) an upgraded 18-hole
championship-quality golf course (ranked "Best of Environmental
Golf" by Audubon International), four tennis courts (three
indoors), and a large full-service spa (opened in 2005); plus dining
and lounge facilities (see listing) and a stylish nearby complex of
specialty shops. Each beautifully decorated, spacious room has a
fieldstone gas fireplace, covered carport, refrigerator, and private
balcony with a view of the nearby golf course, lush forest, or
distant bay and ocean, and two doubles or a king bed.
　　"Premier Room" (18 of these)–spacious, sitting area, gas
　　　fireplace, in-room whirlpool, scenic view of Siletz Bay
　　　from private balcony, king bed.

Sea Gypsy   *(541)994-5266*
　　downtown at 145 NW Inlet Av. - 97367
　　rogueweb.com/seagypsy
　　136 units　　　　*(800)341-2142*　　　　*Low-Expensive*
This modern three-level motel is well situated by a beach in the
heart of town. A large indoor pool and sauna are amenities. Each
comfortably furnished room has a full kitchen and a queen bed.
　　"oceanview unit"–(request third floor), kitchenette,
　　　unobstructed panoramic view of beach.

Sea Horse Oceanfront Lodging   *(541)994-2101*
　　1 mi. N at 2039 NW Harbor Dr. - 97367
　　seahorsemotel.com
　　54 units　　　　*(800)662-2101*　　　　*Moderate*
Blufftop panoramic seascapes are a feature here, along with an
indoor pool and surf-view whirlpool. Each comfortably furnished
room has two doubles, queens, or a king bed. Some units also have
a kitchenette and/or an ocean view.

★ **Siletz Bay Lodge**   *(541)996-6111*
　　3 mi. S at 1012 SW 51st St. (Box 952) - 97367
　　siletzbaylodge.com
　　44 units　　　　*(888)430-2100*　　　　*Moderate-Expensive*
Siletz Bay Lodge is a four-story complex next to the bay, and offers
a complimentary expanded Continental breakfast, a whirlpool, and

a small gift shop. All well-furnished units have a bay and ocean view beyond a picturesque log-strewn sandy beach, refrigerator and microwave, and one or two queens or a king bed.

#110,#108–spacious, in-room two-person whirlpool, large private balcony shares a great view with king bed.

★ **Surfrider Resort**   *(541)764-2311*
10 mi. S at 3115 NW Hwy. 101 (Box 219) - Depoe Bay 97341
surfriderresort.com
50 units   *(800)662-2378*   *Expensive*
High on a bluff overlooking the ocean just north of Fogarty Creek State Park is a handsome contemporary motel with a large indoor pool, whirlpool, sauna, plus an oceanfront restaurant (see listing) and lounge with an awe-inspiring ocean view. Each spacious, well-furnished unit has a refrigerator, microwave, and one or two queens or a king bed. All ocean-view rooms have a private deck.

#69,#64,#78,#74,#70–raised gas fireplace, in-bath whirlpool, semi-private balcony shares splendid ocean view with king bed.

★ **Surftides Inn on the Beach**   *(541)994-2191*
2 mi. N at 2945 NW Jetty Av. - 97367
surftidesinn.com
152 units   *(800)452-2159*   *Moderate-Expensive*
Lincoln City's oldest oceanside resort hotel was fully remodeled and upgraded for the millennium. Amenities of the five-story complex include an ocean-view restaurant and lounge, an indoor pool, whirlpool, sauna, exercise room and steamroom. Each well-furnished unit has a microwave and refrigerator and one or two queens or king bed. All oceanfront rooms have a private balcony.

Waters Edge   *(541)996-9200*
3 mi. S at 5201 SW Hwy. 101 - 97367
watersedgebay.com
56 units   *(877)996-9201*   *Expensive*
This four-story condo complex (circa 1999) is located by Siletz Bay with panoramic views to the nearby ocean. Each well-furnished one- or two-bedroom condo has a full kitchen, gas fireplace, private bay/ocean-view balcony, and one or two queens or a king bed.

★ **Westshore Oceanfront Motel**   *(541)996-2001*
2 mi. S at 3127 SW Anchor Av. - 97367
www.westshoremotel.com
19 units   *(800)621-3187*   *Moderate-Expensive*
A private stairway links this blufftop motel directly with the broad sandy beach. There is an on-site weather station (especially popular with winter storm watchers). Each comfortably furnished studio to two-bedroom unit has a fine ocean view, a fully equipped kitchen, and one or two queen beds. Five of the units have a woodburning fireplace and a private beachfront deck.

McMinnville

McMinnville is the heart of Oregon's Wine Country. Historic brick buildings in an urbane downtown shaded by overarching broadleaf trees provide a lively mix of diversions. A big adjoining park beckons with luxuriant naturalistic landscaping, a major recreation/swim center and library. A small college is within strolling distance. The result is genteel sophistication with deep Eastern roots. Surrounding hills and valleys have a moderate four-season climate ideal for growing classic wine grapes, and for enjoying outdoor activities most of the year.

The town was founded in 1843 by William Newby, a pioneer who came west from McMinnville, Tennessee. He opened a grist mill which became the town's main industry. The substantial business district was built between 1885 and 1912. Happily, most of those buildings are being meticulously preserved by an active preservation effort and continue to serve as shops, residences, and lodgings. Wine grapes, first planted in the area in the 1970s, have become the key to the region's economic future.

McMinnville is now prospering, as appreciation of Oregon premium wines has brought recognition to this burgeoning district with more than fifty wineries. The town's infrastructure has kept up with its success, with colorful gardens, park and recreation facilities, museums and other public buildings blending seamlessly with the historic heritage. Upscale shops, restaurants and lodgings are located both downtown and in environs interspersed with lush vineyards, pastures, and forests in all directions.

McMinnville

WEATHER PROFILE

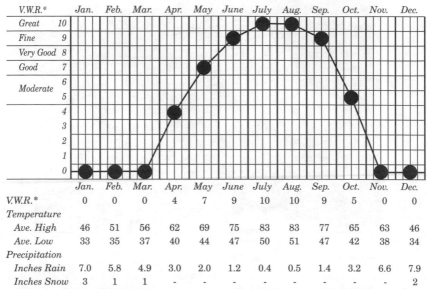

V.W.R.*		Jan.	Feb.	Mar.	Apr.	May	June	July	Aug.	Sep.	Oct.	Nov.	Dec.
V.W.R.*		0	0	0	4	7	9	10	10	9	5	0	0
Temperature													
Ave. High		46	51	56	62	69	75	83	83	77	65	63	46
Ave. Low		33	35	37	40	44	47	50	51	47	42	38	34
Precipitation													
Inches Rain		7.0	5.8	4.9	3.0	2.0	1.2	0.4	0.5	1.4	3.2	6.6	7.9
Inches Snow		3	1	1	-	-	-	-	-	-	-	-	2

* V.W.R. = Vokac Weather Rating: probability of mild (warm & dry) weather on any given day.

BASIC INFORMATION

Population: 26,499
Elevation: 157 feet
Location: 38 miles West of Portland
Airport (regularly scheduled flights): Portland - 45 miles

McMinnville Area Chamber of Commerce (503)472-6196
  downtown at 417 NW Adams St. - 97128
  mcminnville.org
McMinnville Downtown Association (503)472-3605
  downtown at 105 NE 3rd St. (Box 691) - 97128
  downtownmcminnville.com

ATTRACTIONS

★ **Downtown**   *(503)472-3605*
downtown around 3rd & Baker Sts.
downtownmcminnville.com
The historic heart of town includes a wealth of handsome revitalized nineteenth-century buildings. Distinctive shops, restaurants, entertainment spots, coffee houses, a bakery and an ice cream parlor still serve the regular and special-occasion needs of residents and travelers alike. Cascading flower baskets in summer and luxuriant "tree-tunnels" give the district a deja-vu feeling for any one who grew up "Back East." Maps for a self-guided tour are available at the Chamber of Commerce.

★ **Evergreen Aviation Museum**   *(503)434-4180*
3 mi. E at 500 NE Capt. Michael King Smith Way
sprucegoose.org
Looming out of the fields and vineyards by a highway near town is an enormous hanger that is a post-modern architectural tour de force. Here is the new home of the world's largest wood-framed aircraft, Howard Hughes' "Spruce Goose" (his huge–320-foot wingspan–eight-engine HK-1 Flying Boat) along with a wealth of other vintage aircraft and related memorabilia (like "Blackbird," the world's fastest spy plane) and interactive exhibits. The complex also has a cafe and a gift shop. Open 9-5 daily.

★ *Farm Stands*
Surrounding roadside farm stands have collectively evolved into elaborate sources of fresh seasonal fruits, vegies, and related homemade snacks, jams, jellies, pies, etc. Among the best are:
   Farmer John's Produce & Nursery   *(503)474-3514*
   7 mi. SW (on Hwy. 18) at 15000 SW Oldsville Rd.
   Firestone Farms   *(503)864-2672*
   8 mi. NE at 18400 N. Hwy. 99W - Dayton
   firestonefarms.com
   Sweet Oregon Berry Farm   *(503)864-2897*
   7 mi. NE (at jct. Hwy. 18 & Hwy. 99W) at 3005 Dayton Bypass
Food Specialties
★   **Your Northwest**   *(503)554-8101*   *(888)252-0699*
   11 mi. NE (on Hwy. 99) at 110 SW 7th St. - Dundee
   yournw.com
Your Northwest is one of the finest gourmet provisions stores in the Northwest. Located adjacent to Ponzi Tasting Room in Dundee, Your Northwest showcases jams, jellies, sauces, condiments and other foodie delights and related products made in Oregon. The large shop full of attractive displays is enhanced by a number of tasting stations where visitors can experience outstanding limited-production gourmet treats.

★ **Lawrence Gallery Complex**   *(503)843-3633   (800)894-4278*
   7 mi. W (on Hwy. 18) - Sheridan
   lawrencegallery.net
Lawrence is one of the Northwest's quintessential galleries.
Several rooms are full of museum-quality sculptures and wall
hangings in a variety of media. Surrounding grounds are
Northwest and zen gardens showcasing sculpture and fountains
along enticing paths. Upstairs is **Fresh Palate Cafe** (see listing)
with a picture-window view of the gallery below and a rooftop
deck surrounded by gardens. The **Private Reserve Tasting
Room** adjoins the gallery and features premium Northwestern
wines from smaller producers in (fee) flights of several wines.
Across the road is the **Fire's Eye Pottery & Gallery**, and the
Bellevue Market and Oregon Wine Tasting Room ((503)843-
3787) with more wine from 70+ Oregon wineries, plus tasting and
a good display of gourmet jams, jellies and condiments with some
tastes available.

★ **McMinnville City Park**   *(503)434-7310*
   just W at 3rd St. & NW Adams St.
   ci.mcminnville.or.us
Tennis courts, walking trails through dense forest of ancient oaks
and pines, restrooms, and elaborate wood-form play equipment
are features, along with McMinnville Aquatic Center (see listing).
Warm Water Feature
   McMinnville Aquatic Center   *(503)434-7309*
   downtown at 138 NW Park Dr.
   ci.mcminnville.or.us
A large contemporary building at one side of McMinnville's tree-
shaded city park houses two pools (one multi-lane), plus a hot tub
and weight room open to the public year-round.

★ *Wineries*   *(503)646-2985*
   willamettewines.com
McMinnville is the heart of Oregon's premier Wine Country. It is
surrounded by many of Oregon's oldest and most famous
wineries. Among premium varietals prospering here, Oregon
pinot noirs have achieved such international acclaim that even
some French wine makers have developed local vineyards.
   Amity Vineyards   *(503)835-2362   (888)264-8966*
   8 mi. S (via Hwy. 99W) at 18150 Amity Vineyards Rd. SE - Amity
   amityvineyards.com
One of the longest-established wineries in Oregon is high in the
hills above the little town of Amity. Several of their recent
releases are available for tastes, and reserve pinot noirs are also
poured for a fee. The casual little tasting room is in a winery
building surrounded by hillside vineyards. Open 12-5 daily.

Anne Amie   *(503)684-2991*
6 mi. N at 6580 NE Mineral Springs Rd. - Carlton
anneamie.com
Located on one of the most beautiful hilltop sites in Wine County, in 2004 Anne Amie replaced Chateau Benoit, a long-established producer of premium Northwest varietals. A large handsome tasting room features tastes of several recent releases and (fee) tasting for reserve pinot noirs. Wine and picnics can be enjoyed at tables on a lovely deck surrounded by colorful gardens and (as proof of the benign Northwestern climate) small fan palm trees. Open 10-5 daily.

Argyle Winery   *(503)538-8520*   *(888)427-4953*
11 mi. NE at 691 Hwy. 99W - Dundee
argylewinery.com
Argyle Winery is a small gem by the highway with a tasting room in a lovingly refurbished older house with complimentary tastes of two of their notable wines, plus (fee) tastes of outstanding reserve chardonnays, pinots and sparkling wines. The sparklers, most notably brut, are leading Oregon into renown in the "methode champenoise" style. Open 11-5 daily.

Duck Pond Cellars   *(503)538-3199*   *(800)437-3213*
13 mi. NE at 23145 Hwy. 99W - Dundee
duckpondcellars.com
The winery is surrounded by colorful gardens and vineyards and includes a tasting room with pours of several Northwestern wines. The large well-organized tasting room also has related gourmet products and gifts. Outside is seating for picnics. Open 11-5 daily, and open at 10 a.m. in high season.

Elk Cove Vineyards   *(503)985-7760*   *(877)355-2683*
20 mi. N (via Hwy. 47) at 27751 NW Olson Rd. - Gaston
elkcove.com
Tucked away in high rolling hills is the lovely little tasting room and gift shop with a spectacular view of surrounding vineyards. Elk Cove is one of Oregon's oldest (since 1977) and most respected wineries deservedly well known for pinot gris, pinot noir, and riesling. They now have a "methode champenoise" sparkling wine. Picnic tables overlook the undulating vineyards. Open 10-5 daily.

Erath Vineyards   *(503)538-3318*   *(800)539-9463*
12 mi. NE at 9409 NE Worden Hill Rd. - Dundee
erath.com
Erath is one of the oldest and best wineries in Oregon. The winery is high in the Dundee Hills and the tasting room and gift shop is at the crest. In addition to generous pours of their premium Northwest varietals (pinot noir and pinot gris are

especially notable), there is a handsome patio with sunny or shaded tables to enjoy wine and picnics while overlooking lush vineyards and forests. Open 11-5 daily.

Laurel Ridge Winery   *(503)852-7050   (888)311-9463*
10 mi. N at 13301 NE Kuehne Rd. - Carlton
laurelridgewines.com
A stylish contemporary winery complex in the valley includes an expansive tasting room where most of the currently available vintages can be experienced. Their reserve pinot noir and pinot noir port are notable. They also produce "methode champenoise" sparkling wines. Open 11-5 daily.

Ponzi   *(503)554-1500*
11 mi. NE (on Hwy. 99) at 100 SW 7th St. - Dundee
ponziwinebar.com
A stylish neo-Tuscan complex by the highway features Ponzi Tasting Room (the winery is in Beaverton). Flights of regular and reserve premium varietals from four vineyards (the oldest founded in 1970) are poured (for a fee) in the appealing modish facility. Ponzi wines are among top benchmarks for Northwest varietals, and reflect a dedication to sustainable agricultural practices and products. Fine dining (see listing for **Dundee Bistro**) and one of Oregon's best gourmet shops (see listing for **Your Northwest**) complete the complex. Open 11-5 daily.

Private Reserve Wine Shop & Tasting Bar   *(503)843-3900*
7 mi. W at 19702 Hwy. 18 - Sheridan
privatereservewine.us
Sample wines (for a fee) from more than thirty small wineries–many not usually open to the public–at a handsome tasting bar in the Lawrence Gallery building (see listing). Wines are available by the taste, glass, bottle, or case. Open 11-6 daily.

Rex Hill Vineyards   *(503)536-0666   (800)739-4455*
18 mi. NE at 30835 N. Hwy. 99W - Newburg
rexhill.com
One of Oregon's oldest (since 1982) and largest wineries has a big handsome tasting room with a small atmospheric museum and shop, plus overlooks of surrounding vineyards and lush gardens. The pinot noir and pinot gris have earned acclaim. Current releases are offered for (fee) tastes as are premium reserves (with fees refundable with purchase). Open 11-5 Mon.-Thurs. and 10-5 Fri.-Sat.

Sokol Blosser Winery   *(503)864-2282*
9 mi. NE (via Hwy. 99W) at 5000 Sokol Blosser Ln. - Dundee
sokolblosser.com & evolutionwine.com
High on a hill amidst rolling organic vineyards (some dating to 1971) is an oak-shaded tasting room for Sokol Blosser, one of

Oregon's larger premium wine producers. A variety of fee and complimentary tastings are offered. You can also taste and buy their gourmet condiments. A wraparound oak-shaded deck overlooking the vineyards competes for distinction as the best picnic site in Oregon's Wine Country. Open 11-5 daily.

Willakenzie Estate   *(503)662-3280   (888)953-9463*
14 mi. N at 19143 NE Laughlin Rd. - Yamhill
willakenzie.com
High on a ridge surrounded by vineyard-covered hills is an expansive tasting room and shop with indoor and outdoor tables overlooking vineyards for enjoying their notable premium pinot noir and pinot gris varietals. Open 12-5 daily in summer, Fri.-Sun. the rest of the year.

Yamhill Valley Vineyards   *(503)843-3100   (800)825-4845*
6 mi. W (via Hwy. 18) at 16250 SW Oldsville Rd.
yamhill.com
Tucked into folds of gentle hills at the edge of a broad valley, the Yamhill winery is surrounded by fountains, gardens, and great oak trees. Pinot noir, pinot gris, and pinot blanc are offered in the small tasting room above a stainless steel storage area. Oak-shaded picnic tables on a valley-view deck adjoin. Open 11-5 daily from Memorial Day to Thanksgiving; open weekends in spring; closed in winter.

RESTAURANTS

★ **Alf's**   *(503)472-7314*
  just SW at 1250 SE Baker St.
  L-D.   *Low*
More than a dozen hard ice creams are made here like hazelnut crunch or lemon custard. All kinds of luscious shakes and malts (many with fresh fruit) and sundaes are also available, along with highly regarded burgers (the half-pounder is a genuine tasty deal). These and support dishes like onion rings, sweet potato fries, etc. have been served here for over fifty years. Order at the counter to enjoy at booths inside or shaded tables amidst a nifty collection of hanging flowering plants, or to go.

★ **Bistro Maison**   *(503)474-1888*
  downtown at 729 NE 3rd St.
  bistromaison.com
  L-D. No L Fri. Closed Mon.-Tues.   *Expensive*
A short list of French bistro classics like escargot or steak tartare or coq au vin, and housemade desserts like crème caramel, are authentically rendered by French chef/owners. A remodeled house on main street is now outfitted with several simply comfortable dining rooms and an appealing garden courtyard.

★ **The Dundee Bistro** *(503)554-1650*
   11 mi. NE (on Hwy. 99) at 100 SW 7th St. - Dundee
   dundeebistro.com
   L-D.   *Expensive*
The Dundee Bistro is a quintessential Oregon Wine Country dining destination. The menu features top-quality seasonal ingredients of the region in flavorful, light dishes like Oregon wild mushroom soup; salad of Bibb lettuce and honey crisp apples with Rogue River blue vinaigrette, applewood-smoked bacon and hazelnuts; or pan-seared wild salmon entree. Desserts are also delicious, like Oregon cherries jubilee. Dine amid inviting Wine-Country-dining-room decor by a snazzy wine bar.

★ **The Fresh Palate Cafe** *(503)843-4400*
   7 mi. W (on Hwy. 18) at 19706 SW Hwy. 18 - Sheridan
   freshpalatecafe.com
   L only.   *Moderate*
Grilled crab sandwich on homemade bread, or hazelnut-crusted salmon, or wild mushroom ravioli are among regional specialties served in a nifty upstairs cafe overlooking the Lawrence Gallery, and on a sunny deck above the sculpture garden.

Golden Valley Brewery & Restaurant *(503)472-2739*
   downtown at 980 NE 4th St.
   goldenvalleybrewery.com
   L-D.   *Moderate*
The area's biggest and most popular brew pub produces a number of quality beers and ales available as tastes or in support of all kinds of Northwestern pub grub. A vast dining room in an old warehouse is likable because of extensive Craftsman-style dark wood paneling, candles at night, comfortable booths, and a big, ever-popular bar. An enclosed courtyard is also popular when weather permits.

★ **The Joel Palmer House** *(503)864-2995*
   6 mi. E at 600 Ferry St. - Dayton
   joelpalmerhouse.com
   D only. Closed Sun.-Mon.   *Expensive*
The Joel Palmer House, a large 1857 home on the National Historic Register, is now one of Oregon Wine Country's finest dinner houses. Wild mushrooms star, coupled with locally raised ingredients and organically grown vegetables and herbs. The "freestyle" menu showcases culinary adventures like sautéed sea scallops with wild mushroom duxelles and Creole-pinot gris sauce; and for dessert, chocolate hazelnut torte with raspberry sauce. Full linen service enhances the firelit dining room with views of surrounding flowers and an herb garden. A dining patio by the old carriage barn shares the tranquil, romantic setting.

McMenamins Hotel Oregon   *(503)435-3154*
downtown at 310 NE Evans St.
mcmenamins.com
B-L-D.   *Moderate*
Downtown McMinnville's landmark hotel features dining on
three levels. Traditional American comfort foods are served in a
large Old-Western style saloon with a big backbar, a lot of stained
glass, polished wood, brass, and live greenery, plus picture
windows to the main street. Downstairs on weekends, the
romantic little cellar bar is a popular getaway; and upstairs,
weather permitting, the rooftop dining deck is usually full.

★ **Nick's Italian Cafe**   *(503)434-4471*   *(888)456-2511*
downtown at 521 NE 3rd St.
nicksitaliancafe.com
D only. Closed Mon.   *Expensive*
Nick's Italian Cafe has been serving five-course meals that change
daily for more than thirty years. Guests can also order a la carte,
in selections like steamed clams with lemon; pesto hazelnut
lasagne; or roast rack of lamb with fresh artichokes; and for
dessert, chocolate hazelnut brandy torte. The simply comfortable
little wood-trim dining room and bar focus attention on the multi-
course dining adventures.

★ **Red Fox Bakery**   *(503)434-5098*
downtown at 328 NE Evans St.
B-L.   *Moderate*
Red Fox Bakery, opened in 2004, is the area's best source for
artisan breads and other baked goods. A limited selection of
pastries–cinnamon rolls, muffins, etc.–is displayed and sold for
breakfast. Later, assorted artisan breads are used for designer
sandwiches served with soups and cakes here or to go.

★ **Red Hills Provencial Dining**   *(503)538-8224*
11 mi. NE at 276 Hwy. 99W - Dundee
D only.   *Expensive*
An older house has been transformed into a roadside dinner
house with a casually elegant firelit dining room. Northwestern
country cuisine from European roots like sesame-coated oysters
is featured with an appealing view of surrounding garden.

Serendipity Ice Cream   *(503)474-9189*
downtown at 502 NE 3rd St.
L-D.   *Moderate*
An old-fashioned ice cream parlor features Cascade Glacier ice
cream in an 1886 former hotel's lobby transformed to showcase
nifty polished-wood trim and an upright piano.

Thai Country Restaurant   *(503)434-1300*
downtown at 707 NE 3rd St.

L-D. Closed Mon.   *Moderate*

Thai classics like chicken satay appetizer and all sorts of soups, salads, curries and stir fries are given careful attention and served in a big, cheerful dining room with some Thai wall hangings, green plants and interesting objects of art.

★ **Tina's**   *(503)538-8880*
   11 mi. NE at 760 Hwy. 99W - Dundee
   tinasdundee.com
   L-D. No L Sat.-Mon.   *Expensive*

Classic and creative Northwestern cuisine is exalted in a limited selection of expertly prepared entrees like line-caught Oregon chinook salmon filet poached in a white wine and vermouth reduction, or fresh regional wild mushroom risotto with chanterelles, or a double-cut pork chop stuffed with smoky bacon. Similarly delicious seasonal desserts are also made here like peach cobbler or pear-ginger pound cake. Foodies flock to this transformed Craftsman-style cottage with stylish wood-trim tables in cozy rooms separated by a two-sided fireplace for memorable pairings of Oregon Wine Country food and wine.

Trask Brewery & Public House   *(503)435-2382*
   downtown at 527 NE 3rd St.
   B-L-D. No B Mon.-Fri.   *Moderate*

All sorts of pub grub is served in a big casual dining room with a bar, a pool table, and occasional live music on weekends.

★ **Wild Wood Cafe**   *(503)435-1454*
   downtown at 319 N. Baker St.
   B-L. Closed Tues.   *Moderate*

Wild Wood Cafe is the place for breakfast. They specialize in designer or do-it-yourself omelets, assorted scrambles, grilled homemade bread rolled in granola, and other carefully prepared morning delights. Soup, salad and burgers are featured with their bread for lunch amid nostalgic 1950s decor–tables and chairs, booths, walls and ceiling festooned with the era's bric-a-brac.

LODGINGS

In McMinnville, the heart of Oregon's Wine Country, lodgings are still relatively scarce, but range from a historic hotel through contemporary motels to charming bed-and-breakfasts in and near town. In addition to listed properties, several chain motor hotels have lodgings on the highways toward nearby Portland. Rates stay the same year-round but may be reduced 10% on weekdays.

McMenamins Hotel Oregon   *(503)472-8427*
   downtown at 310 NE Evans St. - 97128
   mcmenamins.com
   42 units   *(888)472-8427*   *Moderate-Expensive*

McMenamins Hotel Oregon is McMinnville's landmark lodging. On the National Historic Register, the four-story building circa 1905 was recently fully restored and now includes dining and drinking on the roof, in a pub, or in a cellar (see listing). Worth a tour are the many historic photographs, original art works, and wine-inspired notes in the hallways. Each of the simply furnished, compact rooms has a double, queen or king bed. Some have a private bath; most share.

Paragon Motel   *(503)472-9493*
1 mi. S at 2065 S. Hwy. 99 W - 97128
54 units   *(800)525-5469*   *Low*
This modern bargain motel has a small pool and plain compact rooms with a microwave, refrigerator, and queen or king bed.

Red Lion Inn & Suites   *(503)472-1500*
2 mi. SE at 2535 NE Cumulus Av. - 97128
redlion.com/mcminnville
67 units   *(888)489-1600*   *Moderate-Expensive*
An indoor pool, whirlpool, and exercise room are amenities in this contemporary three-story motor hotel. Expanded Continental breakfast is complimentary. Each well-furnished room has a microwave, refrigerator and one or two queens or a king bed.
    #119,#121–spacious, in-room two-person whirlpool, king bed.

★ **Steiger Haus Bed & Breakfast Inn**   *(503)472-0821*
just S at 360 SE Wilson St. - 97128
steigerhaus.com
5 units   *Moderate-Expensive*
Steiger Haus is a charming European-style bed-and-breakfast in a quiet colorful garden setting a stroll from downtown. Full breakfast with an emphasis on fresh seasonal produce like peaches and hazelnuts is complimentary. Each of the well-furnished rooms has a tranquil view of surrounding trees and gardens, a private bath, and two twins or a queen bed.
    "Fireside Suite"–pressed-wood fireplace, private
        garden-view deck, garden view from queen bed.
    "Morningsun Room"–refrigerator, microwave, in-bath
        two-person whirlpool, garden view from queen bed.
    "Treetop Suite"–soaking tub, bay window
        with garden view shared by queen bed.

Vineyard Inn - Best Western   *(503)472-4900*
1 mi. SW at 2035 S. Hwy. 99W - 97128
bestwestern.com
65 units   *(800)285-6242*   *Low-Expensive*
One of McMinnville's largest lodgings is Best Western's Vineyard Inn. The contemporary four-story complex has an indoor pool, whirlpool and exercise room, and a complimentary expanded

Continental breakfast. Most of the well-furnished rooms have a refrigerator, microwave, and one or two queens or a king bed. Compact rooms without microwave and refrigerator are bargains.

#302,#202–spacious, refrigerator, microwave,
    two-person in-room whirlpool, king bed.

★ **Wine Country Farm**   *(503)864-3446*
11 mi. NE at 6855 Breyman Orchards Rd. - Dayton 97114
winecountryfarm.com
9 units   *(800)261-3446*   *Expensive*

Wine Country Farm lives up to its name in a hill-topping country setting. Hearty farm breakfast is complimentary, as is a tasting room overlooking the vineyards where you can enjoy wines produced here. Surrounded by lush vineyards and orchards, the farm produces five kinds of grapes in addition to raising and showing Arabian horses. Hike or mountain bike the surrounding trails, or (for a fee) take a horse-drawn buggy ride or guided trail ride. Each well-furnished room has a private bath and a queen or king bed.

"Oregon Suite," "Sunset Suite"–fine vineyards view,
    private deck, gas fireplace, canopy king bed.

★ **Youngberg Hill Vineyards & Inn**   *(503)472-2727*
6 mi. SW at 10660 SW Youngberg Hill Rd. - 97128
youngberghill.com
7 units   *(888)657-8668*   *Expensive-Very Expensive*

Oregon's quintessential Wine Country inn crowns the highest hill for many miles. A long and winding road leads to an unsurpassed tranquil setting. The contemporary mansion is completely encircled by covered decks overlooking spectacular panoramas of vineyards, orchards, forests and meadows in every direction. On a clear day, you can see Mt. Adams and Mt. Hood towering along the eastern horizon. Guests are greeted with the owner's award-winning pinot noir from his twelve acre vineyard. By appointment, pinot noir tasting is available to the general public and is complimentary to guests. Guests also enjoy a complimentary full gourmet breakfast with an inspiring Wine Country view. On an estate where luxury and romance are the hallmarks, each of the beautifully rooms has a private bath, a tranquil view, and a queen or king bed.

"Martini"–two-room suite, pressed-wood fireplace in living
    room, in-bath two-person whirlpool, large private porch
    shares spectacular view with king bed.
"Jackson"–sitting area, private view deck,
    two-headed shower, king bed.
"Wadenswil"–fine vineyard view, pressed-
    wood fireplace, queen bed.

Newport

Newport is the keystone of the Oregon coast. The town occupies a favored site bordered by broad sandy Pacific beaches and a calm harbor sheltered by bluffs near the Yaquina River mouth. Beachfronting state parks and harborside marinas provide ample recreation, while Old Town provides a unique commercial hub. A moderate climate supports maritime industries year-round, and attracts vacationers from spring through fall. Winter storm-watching attracts the hearty.

Seafaring and tourism have always been the mainstays of Newport, named in the 1880s after the Rhode Island resort. Initially it was a rustic coastal getaway for Willamette Valley residents who lived in tents in what is now Nye Beach (still one of the city's most intriguing districts). Completion of the splendid Yaquina Bay bridge during the Great Depression opened the entire Oregon coast to tourism.

Today, conventional businesses line the blufftop highway through town. Below, in the bayfront shadow of the bridge, Old Town remains the soul of Newport. An exhilarating hodgepodge of fine regional arts and crafts galleries and specialty shops, restaurants (most featuring local seafoods) and bars share refurbished Victorian buildings amidst unpretentious canneries, seafood markets, and other maritime businesses. Visitors can opt to stay at plush bayside or oceanfront lodgings while exploring Old Town, the Oregon Coast Aquarium, Hatfield Marine Science Center, and diverse recreation on the bay, beaches, ocean and Coast Range mountains.

WEATHER PROFILE

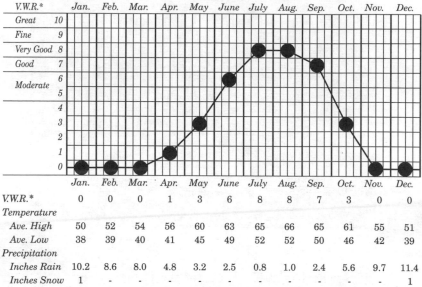

V.W.R.*		Jan.	Feb.	Mar.	Apr.	May	June	July	Aug.	Sep.	Oct.	Nov.	Dec.
Great	10												
Fine	9												
Very Good	8												
Good	7												
Moderate	6 / 5												

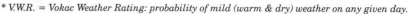

V.W.R.*	Jan.	Feb.	Mar.	Apr.	May	June	July	Aug.	Sep.	Oct.	Nov.	Dec.
V.W.R.*	0	0	0	1	3	6	8	8	7	3	0	0
Temperature												
Ave. High	50	52	54	56	60	63	65	66	65	61	55	51
Ave. Low	38	39	40	41	45	49	52	52	50	46	42	39
Precipitation												
Inches Rain	10.2	8.6	8.0	4.8	3.2	2.5	0.8	1.0	2.4	5.6	9.7	11.4
Inches Snow	1	-	-	-	-	-	-	-	-	-	-	1

* V.W.R. = Vokac Weather Rating: probability of mild (warm & dry) weather on any given day.

BASIC INFORMATION

Population: 9,532
Elevation: 134 feet
Location: 114 miles Southwest of Portland
Airport (regularly scheduled flights): Portland - 120 mi.

Greater Newport Chamber of Commerce (541)265-8801 (800)262-7844
   downtown at 555 SW Coast Hwy. - 97365
   newportchamber.org

ATTRACTIONS

★ **Beverly Beach State Park**   *(541)265-9278   (800)551-6949*
   7 mi. N on Hwy. 101
   oregonstateparks.org
Easy access to a long sandy beach and a four-mile creekside nature loop trail are features. Strung along Spencer Creek is a forest-sheltered campground, the area's largest, with full hookups, abundant tent sites and a separate hiker/biker campground.

★ *Boat Rentals*
   Embarcadero Dock   *(541)265-8521   (800)547-4779*
   just E at 1000 SE Bay Blvd.
   embarcadero-resort.com
For many years, Embarcadero Dock at the Embarcadero Resort Hotel & Marina has been the reliable place to go for boats and kayak rentals, and crabbing and fishing equipment, rented by the hour or day. The promenade extends to a picturesque overlook with a great grey whale sculpture.

   Boat Rides
★ **Marine Discovery Tours**   *(541)265-2600   (800)903-2628*
   in Old Town at 345 SW Bay Blvd.
   marinediscovery.com
The official cruise company of the Oregon Coast Aquarium offers two-hour narrated bay and ocean excursions aboard the 65-foot two-level "Discovery" from March through October. The guides may point out whales, oyster farms and sea and shore wildlife. Aboard "the Oregon Rocket" (a 27-foot rigid-hull inflatable), sixteen adventure-seeking passengers wearing goggles and flotation suits will zip along at up to 45 miles per hour while watching sea life and memorable scenery (from May through October).

★ **Devil's Punch Bowl State Park**   *(800)551-6949*
   8 mi. N on Hwy. 101
   oregonstateparks.org
A huge bowl-shaped rock formation fills from below with a roar at high tide. Scenic picnic sites, a hiking trail, a long curve of clean sandy beach, tidepools, and ocean-carved caves are other features of this unusual day use park.

★ *Fishing Charters*
Salmon fishing is one of the major attractions off the Oregon coast. Newport is home port to several sportfishing charters. Salmon trolling, deep sea fishing, river fishing and whale watching excursions that take from a few hours to overnight can be arranged at a number of places located along the Old Town waterfront. Among the best are:

Newport Marina & Charters *(541)867-4470   (877)867-4470*
2 mi. S at 2122 SE Marine Science Dr.
newportmarinacharters.com
Newport Tradewinds   *(541)265-2101   (800)676-7819*
in Old Town at 653 SW Bay Blvd.
newporttradewinds.com
Sea Gull Charters   *(541)265-7441   (800)865-7441*
in Old Town at 343 SW Bay Blvd.
seagullcharters.com
Yaquina Bay Charters   *(541)265-6800   (866)465-6801*
just E at 1000 SE Bay Blvd.
yaquinabaycharters.com

Food Specialties

★ **Fish Peddler's Market**   *(541)265-7057*
in Old Town at 617 SW Bay Blvd.
The Fish Peddler's Market displays local shrimp, oysters, salmon and more in extensive cases. They can be enjoyed in cocktails, chowder, cioppino or as treats like popcorn shrimp and chips at tables by the deli cases and in a bright little dining room backed by a cannery and a fish processing plants. Cans of salmon, tuna and other fish are also displayed for sale. Closed Wed.

Gino's Seafood & Deli   *(541)265-2424*
in Old Town at 808 SW Bay Blvd.
Gino's is a big basic fish market and deli with a selection of local seafoods for sandwiches, cocktails or chowder. Selections can be enjoyed at a few tables in the bright deli cafe, or to go.

★ **Hatfield Marine Science Center**   *(541)867-0271*
2 mi. S at 2030 SE Marine Science Dr.
hmsc.orst.edu/visitor
Oregon State University operates a large coastal research center on Yaquina Bay. The public wing has marine fish and invertebrates in tanks that simulated their natural environments. At interactive exhibits, visitors can pull up and examine starfish and other intertidal creatures. Other displays and materials in the center's Oregon-oriented bookstore explain coastal geology, tides, weather, and harbor life. Summer marine workshops, field trips, lectures, and films are also offered to the public.

★ **The Lookout at Cape Foulweather**   *(541)765-2270*
9 mi. N on Hwy. 101
The Lookout at Cape Foulweather is one of the highest promontories above the ocean in the Pacific Northwest. Don't miss the lookout point and adjoining historic well-stocked gift shop–real cliffhangers with awe-inspiring panoramic views of the ocean, headlands, coves, beaches, and offshore rocks of many miles of Oregon's central coast.

★ **Newport Marina at South Beach**   *(541)867-3321*
   2 mi. S at 2301 SE Marine Science Dr.
One of the Northwest's largest and most complete marina facilities
is near the outlet of Yaquina Bay. In addition to a huge moorage
and complete marine services, there is a public fishing pier with
fine bay and bridge views, a bait and tackle store, deep sea
charters, a picnic area with barbecues, crab cooking facility, and
brew pub.

★ **Old Town**
   along Bay Blvd. on NW side of Yaquina Bay
Bay Front (or Old Town) is a historic enclave that is the real heart
of Newport. In recent decades, Old Town has unfortunately
attracted tourist traps, t-shirt and trinket parlors. But, the good
news far outweighs the bad. A captivating hodgepodge of specialty
shops, galleries, eateries and bars enlivens refurbished Victorian
buildings amidst a mosaic of unpretentious canneries and other
maritime businesses. Seafood markets, cafes and restaurants do an
outstanding job of showcasing Dungeness crab, Yaquina Bay
oysters, wild salmon, and other local gourmet seafood.

★ **Ona Beach State Park**   *(800)551-6949*
   8 mi. S on Hwy. 101
   oregonstateparks.org
A bathhouse and boat ramp contribute to this day use park's
appeal for swimming and fishing. Many scenic picnic sites on a
lawn with shade trees overlook a creek and a sandy ocean beach.

★ **Oregon Coast Aquarium**   *(541)867-3474*
   2 mi. S (via Hwy. 101) at 2820 SE Ferry Slip Rd.
   aquarium.org
The aquarium opened in 1992, and was soon ranked among the
top ten in the country. Today, there are nearly 200 species of
marine mammals, birds, fish and invertebrates on display. The
theme is following a drop of water from the Coast Range to the
Pacific Ocean. Beyond a first-rate gift shop and cafe, indoor
exhibits feature marine life in wetlands, in sandy and rocky
shores, and in deep waters. The jellyfish exhibit is a must. Acres of
outdoor exhibits feature an underwater cave with a giant octopus;
a rocky pool with sea otters, seals and sea lions; and the largest
walk-through seabird aviary in America. The latest and most
popular exhibit is "Passages of the Deep" featuring three large
ocean habitats connected by a 200-foot underwater acrylic tunnel
with large windows in the floor, and clear walls and ceiling for
viewing sharks, rays, skates, eels, and other deep-sea denizens on
all sides. "Animal Encounters" take visitors behind-the-glass for
unique hands-on experiences (supervised by animal husbandry
staff) with giant octopus, sea otters, sharks, and sea lions.

Oregon Coast History Center   *(541)265-7509*
  just NW at 545 SW 9th St.
The center includes a log cabin, museum, and the 1895 Queen Anne Victorian Burrows House featuring artifacts, photographs, and historical exhibits about the area. A research library, heritage garden and museum stores are also here.

South Beach State Park   *(541)867-4715   (800)551-6949*
  2 mi. S on Hwy. 101
  oregonstateparks.org
Expansive low dunes and a broad sandy beach lie between a full-service campground with picnic facilities and the ocean. Fishing, crabbing, wind-surfing, and beachcombing are popular.

Undersea Gardens   *(541)265-2206*
  in Old Town at 250 SW Bay Blvd.
Thousands of marine creatures can be viewed in their natural habitat through more than 100 underwater viewing windows in this floating aquarium that rises and falls with the tides. There are scuba diving shows several times daily.

★ **Yaquina Bay State Park**   *(541)265-5679   (800)551-6949*
  just SW on Hwy. 101 at N end of bridge
  oregonstateparks.org
Dozens of scenic picnic sites are positioned on a well-landscaped blufftop with panoramic views of ocean beaches and the mouth of Yaquina Bay. Sunbathing, beachcombing, fishing, and swimming (for the hearty) are also popular. The park also features the historic **Yaquina Bay Lighthouse** (1871), Newport's oldest building. This combined lighthouse/residence has been restored and refurnished in period style.

★ **Yaquina Head Outstanding Natural Area**   *(541)574-3100*
  3 mi. N (via Hwy. 101) on Lighthouse Dr.
An interpretive center displays the area's human and natural history. Trails lead from the spectacular coastal headland to beaches, tidepools and overlooks, and a historic lighthouse. Yaquina Head Lighthouse (circa 1873), Oregon's tallest, is on a 93-foot tower.

RESTAURANTS

Agate Beach Inn - Best Western   *(541)265-9411*
  2 mi. N at 3019 N. Coast Hwy.
  agatebeachinn.com
  B-L-D.   *Expensive*
In the hotel's **Starfish Grill Restaurant**, contemporary Northwestern cuisine is featured in a capacious split-level dining room with a window-wall view of a beach and the ocean. **Rookie's Sports Bar** is a big comfortable lounge that shares the view, as does a handsome wood-trimmed umbrella-shaded deck.

★ **April's at Nye Beach**   *(541)265-6855*
  just NW at 749 NW 3rd St.
  D only. Closed Mon.-Tues.   *Moderate*
April's is a deservedly popular destination for some of the finest
cuisine on the Oregon coast. Northwest ingredients are skillfully
prepared into treats like boneless applewood-smoked Idaho trout,
or fresh line-caught wild salmon, or unique creations like seafood
"cannelone" (pasta sheets may be filled with salmon, halibut,
prawns, and/or bay shrimp with ricotta cheese, lemon capers,
spinach, fresh dill and tarragon with a tomato-basil cream sauce).
Innovative delicious desserts also make excellent use of fresh
seasonal fruits. Intimate comfortable dining rooms contribute to
the restaurant's easygoing sophistication.

Black Swan Bookstore & Cafe   *(541)265-7926*
  1 mi. N at 830 N. Coast Hwy.
  blackswanbookstore.com
  L only. Closed Mon.-Tues.   *Moderate*
Light contemporary dishes like muffaletta or spinach salad are
served amid a cheerful melange of live greenery and books in
rooms with comfortable chairs to sit in and enjoy a beverage while
browsing.

★ **Canyon Way Bookstore & Restaurant**   *(541)265-8319*
  in Old Town at 1216 SW Canyon Way
  L-D. Closed Sun.   *Moderate*
For more than thirty years, Canyon Way has been a favorite for
fine food on the Oregon coast. Delicious and unusual specialties,
broiled and sautéed local seafoods, and homemade baked goods
and desserts are served in several stylish dining areas and in a
garden patio. Gourmet beverages of all kinds and food service in
a warm wood-toned lounge are also available. An outstanding
bookstore adjoins.

★ **Champagne Patio Restaurant & Swafford's Oregon**   *265-3044*
  1 mi. N at 1630 N. Coast Hwy.
  L only.   *Moderate*
Delectable fresh-baked bread and rich desserts are served with
creative, flavorful dishes in a cozy, attractive dining room. Their
wine list includes any selection from the expansive wine shop and
outstanding Oregon specialty foods store in the next room.

The Chowder Bowl at Nye Beach   *(541)265-7477*
  just NW at 728 NW Beach Dr.
  L-D.   *Moderate*
Cups, bowls or sourdough bread bowls are filled with thick creamy
clam chowder, the house specialty. Local seafoods are also used for
sandwiches and light entrees in this popular little dining room
with the historic look and feel of Nye Beach.

The Coffee House   *(541)265-6263*
in Old Town at 156 SW Bay Blvd.
B-L.   *Moderate*
In addition to a short list of designer breakfasts, housemade
scones, muffins and bagels on display can be delicious when fresh.
The seven or eight tables have a window-wall view of Old Town.

★ **Embarcadero Resort Hotel & Marina**   *(541)265-8521*
   just E at 1000 SE Bay Blvd.
   embarcadero-resort.com
   B-L-D. Sun. brunch.   *Moderate*
In the resort hotel's restaurant, local seafoods like Yaquina Bay
oysters, Dungeness crab, bay shrimp and salmon can be very good
in a thoughtful selection of hot and cold appetizers, soups, salads
and entrees. There are also several choice steaks of different sizes,
plus housemade desserts. An expansive split-level dining room and
raised lounge share a fine panoramic window-wall view of Old
Town and the bridge, and there is live entertainment on
weekends. Don't miss the last Friday dinner of each month–a
prodigious buffet of gourmet seafoods.

★ **Georgie's Beachside Grill**   *(541)265-9800*
   just W at 744 SW Elizabeth St.
   B-L-D.   *Moderate*
Georgie's Beachside Grill is *the* place to go for a good breakfast
with an ocean view. All-American classics like pecan waffles and
blueberry pancakes; all kinds of four-egg omelets and scrambles;
and specialties like Joe's Special, corned beef hash, and seafood
classics like hangtown fry have made this one of the region's most
popular destinations for early risers. Lunches and dinners
featuring fresh local seafoods are also deservedly popular in this
big handsome split-level coffee shop with window walls on two
sides overlooking the adjacent bluff, beach and ocean.

Mo's   *(541)265-2979*
in Old Town at 622 SW Bay Blvd.
moschowder.com
L-D.   *Moderate*
The original Mo's goes back half a century and still contributes to
the unvarnished charm of Newport's Old Town (the chowder
factory out back attests to the popularity of Mo's clam chowder).
There are now several Mo's along the Oregon coast, but the best
are here and across the street at the annex. Local seafoods
continue to star in all kinds of appetizers, entrees, chowders,
sandwiches and pastas served in the rustic little cafe with the
original garage door that opens to a view of a cannery. The
regional specialty, peanut butter pie, is featured for dessert.

Mo's Annex   *(541)265-7512*
in Old Town at 657 SW Bay Blvd.
moschowder.com
L-D.   *Moderate*
In addition to the touted clam chowder, this best of the little
Oregon chain features seafood stews, steamers, casseroles, bakes
and sautés. The deservedly popular Annex has a tidy, congested
bayfront dining room with close-up views of waterfront activity.

Rogue Ales Public House   *(541)265-3188*
in Old Town at 748 SW Bay Blvd.
rogue.com
L-D.   *Moderate*
Award-winning Rogue brews are showcased in a big, cheerful pub
where they are featured in ale-steamed clams and hazelnut or
garlic ale bread, plus many pizzas and other pub favorites. The
premium Rogue Ale brews from taps or bottles served here are
made at **Brewers by the Bay** at the Marina in South Beach,
where patrons have a view of the kettles and waterfront while
enjoying light pub fare.

★ **Saffron Salmon**   *(541)265-8921*
in Old Town at 859 SW Bay Blvd.
L-D. Closed Wed.   *Expensive*
Saffron Salmon is a post-millennium showcase for contemporary
Northwestern cuisine. Fresh seasonal ingredients from the sea
and land are carefully prepared into traditional and creative
dishes like smoked salmon and pasta flowers tossed with
gorgonzola cream sauce and toasted pecans. Desserts made here
like lemon cake with fresh lemon curd filling and white chocolate
frosting can also be delicious. The snazzy little dining room juts
into Yaquina Bay and has a fine picture-window outlook on three
sides.

★ **Sharks Seafood Bar & Steamer**   *(541)574-0590*
in Old Town at 852 SW Bay Blvd.
sharksseafoodbar.com
D only. Closed Wed.-Thurs.   *Moderate*
Shellfish are poached or steamed–to perfection–thanks to the
chef/owner's skill and unique steam kettles. The big, bold cioppino
is deservedly acclaimed, as are the gumbos, stews, curry, pastas,
pan roasts, and salads served in this spiffy little seafood bar and
steamer cafe.

★ **Tables of Content**   *(541)265-5428*
just NW at 267 NW Cliff St.
sylviabeachhotel.com
D only.   *Moderate*
One of Oregon's most unusual and sophisticated dining venues is

Tables of Content in the Sylvia Beach Hotel. By reservation, four-course family-style fixed-price meals are served at tables set for up to eight people in a warm comfortable dining room that evokes the hotel's decidedly literary bent. Guests can participate in a two-truths-and-one-lie icebreaker verbal game that is both challenging and fun as an intellectual exercise while enjoying delicious Northwestern cuisine beautifully prepared for dishes that use local specialties like line-caught wild salmon and bay shrimp. Each night, the luscious dessert varies (as do the other courses).

★ **Whale Cove Inn**   *(541)765-2255   (866)577-3767*
    11 mi. N at 2345 SW Hwy. 101 - Depoe Bay
    B-L-D.   *Moderate*
In the ultimate foodie hierarchy–*Category: cinnamon rolls; Subcategory: size*–The Whale's Cove Inn rules in America. A cinnamon roll of truly epic proportions has long starred on a customary American menu, along with bountifu l breakfasts. From atop a slope high above the ocean, the simply comfortable dining room features a window-wall view of Whale Cove, a quintessential representation of the bewitching Oregon coast, and a great spot for close-in whale watching. Binoculars are available in-house.

★ **Whale's Tale Restaurant**   *(541)265-8660*
    in Old Town at 452 SW Bay Blvd.
    B-L-D. Closed Wed.   *Moderate*
Breakfasts have been especially notable here since 1976, including unusual treats like poppyseed pancakes from stone-ground flour, and hearty fisherman's omelets with sautéed vegies and two cheeses topped with local grilled oysters. Later, Northwest seafoods, poached or sautéed, are featured along with homemade bread and creative desserts like "mousse in a bag" or apricot baklava that are delicious ways to complete a meal. All kinds of whimsical wall hangings and objects of art enliven the handcrafted wood-toned interior of cozy dining areas.

LODGINGS

Most of the area's best lodgings are near ocean beaches. Low and moderately priced motels are inland along Highway 101 through town. High season is June through September. Rates are reduced as much as 20% at other times.

Agate Beach Inn - Best Western   *(541)265-9411*
    2 mi. N at 3019 N. Coast Hwy. - 97365
    agatebeachinn.com
    148 units   *(800)547-3310*   *Expensive*
Tucked back from picturesque Agate Beach is a modern six-story hotel with a big indoor pool; whirlpool; exercise room; ocean-view

restaurant (see listing), entertainment lounge, and gift shop. Each well-furnished room has a microwave, refrigerator, and one or two queens or a king bed. Most have a standing-only balcony, some with a fine ocean view.

Days Inn   *(541)265-5767*
just W at 544 S. Coast Hwy. - 97365
www.the.daysinn.com
32 units   (800)999-3068   Moderate
The beach is an easy hike from this contemporary motel. Each comfortably furnished room has a microwave, refrigerator, and two doubles, queen or king bed.
   #211–spacious, kitchen, corner window distant ocean view,
      pressed-wood fireplace, in-bath deep whirlpool, king bed.

★ **Elizabeth Street Inn**   *(541)265-9400*
just W at 232 SW Elizabeth St. (Box 1342) - 97365
elizabethstreetinn.com
74 units   (877)265-9400   Expensive
The Elizabeth Street Inn is a fine post-millennium oceanfront motel. The five-story complex crowns a bluff adjoining a broad sandy beach that extends for miles in both directions. Amenities include an indoor pool, whirlpool, exercise room, and complimentary expanded Continental breakfast. Each spacious, well-furnished room has a refrigerator and microwave, a raised corner gas fireplace, and a large private balcony overlooking the ocean, plus two queens or a king bed.
   #110,#112,#114–two-person whirlpool,
      fine ocean view from balcony and king bed.
   #434,#334,#234–outstanding corner
      window ocean view, king bed.

★ **Embarcadero Resort Hotel & Marina**   *(541)265-8521*
just E at 1000 SE Bay Blvd. - 97365
embarcadero-resort.com
80 units   (800)547-4779   Expensive
Nicely landscaped grounds along Yaquina Bay house several three-story contemporary wood-trimmed buildings. The expansive condo complex, an easy stroll from Old Town, has a large indoor bay-view pool, whirlpool, sauna, fishing and crabbing piers, marina with rental boats (see listing) and charter fishing, and a stylish seafood restaurant (see listing) that shares an excellent bay/bridge view with a lounge offering frequent live entertainment. Each spacious, well-furnished room (many with a marina and/or bay view) has a large private balcony and one or two queens or a king bed. One-bedroom suites and two-bedroom townhouses also have a kitchen and gas fireplace.

★ **Hallmark Resort**   *(541)265-2600*
  just W at 744 SW Elizabeth St. - 97365
  hallmarkinns.com
  158 units   *(888)448-4449*   *Expensive*
The Hallmark Resort in Newport is one of the finest lodgings on
the Oregon coast. This five-story motor hotel is on a park-like
blufftop above the ocean. The contemporary complex is just steps
away from miles of broad sandy beach, plus an indoor pool,
whirlpool, sauna, exercise room, surf-view restaurant (see listing
for **Georgie's**), lounge, and gift shop. Each of the attractively
furnished rooms has an ocean view, microwave, refrigerator, and
one or two queen beds. Many spacious newer rooms also have a
private deck, gas fireplace, and a two-person in-room whirlpool.
     #565,#465,#365,#265–spacious, gas fireplace,
        wraparound private balcony, two-person
        whirlpool with ocean view, king bed.
★ **The Inn at Otter Crest**   *(541)765-2111*
  9 mi. N at 301 Otter Crest Loop (Box 50) - Otter Rock 97369
  innatottercrest.com
  120 units   *(800)452-2101*   *Expensive*
Dramatically located in a pine forest high above the ocean, this
long-established condominium resort hotel offers a private sandy
cove, a large ocean-view pool, whirlpool, sauna, exercise room,
nature trails (the Devil's Punchbowl and Beverly Beach are the
reward at the end of a half-mile trail through a Northwestern rain
forest with pines towering above rhododendron bushes twenty feet
high), ocean-view restaurant and lounge, and a gift shop. Each
well-furnished unit has a private deck and a queen or king bed.
Some also have a kitchen and pressed-log fireplace.
  La Quinta Inn & Suites - Newport   *(541)867-7727*
  2 mi. S at 45 SE 32nd St. - 97365
  lq.com
  71 units   *(800)531-5900*   *Moderate-Expensive*
A stroll from the aquarium, this three-story contemporary motel
has a small indoor pool, whirlpool, sauna, and exercise room.
Expanded Continental breakfast is complimentary. Each room and
suite is well furnished and has a queen or king bed.
     "Parlor Suite" (5 of these)–spacious, microwave,
        refrigerator, in-bath two-person whirlpool, king bed.
★ **Little Creek Cove**   *(541)265-8587*
  2 mi. N (via Hwy. 101) at 3641 NW Oceanview Dr. - 97365
  www.littlecreekcove.com
  29 units   *(800)294-8025*   *Expensive*
A secluded beachfront cove was transformed with perfectly scaled
naturalistic buildings and landscaping into a delightful   little

three-story condominium complex. Each (studio to two-bedroom) unit is beautifully furnished and includes a full kitchen, gas fireplace, private deck and queen or king bed. Some have an intimate ocean view.

#29–1 BR, magnificent ocean/beach views, king bed.

#3–studio, magnificent ocean view, Murphy queen bed.

★ **Moolack Shores Motel**   *(541)265-2326*
5 mi. N at 8835 N. Coast Hwy. - 97365
moolackshores.com
12 units   *Moderate-Expensive*

This contemporary single-level motel is in a secluded spot on a bluff above the beach. Each well-furnished room is artistically decorated in a different theme, and has a queen or king bed. Some have a pressed-log fireplace and an ocean view.

#10A–kitchenette, corner ocean view windows,
    private view deck, queen bed.

#4–as above, with Franklin (pressed log) fireplace.

#6,#7–Franklin (pressed log) fireplace, kitchenette,
    private ocean-view deck, king bed.

Newport Belle Bed & Breakfast   *(541)867-6290*
2 mi. S at Newport Marina (H Dock) (Box 685) - South Beach 97366
newportbelle.com
5 units   *(800)348-1922*   *Expensive*

To sleep right on-the-bay, book the Newport Belle, a turn-of-the-century (the 21st century, that is) sternwheeler riverboat designed as a bed-and-breakfast. A gourmet breakfast served in the main salon is complimentary. Each state room has a private bath, a fine view of the famed bridge and/or the Newport Marina, and a queen or king bed.

Newport Motor Inn   *(541)265-8516*
1 mi. N at 1311 N. Coast Hwy. - 97365
newportmotorinn.com
39 units   *Low*

Each comfortably furnished room in this modern, recently remodeled bargain motel has a refrigerator, microwave, and queen bed.

Nye Beach Hotel & Cafe   *(541)265-3334*
just NW at 219 NW Cliff St. - 97365
nyebeach.com
18 units   *(866)865-3334*   *Moderate-Expensive*

The Nye Beach Hotel & Cafe has a rustic, semi-funky look that belies its 1992 vintage. The four-story shingled little hotel has a colorful cafe (B-L-D–Moderate) with an eclectic menu (shrimp and feta sandwich, etc.) that shares an ocean view with an adjoining deck. Each room is nicely furnished and includes a private bath, gas fireplace, standing balcony and some ocean view, plus two doubles or queen bed.

#18,#10–large whirlpool shares ocean view with queen bed.

Oar House Bed & Breakfast   *(541)265-9571*
just W at 520 SW 2nd St. - 97365
oarhouse-bed-breakfast.com
5 units   *(800)252-2358*   *Expensive*
A large house in the historic Nye Beach area is now an appealing bed-and-breakfast inn on a rise a short stroll from a long sandy beach. Full gourmet breakfast is complimentary. Each compact, well-furnished room has a private balcony and a queen bed.

"The Starboard Cabin"– two-person whirlpool, ocean view.

★ **Ocean House Inn**   *(541)265-6158*
3 mi. N (via Hwy. 101) at 4920 NW Woody Way - 97365
oceanhouse.com
8 units   *(800)562-2632*   *Expensive*
The Ocean House Inn is Newport's most romantic bed-and-breakfast. The large gracious inn is surrounded by a beautifully landscaped garden on a high bluff overlooking a sandy beach and dramatic headlands. A private trail leads to the beach which extends for miles to the jetty in Newport. Full gourmet breakfast featuring Northwestern cuisine is complimentary. All of the well-furnished units have a gas fireplace, an intimate ocean view past gardens and towering pines, and a queen or king bed.

"The Overlook"–two-person whirlpool tub,
   fine ocean view from king bed.
"Kelody's"–two-person in-bath whirlpool,
   grand ocean-view four-poster queen bed.
"Rainbow"–spacious, side view of ocean, private
   deck, two-person in-bath whirlpool, four-poster queen bed.
"The Cottage"–sitting room with gas fireplace, kitchenette and
   window-wall view to ocean, in-bath whirlpool, loft king bed.

★ **Schooner Landing**   *(541)265-4293*
4 mi. N (on Hwy. 101) at 201 NW 66th Dr. (Box 703) - 97365
schoonerlanding.com
42 units   *Expensive-Very Expensive*
Amenities of this contemporary condominium complex on a wooded coastal bluff include private hiking paths to the beach, a long indoor pool, whirlpool, sauna, racquetball court, sports court, billiards and ping pong tables, and weight room. Each well-furnished one- or two-bedroom Cape Cod-style unit has a full kitchen, gas fireplace, private deck, two-person whirlpool bath, and one or two queen beds.

#307–1 BR, upstairs, private, coastal/forest view, queen bed.
#306–2 BR, private, coastal/forest view, two queen beds.

Shilo Inn Newport Oceanfront Resort   *(541)265-7701*
just SW at 536 SW Elizabeth St. - 97365
shiloinns.com
179 units   *(800)222-2244*   *Expensive*
Shilo Inn's large four-story motor hotel complex is on a bluff with
easy access to miles of broad sandy beach. There are two indoor
pools, plus an oceanfront restaurant and lounge. Most comfortably
furnished rooms have a fine surf view, microwave, refrigerator,
and one or two queens or a king bed.

★ **Starfish Point**   *(541)265-3751*
3 mi. N (on Hwy. 101) at 140 NW 48th St. - 97365
starfishpoint.com
6 units   *Expensive*
Starfish Point is one of the premier adult getaways on the Oregon
coast. High on the rim of a forested bluff overlooking a broad
sandy beach and surf is a superb example of post-modern
Northwestern architecture perfectly harmonized with nature. A
secluded staircase and path winds down to a sandy beach. Each
romantic, beautifully furnished two-bedroom unit has a designer
kitchen, an unusual octagonal ocean-view study, pressed-wood
fireplace, and a two-person whirlpool bath with an awesome view
of beach and ocean from the tub, and double and queen beds.
Picture windows and a private view deck provide spectacular ocean
and forest views.
   #6,#4,#2–two bedrooms, two decks, octagonal study
      with private ocean view, large whirlpool with superb
      ocean view, double and ocean-view queen bed.

★ **The Sylvia Beach Hotel**   *(541)265-5428*
just NW at 267 NW Cliff St. - 97365
sylviabeachhotel.com
20 units   *(888)795-8422*   *Moderate-Expensive*
Sylvia Beach Hotel, on the National Register of Historic
Landmarks, is a renowned bed-and-breakfast-by-the-sea for book-
lovers. Amenities of the vintage four-story hotel include close
proximity to an ocean beach, a gift shop, a library, plus **Tables of
Content** (see listing) where hearty breakfasts served family-style
are complimentary. Each compact room is individually nicely
furnished with a theme related to a major literary figure and has
a private bath and a choice ranging from twin to king beds.
   "Agatha Christie," "Mark Twain," "Colette"–good ocean view,
      wood-burning fireplace, private view deck, queen bed.

Tyee Lodge Bed & Breakfast   *(541)265-8953*
3 mi. N at 4925 Woody Way - 97365
tyeelodge.com
5 units   *(888)553-8933*   *Expensive*

The Tyee Lodge is a contemporary bed-and-breakfast with an appealing location surrounded by gardens on a forested bluff above a sandy beach and dramatic headlands. A trail leads to the beach which extends for miles alongside Newport. A gourmet breakfast served family-style is complimentary. Each well-furnished room has a gas fireplace, peaceful forest and coastal view, and a queen bed.

"Chinook," "Yaquina"–bay window with
    panoramic coast/forest view, gas fireplace.

Val-U Inn Motel   *(541)265-6203*
just W at 531 SW Fall St. - 97365
valuinn.com
71 units   *(800)443-7777*   *Low-Moderate*
The beach and the historic waterfront are a brisk walk from this modern motel. Expanded Continental breakfast is complimentary. Each comfortably furnished room has a queen or king bed. Kitchen units are available.

"spa room" (4 of these)–in-room two-person whirlpool, king bed.

Waves of Newport   *(541)265-4661*
1 mi. NW at 820 NW Coast St. - 97365
wavesofnewport.com
60 units   *(800)282-6993*   *Low-Moderate*
This contemporary three-level motel is set back across a street from an ocean bluff. Each comfortably furnished room has a microwave, refrigerator, and a queen or king bed. Rooms on the top floor have a fair ocean view.

The Whaler   *(541)265-9261*
just W at 155 SW Elizabeth St. - 97365
www.whalernewport.com
73 units   *(800)433-9444*   *Expensive*
An indoor pool, whirlpool, and exercise room are features of this modern three-story motel across a road from the blufftop above a fine beach. Each well-furnished room has a refrigerator and one or two queens or a king bed. Some rooms (ask for third floor) have a microwave, refrigerator, gas fireplace, or private ocean-view balcony.

Seaside

Seaside is the premier coastal playground of the Pacific Northwest. For more than a century, vacationers have been attracted to the broad sandy beach that links the ocean with a massive forested headland at one of the most dramatic sites on the coast. Summer is the year's only busy season when long warm days and relatively little rain attract capacity crowds. From fall through spring, almost continuous rainfall curtails the area's usability for outdoor recreation, but storm-watching reigns.

Seaside began, in 1806, as the western end of the Lewis and Clark Trail. But settlers weren't attracted to the handsome location until the 1870s when the promenade, amusement facilities and elaborate accommodations began to establish Seaside as the first major coastal resort in the Northwest.

Today, Seaside remains the most appealing fun-oriented destination along the Oregon coast. A well-landscaped pedestrian-and-auto thoroughfare extends from a monumental Lewis and Clark statue at a beachfront turnaround through the heart of town. It is lined with appealing specialty shops, restaurants, atmospheric bars, and an upgraded old-fashioned amusement zone that appeals to all ages (including adults). Ubiquitous rental outfitters offer more ways to peddle, paddle, or putt-putt around town than anywhere else on abundant paths, promenades, sidewalks, byways and waterways. A stylish landmark hotel anchors a two-mile-long pedestrian promenade at the turnaround by the beach. Many other plain-to-plush modern lodgings along the shoreline also serve summer crowds.

WEATHER PROFILE

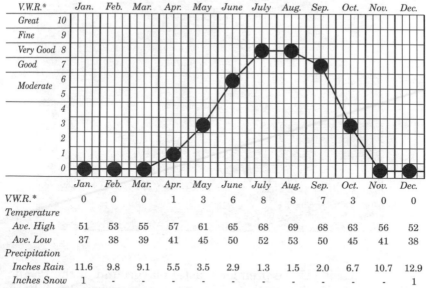

V.W.R.*		Jan.	Feb.	Mar.	Apr.	May	June	July	Aug.	Sep.	Oct.	Nov.	Dec.
Great	10												
Fine	9												
Very Good	8							●	●				
Good	7									●			
Moderate	6						●						
	5												
	4												
	3					●					●		
	2												
	1				●								
	0	●	●	●								●	●

	Jan.	Feb.	Mar.	Apr.	May	June	July	Aug.	Sep.	Oct.	Nov.	Dec.
V.W.R.*	0	0	0	1	3	6	8	8	7	3	0	0
Temperature												
Ave. High	51	53	55	57	61	65	68	69	68	63	56	52
Ave. Low	37	38	39	41	45	50	52	53	50	45	41	38
Precipitation												
Inches Rain	11.6	9.8	9.1	5.5	3.5	2.9	1.3	1.5	2.0	6.7	10.7	12.9
Inches Snow	1	-	-	-	-	-	-	-	-	-	-	1

* V.W.R. = Vokac Weather Rating: probability of mild (warm & dry) weather on any given day.

BASIC INFORMATION

Population: 5,900
Elevation: 10 feet
Location: 80 miles Northwest of Portland
Airport (regularly scheduled flights): Portland - 88 miles

Seaside Chamber of Commerce   (503)738-6391   (800)444-6740
   just E at 7 N. Roosevelt Dr. (Hwy. 101) (Box 7) - 97138
   seasidechamber.com
Seaside Visitors Bureau   (503)738-3097   (888)306-2326
   just E at 7 N. Roosevelt Dr. (mail: 989 Broadway) - 97138
   seasideor.com

ATTRACTIONS

★ *Bicycling*
There is a lot of flat coastal terrain in the area that can be toured on miles of byways and paved separated bikeways. Seaside has one of the Northwest's most comprehensive collections of fun devices for enjoying the bikeways, beach, ocean and river that surround Seaside. Bicycles (beach cruiser or tandem, surrey or deuce coupe), mopeds, electric cars, skates or chariots may be rented for riding around town and on the beach. Offshore water vessels include barracuda, water bee, water skate, kayak, surf bike, or boogie board, and more.
Wheel Fun Rentals   *(503)738-8447*
downtown at 407 S. Holladay Dr. (and other outlets)
wheelfunrentals.com

★ *Boat Rentals*
You can skim across the calm water of the Necanicum River in town in a single or double kayak, pedal boat, barracuda or surfbike rented by the hour or longer at:
Wheel Fun Rentals   *(503)440-1548*
downtown at Convention Center Boat Dock
wheelfunrentals.com

★ **Downtown**   *(503)738-7361*
downtown on Broadway
Seaside was the first town on the Oregon coast to plan and develop a pedestrian-friendly main street by narrowing the roadway. By adding many shade trees, mini-gardens, benches and other street furniture, they effectively narrowed the roadway into a desirable strollway. Broadway between the main highway and the beach has a wealth of tourist-related shops and restaurants. Best of all, skill games, electronic amusements, and rides are still featured in a cluster of commercial entertainment places on Broadway. Some have gone high-tech, but the name of the game is family fun, as it has been for many decades. Success has also brought numerous new lodgings to the lively heart of town.

Food Specialties
★ **Bell Buoy Crab Co.**   *(503)738-2722   (800)529-2722*
1 mi. S at 1800 S. Roosevelt Dr.
bellbuoyofseaside.com
Bell Buoy Crab Co. is one of the West Coast's finest sources for Dungeness crab and salmon. For more than half a century, delicious fresh and canned Dungeness crab, whole or as crab leg meat, and fresh or smoked salmon, have been specialties in an impressive line of seasonally available fresh, smoked, and canned seafoods. Custom smoking or canning can also be arranged. Next door is a tiny cottage cafe with a picnic-table deck by a river.

★ **Fort Stevens State Park**   *(503)861-1671   (800)551-6949*
   17 mi. N via Hwy. 101
   oregonstateparks.org
The park features remnants of military installations that protected the mouth of the Columbia River from the Civil War through World War II. There is an interpretive center and self-guided trails to batteries, guardhouses, and earthworks. Nearby are camping and picnicking facilities, ocean beaches, sand dunes, and bike paths. Swimming areas with sandy beaches are on Coffenbury Lake, which is also popular for boating and fishing.

★ **The Promenade**
   N & S from downtown
Built in 1920, this concrete walkway borders the beach for nearly two miles. It is a delightful place to stroll, skate, or ride a bicycle with sand and surf views on one side and charming beach homes on the other. Near the midpoint, "the Turnaround" at the west end of Broadway (designated "End of the Lewis and Clark Trail") includes an impressive monument to the intrepid explorers.

Saddle Mountain State Park   *(800)551-6949*
   20 mi. E via Hwy. 26
   oregonstateparks.org
A two-and-a-half-mile trail leads to the top of 3,283-foot Saddle Mountain, one of the higher peaks in the Coast Range. From the summit there is an outstanding view on clear days. Unusual alpine wildflowers are tucked amid rocky crags along the way. Picnicking and primitive camping facilities are also available.

Seaside Aquarium   *(503)738-6211*
   downtown at 200 N. Prom
   seasideaquarium.com
The Seaside Aquarium, established in 1937, is one of the oldest aquariums on the West Coast. Today it is involved with contemporary oceanographic activities including giving visitors an opportunity to interact with sea life in an open touch tank. Harbor seals, jellyfish, wolf and moray eels, crabs, lobsters, and salmon are among the critters that can be viewed up-close.

★ **Seaside Beach**
   W of downtown
Bordering the west side of town is a broad beach of hard-packed sand backed by low dunes extending to the Promenade. Lifeguard services are provided in summer. While the inviting surf is inevitably cold, sunbathing and beachcombing are popular activities. One of the most popular surfing "breaks" along the entire Northwest coast is just south off the north side of Tillamook Head (**Cleanline Surf Shop**, (503)738-7888, rents surfboards, boogie boards, and all related equipment). To the

north beyond Gearhart, ten miles of hard sand beach is open to autos when the tide is low. It is an exhilarating scenic drive.

★ **Seaside Historical Society Museum**   *(503)738-7065*
   just N at 570 Necanicum Dr.
   seasidemuseum.org
This museum presents the history of the Northwest's first seaside resort. Displays depict Lewis and Clark saltmakers, and include a collection of early-day photographs, an 1899 diarama of Seaside, plus loggers and Clatsop Indian memorabilia. The Butterfield Cottage in a lovely garden showcases the early seaside resort era in a 1912 beach cottage. There is also a museum gift shop.

Sitka Spruce
   6 mi. SE via Hwys. 101 & 26
The world's (purportedly) largest Sitka spruce (216 feet tall, 53 feet in circumference) is the towering attraction of a little park near the Necanicum River. The monarch of the forest is estimated to be more than 400 years old, and it looks it.

★ **Tillamook Head**
   2 mi. SW via Sunset Blvd.
The area's most impressive landmark is a massive quarter-mile-high cape jutting into the sea between Seaside and Cannon Beach. **Tillamook Head National Recreation Trail** (six miles each way) rewards energetic hikers with memorable coastal panoramas while attaining a height of nearly 1,200 feet above sea level. The trailhead begins at a parking lot at the end of Sunset Road.

RESTAURANTS

★ **Bagels by the Sea**   *(503)717-9145*
   downtown at 210 S. Holladay Dr.
   B-L.   *Moderate*
Bagels by the Sea produces some of Oregon's finest bagels. The wealth of bagels includes some unusual specialties like pretzel, asiago, or cranberry-orange. Plain or with any of their spreads, they can be enjoyed with a wide variety of coffee or ice drinks plus light fare of soups, salads and sandwiches in the big cheerful coffee shop, or to go.

★ **Dooger's Seafood & Grill**   *(503)738-3773*
   downtown at 505 Broadway
   doogersseafoodandgrill.com
   L-D.   *Moderate*
The original (of a small coastal chain of restaurants) has some of the Northwest's best clam chowder. Regional seafoods including (in season) Dungeness crab claws and razor clams are prepared from scratch. Save room for the luscious, ever-popular peanut butter pie. The pleasant dining room overlooking the picturesque main street is an area favorite.

★ **Harrison's Bakery**   *(503)738-5331*
   downtown at 608 Broadway
   harrisonsbakery.com
   B-L.   *Low*
At this full-line takeout bakery, there has been a good selection of
coffee cakes and Danish pastries, plus breads and assorted
desserts, since 1902. Another outlet is by the Prom turnaround.

★ **Kalypso**   *(503)738-6302*
   downtown at 619 Broadway
   D only. Closed Mon.-Tues. off season.   *Moderate*
Kalypso is one of the Oregon coast's best showcases for the
bounty of the local sea and land. Fresh seasonal ingredients
emphasizing the Northwest are presented in creative dishes like
shrimp cakes, pan-fried sesame-seed-studded razor clams, or beer-
battered local rock fish with a caper-dill sauce. Housemade
desserts, similarly delicious, are served in a spacious split-level
dining room that reflects the evolving sophistication of the area.
There is also a nifty little raised, very comfortable lounge
overlooking the dining areas.

★ **Lil Bayou**   *(503)717-0624*
   downtown at 20 N. Holladay Dr.
   L-D. No L off-season. Closed Tues.   *Expensive*
Traditional Louisiana cuisine and some creative detours to take
advantage of fresh seasonal Northwestern ingredients distinguish
appetizers like shrimp remoulade, chicken and sausage gumbo,
shrimp jambalaya, and desserts like sweet potato pecan pie. The
dining areas and lounge have nifty New Orleans artifacts to
complement the flavorful cuisine.

★ **McKeown's**   *(503)738-5232*
   downtown at 714 Broadway
   B-L-D.   *Moderate*
McKeown's serves some of the best breakfasts on the Northern
Oregon coast. Scrambles, omelets and poached egg specialties all
come with delicious housemade scones and banana-nut bread.
Sauces and gravy are also excellent. Later, specialties like shrimp
or crab cobb salad, french-fried artichoke hearts with a lemon-
garlic dipping sauce, black and blue steak fajita quesadilla, or ale-
battered salmon and chips are served in a warm snazzy dining
room.

Norma's Ocean Diner   *(503)738-4331*
   downtown at 20 N. Columbia St.
   L-D.   *Moderate*
Clam chowder, razor or little neck clams, and other seafood, plus
homemade pies, are featured. The long-popular family-oriented
restaurant is in a cheerful dining room with casual nautical decor.

★ **Pacific Way Cafe & Bakery**   *(503)738-0245*
   2 mi. N at 601 Pacific Way - Gearhart
   L-D. Closed Tues.-Wed.   *Moderate*
Outstanding cinnamon rolls, croissants, and other pastries are
served with all sorts of beverages for breakfast in the bakery on
weekends. Spectacular fresh berry pies, crisps, and cakes
accompany designer sandwiches for lunch. Treats like Dungeness
crabcakes and a wide selection of pizzas are served for dinner in
the atmospheric plant-and-wood-trimmed cafe next door with a
lovely garden patio.

Pig 'n Pancake   *(503)738-7243*
   downtown at 323 Broadway
   pignpancake.com/seaside
   B-L-D.   *Moderate*
All kinds of well-made pancakes, including buttermilk,
buckwheat, sourdough and potato, are served along with a variety
of short order American fare. This popular family-oriented coffee
shop, the first of a small regional chain, overlooks the main street
and has a gift shop.

Rob's Family Restaurant   *(503)738-8722*
   1 mi. S at 1815 S. Roosevelt Dr.
   B-L-D.   *Moderate*
Rob's, since 1971, has been popular with natives and families
looking for traditional American comfort foods at all meals served
in a plain little coffee shop by the highway.

Shilo Inn Seaside Oceanfront Resort   *(503)738-8481*
   downtown at 30 N. Prom
   shiloinns.com
   B-L-D. Sun. brunch.   *Expensive*
Updated American dishes featuring regional seafoods in the
evening are served amidst casually elegant decor including unique
Northwestern wall art in the dining room of Seaside's landmark
hotel. The wraparound window-wall view of the Promenade,
beach, ocean and turnaround (shared with a snazzy entertainment lounge) is the best in town.

★ **Vista Sea Cafe**   *(503)738-8108*
   downtown at 150 Broadway
   L-D. Closed Tues.-Wed. except in summer.   *Moderate*
All kinds of designer and do-it-yourself pizzas with dough and
sauce made fresh daily are hand-tossed to order, and there is a
good small selection of salads served with their delicious beer
bread, and sandwiches made with house-baked rolls. Windows on
two sides give diners at high-backed wooden booths a nice outlook
on the main street.

LODGINGS

Among an impressive assortment of lodgings, the best have ocean views and are a stroll from the heart of town. High season is May through September. Prices at other times may be as much as 20% less.

Cannes Microtel Inn & Suites   *(503)738-8971*
1 mi. S at 2455 S. Roosevelt Dr. - 97138
cannesinn.com
60 units   *(866)482-7666*   *Moderate-Expensive*
This newer roadside motel has comfortably furnished units with one or two queen beds. Some have a refrigerator and microwave.
    "whirlpool room" (2 of these)–refrigerator, microwave,
        in-room two-person whirlpool, queen bed.

★ **Comfort Inn Boardwalk**   *(503)738-3011*
downtown at 545 Broadway - 97138
65 units   *(800)226-9815*   *Moderate-Very Expensive*
Seaside's newly remodeled Comfort Inn (built in 1996) is one of America's best representatives of the chain. A small indoor pool, whirlpool and sauna, plus complimentary expanded Continental breakfast, are features of this contemporary motel on the river and four blocks from the beach. Most of the beautifully furnished rooms overlook the peaceful little river and have a private patio or balcony, microwave, refrigerator, and two queens or a king bed.
    #325,#225–windows on two sides, private balcony by
        river, raised gas fireplace and two-person whirlpool,
        balcony with river/town view visible from king bed.

★ **Ebb Tide Motel**   *(503)738-8371*
downtown at 300 N. Prom - 97138
99 units   *(800)468-6232*   *Expensive*
This newly remodeled contemporary oceanfront motel has a large indoor pool, whirlpool, and saunas. Most of the attractively furnished rooms have a surf view, mini-kitchen, gas fireplace and one to three queens or a king bed.
    #200–kitchenette, gas fireplace, partial ocean view,
        two-person in-bath whirlpool, king bed.
    #400–kitchenette, gas fireplace, partial ocean view, two-person
        in-bath whirlpool, small private balcony, two queen beds.

★ **Edgewater Inn on the Prom**   *(503)738-4142*
downtown at 341 S. Prom - 97138
edgewaterinnontheprom.com
15 units   *(866)783-3784*   *Expensive*
The beach and prom adjoin this modern motel. Each well-
̄rnished unit has a full kitchen, gas fireplace and large whirlpool
  ̄h, and a queen bed.
    ̄ceanfront room" (several)–surf view from private balcony.

Gearhart by the Sea   *(503)738-8331*
   3 mi. N (on Marion Av.) at 10th St. (Box 2700) - Gearhart 97138
   gearhartresort.com
   92 units   *(800)547-0115*   *Expensive-Very Expensive*
Two large indoor pools, a whirlpool, and a (fee) 18-hole golf course
are features of this six-story condo complex above expansive low
dunes and a beach. The adjoining **Sandtrap Restaurant** (L-D)
has a golf course view. Each spacious, comfortably furnished one-
or two-bedroom unit (availability varies) has a kitchen, electric or
pressed-wood fireplace, and a private balcony. Most have an ocean
view and a queen or king bed.

Gilbert Inn Bed & Breakfast   *(503)738-9770*
   downtown at 341 Beach Dr. - 97138
   gilbertinn.com
   10 units   *(800)410-9770*   *Expensive*
Gilbert Inn is a handsome 1892 Queen Anne Victorian on a
landscaped site by the heart of town less than a block from the
beach. Hearty breakfasts and afternoon cookies are complimentary. Each cozy room elicits the feeling of yesteryear with
period furnishings and family heirlooms, plus all contemporary
amenities, a private bath and a queen bed.
   "Turret Room"–turret windows with peek
      at ocean, four-poster queen bed.

★ **Hi-Tide Motel**   *(503)738-8414*
   downtown at 30 Av. G - 97138
   hitide.citysearch.com
   64 units   *(800)621-9876*   *Expensive*
This shingled oceanfront motel has a small indoor pool and a
whirlpool. Each well-furnished unit has a gas fireplace, mini-
kitchen and two queens or a king bed. Many also have a private
balcony and an ocean view.
   #305,#205–corner, kitchenette, gas fireplace,
      great beach view from private balcony, king bed.

Holiday Inn Express Hotel & Suites Seaside   *(503)717-8000*
   downtown at 34 N. Holladay Dr. - 97138
   hiexpress.com/seasideor
   79 units   *(800)465-4328*   *Expensive-Very Expensive*
New in 2005, the Holiday Inn Express Hotel & Suites Seaside is
near the beach in the heart of town and has an indoor pool,
whirlpool, sauna and exercise room. Each well-furnished room has
a refrigerator, microwave and two queens or king bed. Some
rooms also have a whirlpool bath or private balcony.

★ **Inn at the Shore**   *(503)738-3113*
   1 mi. S at 2275 S. Prom - 97138

innattheshore.com
18 units   (800)713-9914   *Expensive-Very Expensive*
One of the nicest lodgings on the Oregon coast opened in 1995 at
the quiet end of the Prom on the beach. Use of bikes is
complimentary. All of the beautifully furnished studio-to-two-
bedroom oceanfront suites have a fine view of sand and surf, a gas
fireplace, a private balcony or patio, and two queens or a king bed.
   #301,#201,#302,#202–romantic, corner studio
      with microwave and refrigerator, in-bath two-
      person whirlpool, gas fireplace, private balcony,
      terrific ocean/Tillamook Head view from king bed.

★ **Inn of the Four Winds**   *(503)738-9524*
   just N at 820 N. Prom - 97138
   innofthefourwinds.com
   14 units   (800)818-9524   *Expensive*
The Prom and beach are right in front of this skillfully upgraded
contemporary inn. Each of the well-furnished units has a wet bar,
refrigerator, microwave, raised gas fireplace, and one or two
queen beds. Many have a fine ocean/Prom view from a private
balcony.
   #206–outstanding alcove window view of Prom, beach,
      and ocean, private partial ocean-view balcony, queen bed.

The Lanai at the Cove   *(503)738-6343*
   2 mi. S at 3140 Sunset Blvd. - 97138
   seasidelanai.com
   18 units   (800)738-2683   *Moderate*
On Sunset Beach, this modern condominium motel has a small
outdoor pool. Each spacious, individually comfortably furnished
unit has a refrigerator or kitchenette and a double or queen bed.
Ocean-view units have lanais or patios by the beach.

Motel 6   *(503)738-6269*
   1 mi. S at 2369 S. Roosevelt Dr. - 97138
   motel6.com
   53 units   (800)466-8356   *Moderate*
This recent addition to the moderately priced chain has
comfortably furnished units with one or two queen beds.
   "whirlpool room" (2 of these)–in-room
      two-person whirlpool, king bed.

★ **Ocean View Resort - Best Western**   *(503)738-3334*
   downtown at 414 N. Prom - 97138
   oceanviewresort.com
   107 units   (800)234-8439   *Expensive-Very Expensive*
The beach and Prom border this contemporary five-story motor
hotel with an indoor pool, whirlpool, restaurant and bar. Many of
the recently renovated, beautifully furnished rooms have a

refrigerator and microwave, private ocean-view balcony or patio, gas fireplace, and one or two queens or a king bed
  #504,#404,#304,#204,#503,#403,#303,#203–
    spacious, raised gas fireplace, kitchenette, private
    balcony that shares spectacular ocean view with
    two-person whirlpool, king bed.

Royale Motel   *(503)738-9541*
  downtown at 531 Av. A - 97138
  royalemotel.com
  26 units   *(888)345-1012*   *Low-Moderate*
This motel by the river is an easy stroll to downtown and the beach. Each comfortably furnished room has one or two doubles or one or two queen beds.

Sand and Sea Condominium   *(503)738-8441*
  downtown at 475 S. Prom (Box 945) - 97138
  sand-and-sea.com
  30 units   *(800)628-2371*   *Expensive-Very Expensive*
This modern six-level oceanfront condominium/motel has a small round indoor pool and saunas. Each individually comfortably furnished one- or two-bedroom condo has a floor-to-ceiling window, kitchen, private view balcony, gas fireplace, and a queen or king bed.
    "oceanfront"–one bedroom, kitchen,
      gas log fireplace, floor-to-ceiling windows,
      private balcony, ocean view.

★ **Sea Side Inn**   *(503)738-6403*
  downtown at 581 S. Prom - 97138
  15 units   *(800)772-7766*   *Expensive-Very Expensive*
One of the area's newer oceanfront bed-and-breakfasts is in a four-story building with a clock tower that opened in 1994 on the Promenade. Full breakfast is complimentary. Each well-furnished themed room features an eclectic mix of antiques and contemporary furniture and a plethora of knickknacks, refrigerator, and contemporary amenities like a private bath. Some also have a gas fireplace, one- or two-person whirlpool bath, and a queen or king bed.

The Seashore Inn   *(503)738-6368*
  downtown at 60 N. Prom - 97138
  seashoreinn.com
  54 units   *(888)738-6368*   *Expensive*
By the beach and prom in the heart of town, this modern three-story motel has a large indoor pool, whirlpool and sauna. Each room is nicely furnished and has one or two queens or a king bed.
    third floor oceanfront–small balcony overlooking
      prom/ocean, two queens or king bed.

★ **Shilo Inn Seaside Oceanfront Resort**   *(503)738-9571*
downtown at 30 N. Prom - 97138
shiloinns.com
    112 units   *(800)222-2244*   *Expensive-Very Expensive*
Seaside's most complete hotel has a choice site by the beach and
Promenade at the turnaround. Other features of the recently
remodeled and upgraded contemporary five-story complex include
an indoor pool, whirlpool, steam room, sauna, exercise room, and
gift shop, plus a view restaurant (see listing) and lounge with live
entertainment. Each room is beautifully furnished, and has a
microwave, mini-refrigerator, and two queens or a king bed.
    "deluxe oceanfront suite" (several)–ocean/Prom
       view, private balcony, kitchenette, gas fireplace,
       two queens or king bed.
The Tides   *(503)738-6317*
1 mi. S at 2316 Beach Dr. - 97138
thetidesbythesea.com
    53 units   *(800)548-2846*   *Moderate-Expensive*
This modern motel/condominium has some fine beachfront units
just beyond the south end of the Prom. There is a large outdoor
pool. Each spacious, nicely furnished studio-to-two-bedroom unit
has a refrigerator and microwave, and one or more double, queen
or king bed(s). Full kitchen and pressed-wood fireplace units are
available.

Sisters

Sisters is a celebration of the artistic sensibilities and natural grandeur of the Old West. Dramatically overseen by the three "sister" peaks (Faith, Hope, and Charity) from which its name is derived, this unassuming village is clearly inspired by its favored natural setting. A full four-season climate provides all sorts of recreation opportunities amid idyllic alpine settings. In addition, townsfolk hail the arrival of warm weather with luxuriant seasonal floral displays throughout the stylish downtown.

Sisters was given its distinctive name in the 1880s when trappers and loggers settled here to take advantage of abundant resources in surrounding forests. Growth was slow–and set back when major fires destroyed much of the town. In recent years, improvements in recreation equipment and clothing have boosted travelers' interest in Sisters toward its ultimate role as a major tourist destination.

Copious local pine wood and sensitivity of locals to the special site has fostered a woodsy Old West architectural style perfectly attuned to the alpine setting. The charming downtown now showcases art galleries; specialty shops featuring local arts, crafts and foods; good restaurants; and delightful bed-and-breakfast inns. Lodgings in the pines provide another way to enjoy the unspoiled setting. Outdoor recreation is passionately embraced, with opportunities galore to use surrounding forests, rivers, and mountains. The infectious beauty of the setting is reflected in a uncommon prevalence of friendly villagers in a place where peo choose to live just because they really like being here.

WEATHER PROFILE

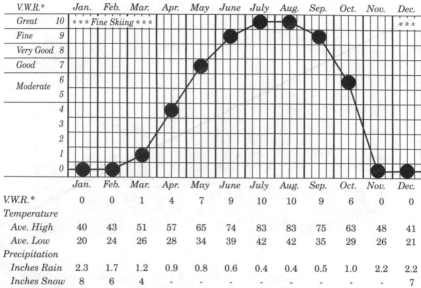

V.W.R.*		Jan.	Feb.	Mar.	Apr.	May	June	July	Aug.	Sep.	Oct.	Nov.	Dec.
Great	10	*** Fine Skiing ***											***
Fine	9												
Very Good	8												
Good	7												
Moderate	6												
	5												
	4												
	3												
	2												
	1												
	0												

	Jan.	Feb.	Mar.	Apr.	May	June	July	Aug.	Sep.	Oct.	Nov.	Dec.
V.W.R.*	0	0	1	4	7	9	10	10	9	6	0	0
Temperature												
Ave. High	40	43	51	57	65	74	83	83	75	63	48	41
Ave. Low	20	24	26	28	34	39	42	42	35	29	26	21
Precipitation												
Inches Rain	2.3	1.7	1.2	0.9	0.8	0.6	0.4	0.4	0.5	1.0	2.2	2.2
Inches Snow	8	6	4	-	-	-	-	-	-	-	-	7

* V.W.R. = Vokac Weather Rating: probability of mild (warm & dry) weather on any given day.

BASIC INFORMATION

Population: 959
Elevation: 3,160 feet
Location: 150 miles Southeast of Portland
Airport (regularly scheduled flights): Redmond - 20 miles

...sters Area Chamber of Commerce   (541)549-0251
...owntown at 164 N. Elm St. (Box 430) - 97759
...terschamber.com

ATTRACTIONS

★ *Bicycling*

In summer bicycles can be rented by the hour or longer to enjoy numerous scenic byways and separated bikeways. Mountain bikes are also available for use on a vast network of forest and logging roads, especially in the expansive Black Butte Resort where gentle grades make touring easy through luxuriant forests, along tranquil streams, and past small ponds and lakes with snow-capped volcanic peak backdrops. For rentals and info, contact:

Black Butte Ranch   *(541)595-1258*
8 mi. W via Hwy. 20

★ **Deschutes National Forest**   *(541)549-7700*
surrounds Sisters
fs.fed.us/r6/deschutes

This luxuriant pine forest is one of the West's largest and most scenic alpine playgrounds. A series of volcanic peaks is topped by Mt. Jefferson 10,497 feet above sea level. Shimmering glaciers and abundant waterfalls, clear streams, and small lakes are the reward for hikers on hundreds of miles of alpine trails. Backpacking, horseback riding and pack trips are ways to access the spectacular wilderness portions of the forest. Roads provide access to trailheads, picnic sites, and campgrounds with outstanding views of nearby peaks and streams famous for fishing, river running, kayaking and canoeing (see listings).

★ **Downtown**
on and around Hwy. 20 (Cascade Av.)

Here is a genuine Western village that took its tiny origins as a stage stop/hotel seriously. For years, downtown Sisters has fostered distinctively Old West-style architecture and decor, making maximum use of surrounding pine forest materials. Today, the main street (Cascade Avenue–Highway 20) is a picturesque collection of specialty shops, arts and crafts galleries, restaurants and bakeries in wood-trim buildings surrounded by colorful gardens and flower baskets in summer.

★ *Fishing*

The Fly Fisher's Place   *(541)549-3474*
downtown at 151 W. Main Av.
theflyfishersplace.com

"Home water" guides for the Metolius River and other nearby streams have the latest in fishing reports and equipment to improve visitors' luck year-round. Professional guides will make all arrangements for half-day to multi-day trout fishing trips by drift boat or on foot into surrounding forests.

Food Specialties

★ **Sisters Coffee Company**   *(541)549-0527   (800)524-5282*
downtown at 273 W. Hood Av.
sisterscoffee.com
Sisters Coffee Company is a long-established source for premium brews. The tiny outlet expanded in 2005 to a much-larger adjacent space where guests can enjoy assorted coffee with light fare at indoor and outdoor seating or to go.

★ **Head of the Metolius Observation Point**   *(541)595-6117*
14 mi. NW via Hwy 20 & SW F.S. Rd. 1419 - Camp Sherman
metoliusriver.com
A quarter-mile hike down a paved forest trail ends at an overlook of a river with a grand view of glacier-shrouded Mt. Jefferson towering above the broad clear stream and the forest beyond. Looking to the left at the Observation Point you become aware that the full-size stream has abruptly appeared out of the adjoining hillside. (See listing for **Metolius River Recreation Area** for other features in this area.)

★ **McKenzie Pass-Santiam Pass National Scenic Byway**
86 mile loop via Hwys. 242 & 126 through town
This paved loop road (closed in winter, and to vehicles over 35 feet) showcases the greatest concentration of snow- and glacier-shrouded volcanic peaks in the coterminous United States. The highway crosses the National Pacific Crest Trail twice, and numerous other trailheads lead to hundreds of miles of trails into the forest and wilderness areas. Sahalie Falls and several others are on this route, as are several picturesque lakes–like Clear Lake. Spectacular overlooks are also numerous, including the panoramic scene from Dee Wright Observatory, Windy Point Overlook, and Belknap Crater viewpoint.

★ **Metolius River Recreation Area**   *(541)595-6117*
13 mi. NW via Hwys. 20 & 14 - Camp Sherman
metoliusriver.com
From where it begins in a pine-shaded hillside, the Metolius (a designated National Wild and Scenic River) flows crystal-clear for miles through a luxuriant pine forest backed by volcanic peaks. It is one of the nation's most popular fly-fishing-only streams with a variety of trout, plus kokanee. Several cabin complexes (see listings), a fine restaurant, full service campground, and a general store line the banks of this picturesque stream.

★ ***River Running***
Sisters has two major outfitters offering half-day to two-day trips on the cold, crystal-clear McKenzie River with exciting (Class II and Class III) rapids and fine mountain scenery near the Three Sisters Wilderness for rafters from March to October.

Destination Wilderness   *(541)549-1336   (800)423-8868*
downtown at 101 W. Main Av. (Box 1965) - 97759
www.wildernesstrips.com
McKenzie River Adventures *(541)822-3806 (800)832-5858*
downtown at Cascade Av. & Pine St. (Box 567) - 97759
mckenzieriveradventures.com

★ *Sculpture*
1 mi. E on Hwy. 20
Life imitates art close to Sisters' eastern city limits where a handsome herd of horses gathers near a fence by the highway. Beyond, in the same broad pasture, cowboys gallop after horses running free in a dramatic tableau of iron sculptures. The far horizon punctuated by glacier-clad volcanic peaks completes the spellbinding "Old West" scene.

★ *Specialty Shops*
The Gallimaufry   *(541)549-9841*
downtown at 111 W. Cascade Av.
The Gallimaufry is a large, diverse gift store that features a wide selection of Oregon-related gifts, Sisters' best selection of premium Oregon wines, and some Oregon-made specialty jams and food products.

The Oregon Store   *(541)549-6700   (800)541-5797*
downtown at 271 W. Cascade Av.
theoregonstore.com
The Sisters outlet of a first-rate chain of stores features premium-quality arts, crafts, food products, books and more about Oregon in handsome displays. Samples of gourmet products are offered on summer weekends.

Sisters Drug & Gift   *(541)549-6221*
downtown at 211 E. Cascade Av.
This is the home of **Truly Oregon** & **Cooks Nook** in addition to a full-service drug store. All three sections have a generous spirit regarding samples and extensive collections of gifts made in Oregon and items related to Sisters.

Winter Sports
Hoodoo Ski Area   *(541)822-3799*
22 mi. NW via Hwy. 20
hoodoo.com
This small ski area appeals to whole families with a vertical drop of 1,035 feet and a top elevation of only 5,700 feet served by five chairlifts. Downhill, snowboard and cross-country skiing are popular. The Hoodoo's Autobahn takes you and your tube to the top of a hill with sixteen 800-foot runs for an exciting, fun alternative to skiing and snowboarding. The season is normally late November to mid-April.

RESTAURANTS

Angeline's Bakery & Cafe   *(541)549-9122*
downtown at 121 W. Main Av.
B-L.   *Moderate*
A limited selection of delicious muffins and scones is available for breakfast; along with bagels and breads with designer spreads for lunch with desserts like lime bars. They can be enjoyed at the few tables inside, out back in a tree-shaded grassy courtyard, or to go.

★ **Black Butte Ranch**   *(541)595-1260*
   8 mi. NW(via Hwy. 20)at 12930 Hawks Beard Rd.-Black Butte Rch.
   blackbutteranch.com
   B-L-D. Sun. brunch.   *Moderate-Expensive*
The **Restaurant at the Lodge** (B-L-D–Expensive) features, appropriately, ranch favorites like locally farmed elk, slow-roasted prime rib, a center-cut Porterhouse pork chop topped with blueberry cream sauce and hazelnuts, and housemade desserts. The dining room is a multilevel architectural gem with tall window views of spectacular nearby volcanic peaks. Each table is set with fresh flowers, candles and full linen to further enhance the special-occasion feeling of the restaurant. Upstairs is a mountain-view lounge. The **Restaurant at Big Meadow Clubhouse** (B-L-D. Sun. brunch–Moderate) offers upscale Northwestern comfort foods from steamer clam appetizers to wild-caught salmon in a stylish dining room with a panoramic view from the clubhouse and terrace of splendid volcanic peaks and a golf course.

★ **Bronco Billy's Ranch Grill & Saloon**   *(541)549-7427*
   downtown at 190 E. Cascade Av.
   broncobillysranchgrill.com
   L-D.   *Moderate*
Old-time Western grub is updated with some nifty flourishes at Bronco Billy's. Flavorful dishes are served in a dining room distinguished by Western artifacts and a large movie poster of Bronco Billy (a.k.a. Clint Eastwood). Don't miss the adjoining saloon through swinging wood doors. It's a nostalgic treat all the way, and is deservedly popular as the town's gathering place as it has been from a century ago when a hotel was upstairs.

Coyote Creek Cafe   *(541)549-9514*
   just NW (in Three Winds Shopping Ctr.) at 497 Hwy. 20 W
   B-L-D.   *Moderate*
Concern for fresh seasonal ingredients elevates this coffee shop's traditional American and Southwestern dishes. The comfortable wood-trimmed split-level dining rooms have a pleasant peek-a-boo view of mountains through the pines. There is also a sports bar, and live entertainment on weekends.

Depot Deli & Cafe   *(541)549-2572*
downtown at 250 W. Cascade Av.
B-L-D.   *Moderate*
Casual comfort foods are served at all meals in a room with a
train running around the walls, out back under a shade tree, or
on a front porch overlooking main street.

El Rancho Grande   *(541)549-3594*
downtown at 150 E. Cascade Av.
L-D.   *Moderate*
A wide selection of traditional and innovative Mexican dishes is
offered here including shrimp in nearly a dozen dishes served in
several comfortable little dining areas.

★ **The Gallery Restaurant**   *(541)549-2631*
downtown at 171 W. Cascade Av.
B-L-D.   *Moderate*
The long-established Gallery Restaurant offers a wide assortment
of traditional American dishes including housemade specialties
like applesauce and cinnamon rolls for breakfast, and pies for
dessert. A large dining room with a choice of padded booths or
counter chairs reflects the "Sisters style" of knotty pine, wood
trim and interesting use of Western artifacts for accents, plus
picture-window views of a park and main street.

★ **Kokanee Cafe**   *(541)595-6420*
15 mi. NW at 25545 SW F.S. Rd. 1419 - Camp Sherman
D only. Closed Nov.-mid-Apr.   *Expensive*
One of the most renowned dining destinations in the region is
Kokanee Cafe. Northwestern cuisine is given skilled careful
attention in dishes ranging from wild forest mushroom ragu
through Oregon-grown buffalo burger to roasted rack of lamb, or
grilled rainbow trout with citrus tarragon stuffing. Delicious
desserts made here include marionberry crisp and kokanee mud
pie. A lodge in the pines offers indoor seating with a working fireplace (seasonally), or on an enclosed deck when weather permits.

★ **The Lodge at Suttle Lake**   *(541)595-2628*
14 mi. NW at 13300 Hwy. 20
thelodgeatsuttlelake.com
L-D.   *Moderate*
In the **Boathouse Restaurant**, Northwestern cuisine is featured
in dishes like wild salmon with strawberry balsamic reduction
served with an outstanding house salad (blue cheese, chili roasted
walnuts, dried cranberries, grilled apple and balsamic vinaigrette)
and a fresh multi-fruit cobbler for dessert. The knotty-pine
interior of a handsome rustic lodge is oriented toward picture-
window views of the tranquil little lake amid gentle pine-shrouded
mountains.

Martolli's *(541)549-8356*
 downtown at 220 W. Cascade Av.
 L-D. *Moderate*
Designer meat and vegie pizzas or create-your-own pizza and calzone prepared from dough and sauces made fresh daily are served in a plain popular little parlor at picnic tables overlooking main street.

★ **Sisters Bakery** *(541)549-0361*
 downtown at 251 E. Cascade Av.
 B-L. *Moderate*
Sisters Bakery is a long-established foodie landmark with world-class baked goods. Multi-layered cases display a plethora of decadent delights ranging from huge cinnamon rolls or scones made with fresh seasonal berries through all sorts of donuts to the finest delicate pastry–apple dumpling–anywhere. Assorted breads are also made here. Locals and tourists alike wait happily in line for the tasty treats to be enjoyed at a few tables by the displays or in a nifty landscaped alcove beside the building, or to go.

Sno-Cap Drive In *(541)549-6151*
 downtown at 380 W. Cascade Av.
 redmondcommunity.com/snocap.html
 L-D. *Moderate*
Many flavors of their homemade ice cream like cascade blackberry can be enjoyed by the scoop or in a shake, along with popular burgers made here and other drive-in fare in your car, in their cafe, or on an umbrella-shaded patio.

LODGINGS

Lodgings are relatively scarce, but invariably in keeping with the "alpine backcountry" motif. Motels, bed-and-breakfasts, and resorts are each represented by one or more world-class lodgings. High season is May through September. Rates may be reduced by 10% or more at other times. Overflow bargain lodgings are available in Redmond (19 miles east) and also in Bend (30 miles east).

Aspen Meadow Lodge *(541)549-4312*
 1 mi. E at 68733 Junipine Lane (Box 912) - 97759
 sisterslodging.com
 5 units *(866)549-4312* *Moderate-Expensive*
Aspen trees and Ponderosa pines border Squaw Creek and shade this contemporary motel/lodge-and-breakfast. Full breakfast is complimentary, as is use of a whirlpool. Each well-furnished unit has a private bath, refrigerator, microwave, and queens or a king bed.

★ **Black Butte Ranch**   *(541)595-6211*
8 mi. NW (on Hwy. 20) (Box 8000) - Black Butte Ranch 97759
blackbutteranch.com
130 units   (800)452-7455   Moderate-Expensive
A small spring-fed lake in a high country meadow, surrounded by a Ponderosa pine forest backed by a trio of snow-capped peaks, is the site of this superb condo/home resort. Recreation facilities include a large pool by the lake (plus three others), whirlpools, saunas, hiking and jogging trails, a recreation center, and (for a fee) two scenic 18-hole golf courses, many tennis courts, bicycles, horseback riding and canoes. The handsome wood-toned lodge has a plush dining room (see listing) and lounge with spectacular views. Units range from well-furnished lodge rooms to spacious beautifully furnished condominiums and private houses. All have a private view deck and queen or king bed. Many have a kitchen and fireplace.
   "Lodge condominium"–one-bedroom, spacious, kitchen, (pressed or woodburning) fireplace, (many have) lake and mountain view.
   "Deluxe bedroom"–in lodge, spacious, fireplace.

★ **Blue Spruce Bed & Breakfast**   *(541)549-9644*
downtown at 444 S. Spruce St. (Box 1904) - 97759
www.blue-spruce.biz
4 units   (888)328-9644   Expensive
Blue Spruce is one of central Oregon's best bed-and-breakfasts. A large wood-trim ranch house-style building designed as a bed-and-breakfast opened in 1999 in a quiet residential area a stroll from the village center. A full gourmet breakfast (like lemon souffle pancakes with blueberries), and fresh cookies and ice cream, are complimentary. Each spacious, Western-themed room is beautifully furnished and includes extra amenities, a small refrigerator, gas fireplace, a sitting area, private bath with towel warmers, rain-bath shower, two-person whirlpool tub, and a king bed.

Comfort Inn at Sisters   *(541)549-7829*
just NW at 540 Hwy. 20 W (Box 938) - 97759
comfortinn.com
50 units   (800)228-5150   Moderate
An indoor pool and whirlpool are features of this contemporary motel with an adjoining RV park. Each unit is comfortably furnished and has two queens or a king bed.

★ **Conklin's Guest House**   *(541)549-0123*
1 mi. E at 69013 Camp Polk Rd. - 97759
conklinsguesthouse.com
5 units   (800)549-4262   Moderate-Expensive

A historic Craftsman-style home in a tranquil pastoral setting is surrounded by colorful gardens, a heated pool and expansive lawns extending to a gazebo, two stocked ponds with fishing and splendid views of the Cascades. A full country breakfast and evening refreshments are complimentary. Each room showcases country charm with beautifully individualized furnishings and has a private bath, one or two twin beds and a queen bed. In 2006, the name will change, and the property will become an inn with new upscale amenities and cottages.

"Morning Glory"–spacious, view balcony, in-room
  clawfoot tub with mountain view, twin and queen bed.
"Forget-Me-Not"–pastoral view, gas fireplace, view
  deck, in-bath clawfoot tub, twin and queen bed.

Grand Palace Hotel   *(541)549-2211*
downtown at 101 E. Cascade Av. (Box 2251) - 97759
grandpalacehotelsisters.com
5 units   *Moderate-Expensive*
Check in at Helen's Antique Store and go upstairs to a Western-themed suite in a little Old West-style hotel that opened in mid-2005 in the heart of town. All of the units have a full kitchen or kitchenette, a private bath, and one or more queen beds. Most are spacious including quality antiques (for sale), are individually well furnished, and have close-up village views.

★ **Lake Creek Lodge**   *(541)595-6331*
14 mi. NW at 13375 SW F.S. Rd. 1419 - Camp Sherman 97730
lakecreeklodge.com
18 units   *(800)797-6331*   *Expensive*
Rustic cabins on the banks of the beautiful Metolius River share pine-shaded grounds with a large pools, two tennis courts, a basketball court, hike-and-bike path, and a game room with pool and ping pong. The **Lodge Dining Room** (B-D–Moderate) features country buffet dinners in summer, and hearty breakfast in the wood-trim lodge on a forest-view deck. All comfortably furnished one- to three-bedroom cabins have knotty-pine wood trim, a full kitchen or kitchenette, private porch, and twins and/or queen beds. Most have a gas fireplace or wood stove.

"Cabin #1," "Cabin #2"–two bedrooms, fine view
  of creek and pond, gas fireplace in living room,
  full kitchen, two twins and one queen bed.

★ **The Lodge at Suttle Lake**   *(541)595-2628*
14 mi. NW at 13300 Hwy. 20 - 97759
thelodgeatsuttlelake.com
25 units   *Moderate-Very Expensive*
This complex is tucked into a dense pine forest along the shore of pretty little Suttle Lake with opportunities for swimming, fishing,

hiking on a trail around the lake, and mountain biking (rentals available here), plus rentals of paddleboats, rowboats, canoes or kayaks in summer. In winter, cross-country skiing and snow-mobiling from here are popular. New in 2005 is a handsome new lakefront lodge building with a classic look of elegant Western rusticity. The grounds also include a restaurant (see listing), general store and marina. Rooms (up to two bedrooms) feature mountain cabin decor ranging from rustic to plush, and from simply furnished to beautifully furnished.

"Deluxe Suite" (4 of these)–studio with fine view
    of lake, state-of-the-art amenities, exclusive use
    of private beach, gas fireplace, in-bath whirlpool
    tub, queen sofabed and king bed.

"Cabin Fever," "Northern Exposure," "Bear Hollow,"
    "Trapper's Retreat"–lake-view luxury one-bedroom
    cabins (many with flagstone/wood touches), stone
    gas fireplace, full kitchen, gas barbecue grill on private
    private porch, queen sofa sleeper, loft with twin beds,
    queen bed.

"The Pointe"–two bedrooms, two baths, kitchen,
    spectacular lake view, private dock, two twin beds
    and two queen beds.

★ **Metolius River Lodges**   *(541)595-6290*
    15 mi. NW at 12390 SW F.S. Rd. 1419 (Box 110)-Camp Sherman 97730
    metoliusriverlodges.com
    13 units   *(800)595-6290*   *Moderate-Expensive*
Rustic cabins and studios in the pines are strung along the banks of the crystal-clear Metolius River, famous for fly-fishing. Trails lead along the river and into the nearby lush Ponderosa forest. All of the comfortably furnished knotty-pine-trimmed units have a microwave and refrigerator, and most also have a woodburning fireplace and doubles or a queen bed.

"Dragonfly"–two bedroom, fireplace in living room,
    full kitchen, private deck by river, double and queen bed.

★ **Ponderosa Lodge - Best Western**   *(541)549-1234*
    just NW at 505 Hwy. 20 West (Box 218) - 97759
    bestwesternsisters.com
    77 units   *(888)549-4321*   *Expensive*
Ponderosa Lodge is one of the Pacific Northwest's finest motels. The contemporary two-story complex on expansive pine-shaded grounds surrounds a large garden courtyard with a pool and whirlpool. Some of the owner's gentle llamas are in an adjoining pasture. Hiking paths extend into the adjacent national forest, and to the nearby heart of the village. Expanded Continental

breakfast is complimentary. Each spacious room is beautifully furnished with all contemporary and extra amenities, refrigerator, microwave, a private balcony or patio overlooking the courtyard, and two queens or a king bed.

"Aspen Suites" (20 of these)–opened 2004, spacious, romantic, corner river-rock raised gas fireplace, large TV/DVD, overstuffed leather armchair and ottoman, walk-in rain-bath shower, oversized whirlpool tub in view of king bed.

Sisters Motor Lodge *(541)549-2551*
just W at 511 W. Cascade Av. (Box 28) - 97759
11 units *Moderate-Expensive*

One of the oldest motels in Oregon is this single-level motor lodge dating from 1942. It has been delightfully upgraded over the years. Full breakfast is complimentary in summer. Beautifully landscaped grounds surround comfortably furnished units (up to two bedrooms) with queen or king beds.

"Honeymoon Suite"–vaulted ceiling, private deck with spectacular mountain view, refrigerator, queen bed.

"Oregon Lodge"–spectacular mountain views, full kitchen, queen bed.

Quality of Life in the Great Towns

The preceding pages have all of the information you need to transform your ideas and dreams into fun-filled travel adventures and vacations. But, suppose you fall in love with one of the great towns of Oregon after a memorable visit. What if you decide that you might want to live there?

The following pages will help you consider relocation to a great town. To support easy consistent comparisons, numbers shown in most categories are a percentage of the national norm. Data sources included: U. S. Bureau of the Census; U. S. Department of Commerce, Comparative Climatic Data for Oregon; County and City Data Books; local police and sheriff departments and Federal Bureau of Investigation Uniform Crime Reports; local publications in each town featuring real estate information; each great town's chamber of commerce and/or convention and visitors bureau, plus extensive field research.

Seven indicators summarize key aspects about quality of life. A final chart addresses demographics through selected basic characteristics of the population of each town.

(1) Most would agree that a great town should have certain amenities and services that we take for granted in big cities. Towns are checked for each of twelve "Basic Facilities" (airport, hospital, library, etc.).

(2) Downtown Vitality reflects the way a town charms us with places to go and things to do day and night in a compact, engaging central business district.

(3) Crime concerns everyone. While recent data suggest that major cities are becoming safer, most great towns continue to be substantially safer than cities.

(4) Weather in Oregon's great towns ranges from mild (supporting semi-tropical palms and flowers) year-round, to classic four seasons (including heavy winter snow) to official "rain forest" status (along the northern Oregon coast).

(5) The Overall Livability Rating is a composite of the above factors plus extent of: independence from other places; a notable geographic setting; and cultural amenities.

(6) Housing Affordability compares housing cost in each town to the national median.

(7) In the final table, the Vokac Index of Livability and Affordability (VILA)© is used to quantify the relationship between Quality of Life and Housing Cost. An ideal town with a "perfect" Quality of Life and the nation's median housing cost would score "100." How well do you suppose Oregon's great towns did? Their ranks and scores are presented in the Livability/Affordability Table.

Basic Facilities

	Airport Nearby	Hospital	Library	High School	College	Lodging Landmark	Live Theater	Movie Theater	Park	Swimming Pool	Newspaper	Radio Station
Ashland	✓	✓	✓	✓	✓	✓	✓	✓	✓	✓	✓	✓
Astoria		✓	✓	✓	✓	✓	✓	✓	✓	✓	✓	✓
Baker City		✓	✓	✓		✓	✓	✓	✓	✓	✓	✓
Bandon		✓	✓	✓		✓	✓	✓	✓			
Bend	✓	✓	✓	✓	✓				✓	✓	✓	✓
Brookings			✓	✓			✓	✓	✓	✓	✓	✓
Cannon Beach		✓	✓				✓	✓	✓			
Florence		✓	✓	✓			✓	✓	✓	✓		✓
Gold Beach		✓	✓	✓		✓			✓			✓
Grants Pass	✓	✓	✓	✓	✓	✓	✓	✓	✓	✓	✓	✓
Hood River	✓	✓	✓	✓		✓	✓	✓	✓	✓	✓	✓
Jacksonville	✓	✓	✓				✓	✓				
Joseph		✓	✓	✓		✓				✓	✓	
Lincoln City		✓	✓	✓		✓	✓	✓		✓	✓	✓
McMinnville	✓	✓	✓	✓	✓	✓	✓	✓	✓	✓	✓	✓
Newport		✓	✓	✓	✓	✓	✓	✓	✓	✓	✓	✓
Seaside		✓	✓	✓		✓	✓	✓	✓	✓	✓	✓
Sisters	✓		✓	✓		✓			✓	✓	✓	

To be viewed as "complete and convenient," a community needs easy access to important amenities and services. Easy access to an airport (within a half-hour drive) and a hospital (within fifteen minutes) are conveniences that people do not want to give up when they leave the big city. Other facilities are important to have right in town in order to foster community identity and spirit. Those include a library (preferably located downtown), high school (within town limits), college or university, landmark lodging (preferably downtown), live and movie theaters, public park, and swimming pool. Local media (newspaper and radio station) provide a fundamental communication link among residents, and an important local perspective. For any of these facilities not available locally, there is a price to pay in loss of town character and fellowship. The table displays a check mark for each key facility in town or, in the case of airport and hospital, nearby within a reasonable distance.

Downtown Vitality

Rank		Total Score*
1	Ashland	100
2	Bend	97
2	Seaside	97
4	Astoria	94
4	Grants Pass	94
6	Cannon Beach	92
6	Hood River	92
6	McMinnville	92
9	Baker City	91
10	Newport	87
11	Jacksonville	82
12	Bandon	76
13	Florence	75
14	Lincoln City	68
14	Sisters	68
16	Gold Beach	60
17	Joseph	56
18	Brookings	50
-----	--------------------------	-----
(6)	Portland	92

Total Score=% of a "perfect" downtown (expressed as 100).

Vitality of the heart of town is a keystone of any community. Each downtown was evaluated on more than two dozen attributes related to the cohesion and completeness of the central business district. Library architecture, book collection, length of operating hours and special facilities were considered. Since a lodging landmark often provides a central place for meetings, dining and drinking as well as overnight lodgings, the facilities of the principal hotel were reviewed. Quality and quantity of restaurants were rated since dining is both a necessity and a pleasure. Another favorite pastime, shopping, was rated for distinctiveness and breadth. The location and scope of movie and live theaters were reviewed, along with choices of both day and nighttime leisure pursuits. Availability of free (non-metered) parking both on the street and in lots; quality of parks; and scenic, usable water features were also given careful attention. The composite score represents the extent to which a downtown succeeds as an exciting, pedestrian-friendly center appealing to both residents and visitors for business and leisure-time fun.

Crime

Rank		Risk of Violent Crime*
1	Joseph	21
2	Brookings	25
3	Jacksonville	28
4	Hood River	29
5	Baker City	31
6	Ashland	33
7	Sisters	39
8	Cannon Beach	40
9	Astoria	42
10	McMinnville	43
11	Bandon	44
12	Gold Beach	46
13	Bend	47
14	Grants Pass	51
15	Newport	80
16	Seaside	82
17	Florence	84
18	Lincoln City	85
------	------	------
(20)	Portland	184
(19)	United States	100

Violent Crime Risk=violent crime (homicide, rape, robbery, aggravated assault) rate of each town compared to the norm (expressed as 100) for the United States as a whole.

One of the top reasons people give for leaving big cities is the search for kinder, gentler places where people can still leave their doors unlocked, and where anyone can fearlessly stroll downtown in the evening. While there are no guarantees of complete safety anywhere, there are fortunately many places where law and order uniformly prevail. The above chart ranks the great towns based on relative personal safety. There are, of course, limitations to the validity of any data on crime due to unknowns about the extent to which crime is actually reported. Comparable information about criminal activity is based on reports prepared for the Federal Bureau of Investigation by city police and county sheriff departments, who provided data for the above table. To make great towns and cities comparable, raw data were converted into a percentage of the crime rate for the nation as a whole. For example, Joseph's violent crime rate is remarkably low–merely one-fifth that of the nation. All of the Oregon great towns are safer than the nation as a whole, and all are substantially safer than Portland.

Weather

Vokac Weather Rating*

Rank		VWR	Good-to-Great Weather Span
1	Ashland	5.4	April through October
2	Grants Pass	5.3	April through October
3	Jacksonville	5.1	April through October
4	Hood River	5.0	May to early October
5	Baker City	4.9	May to early October
6	Bend	4.8	mid-May to early October
7	Sisters	4.7	mid-May to early October
8	Joseph	4.6	mid-May to early October
9	McMinnville	4.5	mid-May to early October
10	Brookings	4.2	June to early October
11	Gold Beach	3.8	June to early October
12	Florence	3.7	June through September
13	Bandon	3.6	June through September
14	Lincoln City	3.2	late June to mid-September
15	Newport	3.0	late June to mid-September
16	Cannon Beach	3.0	late June to mid-September
17	Seaside	3.0	late June to mid-September
18	Astoria	3.0	late June to mid-September
(10)	Portland	4.4	

Vokac Weather Rating© (VWR) =The average of monthly ratings for the year where #10 is "perfect weather"–mild, warm and dry.

Residents and visitors alike talk about the weather–a lot. It is one of the most distinguishing elements of any place. Oregon is said to be a rainy state. However, the state actually enjoys drier summers than most of the rest of the country. Most of Oregon's great towns have fairly dry, uniformly warm and sunny summers, while winters typically have substantial rainfall but (apart from the mountain towns) only light snowfall.

Since 1985, the Vokac Weather Rating © has served as one of the most popular features of the "great towns" guidebook series, using historical data about climate to predict the probability of pleasant (warm and dry) weather during each month of the year. The table above averages the Vokac Weather Rating © for each town in all twelve months, yielding a score on a basis of 0 to 10, where 10 is "perfect" weather. The highest scoring locales in Oregon are the three Rogue Valley towns inland near the California border, followed by Central Oregon towns. McMinnville's weather is very similar to that of nearby Portland, while Hood River (in the Columbia Gorge) has Oregon's longest run of "perfect weather." The nine coastal towns scored lowest due to pleasant-but-brief summers and long, very wet winters.

Livability

Rank		Overall Livability Rating*
1	Ashland	90
2	Bend	88
3	Grants Pass	86
4	McMinnville	82
5	Hood River	81
6	Baker City	80
7	Seaside	78
8	Newport	78
9	Astoria	77
10	Cannon Beach	75
11	Jacksonville	74
12	Bandon	73
13	Sisters	70
14	Florence	70
15	Lincoln City	69
16	Gold Beach	68
17	Joseph	66
18	Brookings	64
------	--------------------------------	------
(12)	Portland	74

Overall Livability Rating=Average score of all elements of livability (where 100 would be perfect).

This is the list everyone has been waiting for–which town has the "best" quality of life! Keep in mind that the competition is intense–these eighteen towns are the authors' perception of Oregon's best blends of small town independence; scenic, recreation-oriented locales; and notable cultural amenities. The overall rating is based on the following elements: independent identity far enough from large cities to escape their congestion; proximity to significant natural attractions like an ocean, lake, river, or mountains offering recreation opportunities and scenic grandeur; basic facilities like hospitals, libraries, and newspapers; safety; weather; and downtown vitality. The top-rated great town, Ashland, scored a "90" out of a possible "100"–a nearly perfect place! Bend follows closely behind as an idyllic locale with a delightful setting and unlimited year-round recreation choices. Grants Pass shares Ashland's favored climate–its third place rank reflects evident ongoing development of its river-oriented appeal to visitors. As a tribute to Portland, while it was penalized in points for its size (and does not qualify as a "town"), it scored tter than several great towns. In fact, Portland would have ked among the dozen most livable great towns in the region.

Housing Cost

Rank		Housing Cost*
1	Baker City	$145,000
2	Joseph	$200,000
3	McMinnville	$245,000
4	Lincoln City	$250,000
5	Gold Beach	$260,000
6	Newport	$265,000
7	Astoria	$270,000
8	Florence	$320,000
9	Hood River	$330,000
10	Seaside	$340,000
11	Brookings	$350,000
12	Grants Pass	$360,000
13	Bend	$380,000
14	Bandon	$390,000
15	Sisters	$510,000
16	Ashland	$520,000
17	Jacksonville	$560,000
18	Cannon Beach	$650,000
(8)	Portland	$280,000
(3)	United States	$200,000

* Housing Cost=Median price (in thousands of dollars) of all houses and condos for sale (Spring, 2005)

Oregon has a lot of desirable towns, but can people still afford to move there? The state is known for its great natural beauty, recreation options, and gourmet foods; and good weather from spring to fall–migrating Californians have already escalated prices in the warmest areas. Compared to average costs in the rest of the nation, housing is typically more expensive.

This is not surprising. Great towns are compact, and are the most desirable townsites. The limited supply of residential land and ever-growing demand for these popular locales explain the higher cost of housing. Beautiful Baker City and Joseph lag behind the price escalation thanks to their isolation and relatively long winters. All other Oregon coast towns are more expensive than the national average (in spite of long, wet winters) due to the coast's renowned beauty and desirability as a second home. The mountain towns of Bend and Sisters are relatively expensive due to their four-season appeal. It is not surprising that two of the most expensive towns are in the Rogue Valley where a moderate year-round climate prevails. Ashland and Jacksonville also offer fine theater, exquisite dining venues, and easy access to skiing, river and wilderness recreation.

Livability/Affordability

Rank		VILA*
1	Baker City	414
2	McMinnville	256
3	Newport	209
4	Bend	200
5	Grants Pass	200
6	Astoria	198
7	Hood River	189
8	Seaside	166
9	Joseph	162
10	Ashland	155
11	Lincoln City	152
12	Gold Beach	135
13	Bandon	116
14	Florence	113
15	Jacksonville	85
16	Sisters	79
17	Brookings	78
18	Cannon Beach	77
(13)	Portland	123
(15)	United States	100

* VILA© (Vokac Index of Livability and Affordability)= the ratio of quality of life to housing affordability compared to the national average (expressed as 100)

Oregon's biggest "bang for the bucks," or quality of life value for the money, is clearly Baker City. Remarkably, this charming town with abundant outdoor recreation, historic significance, and well-endowed infrastructure still offers housing stock at less than the national average cost. Don't expect these bargains to last!

McMinnville, sophisticated gateway to a burgeoning Wine Country, offers great value considering its proximity to Portland and stunning main street. Newport and Bend, in spite of their fame, have not yet experienced the price escalation seen by other nationally famous towns. Both Grants Pass and Astoria are about to reap the rewards of recent significant private investments as both towns' desirability increases. Hood River and Joseph, stellar but remote gems, are ideal places to get away from big city life, while Seaside appeals to families who enjoy coastal fun. Ashland, the prototypical nearly "perfect" town, is still priced well below its comparable competitors in California.

Only Cannon Beach, Brookings, Sisters and Joseph have es below the national average–because their housing costs are even greater than their impressive quality of life attributes. ver, for those able to afford them, they remain good choices.

Demographics

	2000 Population	Age % under 21	Age % over 65	Housing % owner-occupied
Ashland	19,522	27	15	52
Astoria	9,813	28	16	51
Baker City	9,860	28	20	67
Bandon	2,833	22	29	60
Bend	52,029	29	12	63
Brookings	5,447	26	24	57
Cannon Beach	1,588	25	17	61
Florence	7,263	19	38	68
Gold Beach	1,897	24	19	66
Grants Pass	23,003	30	19	53
Hood River	5,831	30	13	48
Jacksonville	2,235	21	25	77
Joseph	1,054	28	21	67
Lincoln City	7,437	26	19	46
McMinnville	26,499	33	14	60
Newport	9,532	26	17	52
Seaside	5,900	25	19	48
Sisters	959	30	14	58
Portland	529,121	25	12	56
Oregon	3,421,399	29	13	64
United States	281,421,906	30	12	66

Demographics

	% White	% Black	% Indian	% Asian	% Hispanic
Ashland	92	1	1	2	4
Astoria	91	1	1	2	6
Baker City	95	-	1	1	3
Bandon	93	-	2	1	3
Bend	94	-	1	1	5
Brookings	91	-	2	1	5
Cannon Beach	93	-	1	-	11
Florence	96	-	1	1	2
Gold Beach	93	-	2	1	3
Grants Pass	93	-	1	1	5
Hood River	81	1	1	1	23
Jacksonville	96	-	1	-	2
Joseph	95	-	-	-	1
Lincoln City	88	-	3	1	8
McMinnville	86	1	1	1	15
Newport	89	-	2	2	9
Seaside	93	-	1	1	6
Sisters	96	-	2	-	5
Portland	78	7	1	6	7
Oregon	87	2	1	3	8
United States	75	12	1	4	13

* Percentages will not add up to 100 because "% Hispanic" can also
  be in other categories, and there are other minor categories.

Demographics

	%with high school degree	% with college degree	Vote for President % for Bush	Vote for President % for Kerry
Ashland	95	51	56	44
Astoria	86	22	44	55
Baker City	77	15	70	29
Bandon	88	19	55	43
Bend	90	29	57	42
Brookings	85	24	58	41
Cannon Beach	92	35	44	55
Florence	85	17	41	58
Gold Beach	77	19	58	41
Grants Pass	82	14	62	36
Hood River	83	31	42	57
Jacksonville	92	38	56	44
Joseph	88	17	70	29
Lincoln City	85	16	42	57
McMinnville	82	21	57	42
Newport	85	27	42	57
Seaside	83	18	44	55
Sisters	90	21	57	42
Portland	86	33	27	72
Oregon	85	25	48	52
United States	80	24	51	48

Note: percent for Presidential votes is based on county data.

Index

Index

Index

Index

Index

Index

Index

Index

About the Authors

David Vokac was born in Chicago and grew up on a ranch near Cody, Wyoming. He served as the first airborne fire-spotter for the forest next to Yellowstone National Park. Later, he taught land economics while completing a Masters degree in geography at the University of Arizona. In Denver, David headed the City's economic base analysis and the Neighborhood Planning division. He moved to Southern California in 1974 to direct San Diego County's local parks program. David is the author of ten guidebooks, including the acclaimed *Great Town of America* series.

Joan Vokac was born and raised in New Jersey, and completed her Bachelors degree at Bucknell University and her Masters degree at the University of Michigan. She recently completed a thirty-year career as a planner for unincorporated towns in San Diego County, heading projects like village revitalization and redevelopment programs, incorporation studies, and facilities planning. For the past year, she has joined David as co-author of this guidebook. She is the webmaster for *www.greattowns.com*.

The Vokacs presently reside in San Diego, California. When they're not researching, writing, speaking, or producing updates and photographs for the website, you might pass them on a road they're traveling for the sheer joy of it somewhere in America.

The "Great Towns" Series

Over the years since 1985, David Vokac's guidebooks have delighted travelers nationwide and earned critical acclaim.

The "Great Towns" series of travel guides offers accurate, comprehensive information about the most scenic and civilized communities throughout America. All noteworthy attractions, lodgings, restaurants, and more (like the weather) are described and rated by the author for each exciting locale.

The Great Towns of America (released in 1998) featured for the first time the 100 most delightful towns from coast to coast and added a chapter about livability for anyone considering relocation to one of these welcome havens.

The Great Towns of Northern California, the second subregional book, made its debut in 2003 featuring updated and expanded descriptions and ratings for restaurants, attractions and lodgings in the eleven towns that were included in the 1998 book, plus seven additional places that qualified as great towns in Northern California. The livability chapter was expanded and refined to identify and rank each locale's quality of life based on weather and safety, plus natural and cultural amenities.

The Great Towns of Southern California, released in 2002, is the companion book which provides the same information for the southern half of the Golden State.

The Great Towns of Oregon, released in 2005, is the timely addition to the series, and introduces nine great towns that have achieved "great town" status since the original 1998 work.

Information will stay current through websites included for all listings in these books, and with updates presented in our website:

greattowns.com

This vital internet portal to great towns throughout America is West Press' ongoing tribute to the United States' best getaways for a vacation or a lifetime. With it, you can link directly to each town; enjoy detailed updates and color pictures of restaurants, attractions and lodgings in featured great towns; and discover new ways to enjoy these special getaways.